JUST A SAILOR

A Navy Diver's Story of Photography, Salvage, and Combat

Steven L. Waterman

Steven L. Waterman

Ballantine Books • New York

This book is dedicated to all the men and women who have served our country. Without their sacrifices, we could not appreciate the quality of life we experience in America today. I would also like to express my deepest gratitude to the late Roland G. Ware, who was more of a father than a father-in-law; Comdr. Jerry Pulley, USN (Ret.), who gave me every opportunity to further my career in the Navy as a photographer and diver; and to my great friend Capt. George W. Kittredge, USN (Ret.), who remains my constant mentor.

A Ballantine Book
Published by The Ballantine Publishing Group
Copyright © 2000 by Steven L. Waterman

www.randomhouse.com/BB/

Library of Congress Catalog Card Number: 00-105352

ISBN 0-8041-1937-6

Front cover photos: top, BM3 Dan Sager, UDT-13; middle, PH1 Dave Graver, AFCCG; bottom, PH1 Steven L. Waterman
Back cover photo: PH1 Steven L. Waterman

Manufactured in the United States of America

First Edition: October 2000

10 9 8 7 6 5 4 3 2 1

Contents

Introduction   iv
1   Why Not Join the Navy?   1
2   Boot Camp   9
3   Boot Leave   19
4   Pensacola   22
5   Photo School   31
6   Naval Air Station, Oceana   43
7   More Time at Oceana   55
8   Underwater Swimmers School   69
9   Combat Camera Group   77
10 Panama City   91
11 Back Home from the Azores   105
12 Heading for the West Coast   111
13 Reporting for Duty with UDT-13   114
14 Overseas with Team-13   118
15 Back in the States, San Diego   154
16 Combat Camera Group Again   168
17 NavSpecWarGruLant   191
18 The SHAD Project   209
19 Italy   224
20 Naval School, Diving and Salvage   233
21 USS *Ortolan*, ASR-22   256

Introduction

This is my first book. There may be more.

Most of my life, I have wondered what it would take to have a book published. I've always felt those who could accomplish this were far and above the level of my abilities. After attending a writing workshop some years back that left me with the feeling that being published was hopeless—something akin to winning the lottery—I developed an attitude.

One feminist New York editor stated, "You have to pay your dues and run the gauntlet of New York's young male editors." According to her, a writer has to look forward to being rejected many times, and one would have to make the rounds and talk the talk, taking full advantage of the old-boy network as much as possible. This attitude sank in and caused me to doubt my abilities and the very worth of what I had to say. I had some articles published in magazines, but I never felt that I would be published in the way I had envisioned in my pipe dreams. I made my thoughts clear on this to my wife, Mary, on many occasions. She encouraged me to "just sit down and start writing."

One day my cousin Denny Davis, a longtime lobster fisherman, childhood playmate, and classmate, said to me, "Most of us lead relatively boring lives, Steve. You have done things that others can only read about."

Well, now they can read about it. I think it takes only three things to get a book published: You need to have something to say, be able to say it, and have a publisher who believes that there are people who want to read what you have said. Let's hope so.

Steve Waterman
June 2000

CHAPTER ONE

Why Not Join the Navy?

It was New Year's Eve, 1963. I was seventeen years old, and Bill Swanson, a high school classmate, and I were out roaming the streets of Rockland, Maine, trying to find somebody who would buy two underage boys some alcohol. Our goal was Gluek Stite, a rank but strong malt liquor that came in small six-ounce cans. The stuff would gag a maggot, but it would get us drunk in minimum time. All of us who drank for the sole purpose of getting hammered used it.

Earlier in the evening, as I left my house in Spruce Head, I had asked my mother for some money so I could get something to eat and go to the movies. Needless to say, I did neither that night.

Bill knew a Coast Guard sailor called Reb who would buy kids beer. We found him in his room, above the Oasis Lounge in Rockland. We walked up the outside stairs to Reb's room and gave him the money. He went to the market across Park Street to make our purchase.

Reb came back to the room, handed us the brown sack, and we drank down the malt liquor and waited for the buzz that would signify the first stages of adolescent intoxication. Reb just lay back on his bed reading a magazine, every once in a while looking at us with a big grin as we drank.

A few minutes after having downed our six-packs, we left Reb's room for our first stop, the barroom downstairs. The operators of the place didn't question our ages. I proposed to one woman that she might dance with me. She gave me a quizzical look and impolitely declined the offer.

We then strode valiantly, however unsteadily, out into the street. I was walking toward Park Street along Main when I was overcome by nausea. Right in front of Phil's Corner, a small luncheonette, I felt the immediate urge to throw up. To steady myself, I grabbed firmly onto a parking meter (a long since discarded

1

fixture on Rockland's Main Street) and proceeded to spray yellow Gluek Stite all over my shoes and the surrounding sidewalk. Just then a Rockland cop, Officer Hanley, walked up and asked if I was all right. Bill had seen Hanley walking down the street and had put some distance between us, and he shouted at me to run. In an alcohol-induced haze, I ran as fast as I could south down Main Street. Figuring Hanley was hot on my tail, I ducked behind Phil's and then back out onto Park Street. Of course it wasn't the brightest choice; Phil's Corner was only about fifty feet square and there were no buildings around it. As I ran around the building, trying to look back and see if Hanley was following me, I blasted around a corner and ran directly into him. He hadn't moved an inch.

"Better come with me, son," were his next words.

We drove to the Rockland Police Department, where I was placed in a cell painted therapeutic green. It had a hole in the floor and no mattress on the bed. My mother's cousin, Bruce Gamage, was on duty that night and he saw some degree of humor in my situation. I *knew* he had done more bad shit when he was young than I ever had, so I was quite sure I was not the first adolescent to have this experience.

My father and Sonny Drinkwater, a lobsterman friend of his, came to bail me out. It required some surety to obtain my release so Sonny put up his house for bond. In those days, drinking as a minor was quite a serious offense.

I was unceremoniously dumped into the back of Sonny's car and we drove to Spruce Head. I made some comment to my father about never being thought of by anybody as much more than a waste. That drew a hard slap across the face. That was the last time I ever gave him reason to hit me.

At the time, I lived in a rented house in Spruce Head with my mother, stepfather, and two sisters, Heather and Cheryl. My parents divorced when I was ten years old, and I had lived with each of them for a while as they still lived in the same town. That way, I did not have to change schools.

My father shoved me through the door with a comment directed at my mother that he had brought "her little boy" home. I went to bed with thoughts of impending death running through my mind. The next day I got up early and my mother ordered me to saw a cord of firewood into stove lengths, and then split and stack it.

The legal system in those days was not as understanding as it is now. I was fined thirty-five dollars, given a suspended fifteen-day jail sentence, and placed on one year's probation for my heinous crime. And I had to visit my probation officer every week. I had visions of never being able to get a job or vote or do any of the other things people take for granted, and in my own mind I felt like a convict.

When I returned to school after holiday vacation, word had spread about my run-in with the law. The Key Club (junior version of Kiwanis) had taken a vote and expelled me from it.

To get to my probation officer in the Post Office building, I had to pass by the military recruiters' offices. Most of the time the recruiters were not in and a sign on the door announced when they would be. One afternoon, a few months after my "conviction," the Navy recruiter happened to be in, a first class boatswain's mate in a blue uniform bedecked with ribbons and gold hash marks. A sign on his desk read "BM1 Allen, USN." I kind of liked that. A title in front of your name. A uniform and that look in the eye that told others you had seen things they could only dream about or see in movies. I walked in. He looked up from filling out some forms and asked if he could help me. I told him I was considering joining the service and wanted to see what the Navy had to offer. He asked me if I was still in high school. I said I was for the moment, but that it might not last much longer. He pointed to a chair and said he would be right with me.

I looked around the room. Posters from the World War II era were all over the walls, one showing an attractive girl and another a girl in dress blues saying her man was in the Navy—that sort of thing. I didn't know if she was making an offer to other sailors who weren't at sea, or if she was just a prop to attract dumb high school kids like me into signing on the dotted line. Around a recruiter's office there is always the implication that you are going to have more fun, get laid more, and see more exciting places and things in the military. They always seem to leave out information about fighting wars, getting your ass shot off, scrubbing pots and pans, and cleaning heads.

After a few minutes Bosun's Mate First Class Allen looked up from his paperwork. He stood and with a smile reached out and shook my hand, and we introduced ourselves. He asked me what I meant about not being in high school for long. I told him I was fed up with the place and going to quit. He said that was not a good idea because he could not guarantee me a school if I did that. He said that he would enlist me if I passed the Armed Forces Qualification Test, but it would be much better if I didn't quit. Also, the Navy would give me E-2 (Airman Apprentice) out of boot camp if I had a high school diploma. I didn't know what that meant, but I figured it might translate into more money.

I looked over the brochures he had that described navy career fields and told him I would like to be a photographer's mate. I was interested in photography and diving, but I understood the Navy didn't enlist you and send you directly to diving school.

Allen told me to talk my decision over with my parents and then come back in a couple of days. Even though I would be eighteen when I joined, it was always good to have the approval of the parents. I knew my chances of going to college were just short of nonexistent. Even if I'd had the financial means, I hated school and would never have graduated. I wouldn't have been able to bring myself to go just to keep from being drafted. In the 1960s the draft was in full swing and many of my schoolmates were discussing ways to avoid serving their country in the military.

The next time I went to sign in with my probation officer, I stopped by the Navy recruiter's office. Allen had some papers laid out on the desk. He asked me to fill in the blanks so he could start the paperwork. I would not be obligated to join, he just wanted to lay out the groundwork. Then he gave me the Armed Forces Qualification Test. The test was multiple choice and made up of questions about mechanical things, electricity, math, language comprehension, abstract thinking, and so on. I finished it in rapid fashion and was told I had scored a 94 percent out of a possible 99, which seemed to impress the recruiter. He told me that once I got in I could go to any school I could physically qualify for. He then asked if I was on probation or anything like that. I told him I was—for drinking under age. He smiled and said that wouldn't be a problem. He would get the judge to erase my record and it would be as though it had never existed. That happened a lot in those days. Many young men who might otherwise have ended up in jail joined the service. The vast majority of them never had trouble with the law again.

The next day in school, I went to the guidance office and asked to see the catalogs on Navy training. In Maine back then, the military was still seen as an honorable profession, not looked down upon as a place where people served who couldn't make it anywhere else. The guidance counselor gave me the books I asked for, and I sat down at a desk in his office and looked them over.

That evening I went to my girlfriend Mary's house. Her father, Roland Ware, was always glad to see me and would drop whatever he was doing to sit and talk with me. For some reason I seemed to spend as much time talking to him as I did with Mary. I imagine the conversations probably did me more good. I couldn't figure out why a man of his stature would want to sit and talk with me. Roland always gave good advice. He was well-thought-of in the community and had started and still operated a local petroleum products distribution company, Maritime Oil Company. At that time I owned exactly four changes of clothes and two pairs of shoes, not counting my rubber boots. I was the son of a chicken farmer and the stepson of a lobster fisherman, neither one very successful, and came from a broken home.

Roland said he thought it might be good for me to go into the Navy. I explained that I thought I could get training in photography and travel a little and possibly learn enough so I could make a living when I got out. He agreed that for a young man it was not the worst of options.

My next stop was to get the probation officer to expunge my record of all criminal activity. That was not a problem. It lightened his workload and would get another troublemaker out of town.

On June 11, 1964, I graduated from Rockland District High School about number 80 out of 140 or so. I did not consider it a momentous occasion, but I felt many of my classmates thought this would be the apex of their careers. I couldn't wait to get the hell out of our little seacoast community and get on with my life. From my standpoint, Rockland and its surroundings had very little to offer, and I would just as soon see them in the rearview mirror for the last time.

I still had to take a physical and this required me to go to Bangor, Maine, to the military medical facility there, where Army and Navy medical personnel gave preinduction physicals to draftees and volunteers. Volunteers were quickly becoming the minority as the draft was beginning to crank up for the Vietnam War.

The recruiter provided a Greyhound Bus ticket to Bangor and

handed me an envelope with some papers in it. He told me to answer "no" to anything I didn't understand. During my childhood and up into my teens I had been bothered with asthma on occasion. There were times when I couldn't go to school, it was so bad. He said it sounded like hay fever to him and that's what I probably would answer on the sheet when they asked me. I took his advice.

The physical was a typical walk-through. They noted that I had slightly flat feet and blue eyes, and that was about it. One potential recruit had a big scar on his chest from open-heart surgery. The corpsmen asked him some questions and then told him he was okay. Another kid wanted to join the Marines. He had high blood pressure, and they rejected him. I passed with flying colors and went home on the next bus. It was almost like a dream. All I did was sign my name on some papers and all this stuff started happening to me. Somebody wanted to hire me and was willing to pay to have me work for them. They would give me clothes, fly me around, educate me, and even let me eat all I wanted. Christ, what a deal!

The day before I was to hop the "many windows" to Portland, where I would be sworn in, I ran across Mike McNeil and David Cooper, friends of mine from high school. They proposed we get some Gluek Stite, go to Samoset Resort Road, and slam a few down as a going-away party for me. Sounded like a good idea. The usual formalities of obtaining the brew were quickly dispensed with and we were on our way to getting drunk. We drove back into Rockland and parked on Main Street near the Central Maine Power Company building. An alley that ran between that building and the one next to it was a favorite place to piss. As I stood there writing my name on the wall, just getting ready to cross the T's, I felt a tap on my shoulder. I looked quickly around and there was Bert Snow, a Rockland cop. "Oh Christ," I thought, "here I go again." I told Bert I was going into the Navy the next day, the mother of one of the other guys was extremely sick and was probably not going to live much longer, and I can't remember the other horrible things we told them, but he let us go. David Cooper's mother, Winola, came to the police station and got us and drove me home. She had been my music teacher my whole career in the school system and I was quite embarrassed to have her come and take us away in that shape. She didn't have much to say to me on the ride to my house.

At this time I was living with my stepfather, "Tint" Drink-water, and my mother and two sisters. We lived in a Cellotex hunting camper that measured about eight feet by twelve. Winter had started out with me sleeping in the top bunk, the grown-ups on the bottom, and my sisters on the floor in sleeping bags. I didn't think we were poor, I just thought we didn't have a pot to piss in and hardly a window to throw it out of. I got pretty tired of the sleeping arrangements and started wheezing as it was so damned hot inside that tiny one-room structure.

My grandfather gave me an old Army wall tent he had bought at a surplus store. I set it up on a wooden platform I got from one of the hen pens and put a bed in it. That made for a comfortable outdoor bedroom. It could be embarrassing to live there. I re-member getting a ride home from school one day with Tommy Painter, one of those guys who always seemed to "have" things, like cars. When he dropped me off in front of the place he asked me if that was where I lived. I said it was. He looked at me and said, "You're shitting me."

After that, whenever I got a ride, I would get out up or down the road in front of a "real" house and walk the rest of the way home.

The next morning I woke with no hangover; we hadn't con-sumed all that much beer. My mother had packed some of my stuff in a small gym bag and I put on a pair of Levi's and a shirt. I'd already purchased a pair of black shoes, standard black low-cuts like the dress shoes worn in all the services. My mother gave me a ride to the Greyhound Bus station in Rockland. Mary, my girlfriend, was there. Both of them kissed me good-bye. I got on the bus, sat down, and we started up the street. As we passed out of Rockland I thought to myself, I guess I won't be seeing this place for a while.

I didn't have a clue as to what lay in store for me. What sort of adventures were ahead? Would I fit in with the crowds I would meet? Where would I end up being stationed? Would the Navy give me what I wanted for training or had the recruiter been blowing smoke to suck me in?

All the way to Portland I thought about what I had done so far in my life and how it hadn't amounted to much. I was never able to make any amount of money, most girls wouldn't give me the time of day, and my parents couldn't seem to decide where they wanted me to live. Ah, what the hell, it was my chance to punch the reset button and start from scratch.

I reminisced about the days when I lived on Hewett's Island in the summer and went lobstering with my stepfather, but all I could remember about it was being seasick out by Two Bush Reef and puking over the side. The waves would come up and nearly touch my face as I watched my reflection in them, my glasses being full of tears from the strain of heaving my guts out.

Nope, I thought to myself, I am doing the right thing.

CHAPTER TWO

Boot Camp

The bus pulled up to the terminal in Portland and I got off. The recruiter had lined up a room at the YMCA, where I would stay that night. I stopped by there and signed in. The person at the desk told me the rules and that I had to be in my room by a certain time, midnight I think.

After a brief visit with a girl I knew from Rockland High, and a few beers, and a brief run-in with the local cops, I found my way to my tiny room and went to bed. The next morning I walked to the Portland recruiting office. It was June 24, 1964.

There were about forty of us heading for boot camp from the State of Maine. I don't remember any of them at all; they were generic Maine boys. Most of them were joining to avoid the Army or get the hell out of an economically depressed area. I could relate to that. Some had been in trouble with the law. I could relate to that, too, although I didn't consider myself a criminal by their standards.

We went through the swearing-in process and signed more papers. Then we were loaded onto a bus and driven to Portland Airport, where we boarded a plane for O'Hare International Airport. This was my first ride on a jet airliner. Before that I had been out of Maine only twice, once when I flew to Nova Scotia with a local pilot out of Owl's Head Airport to deliver some engine parts for a Maine boat that had broken down in Yarmouth, and once when I went someplace in New Hampshire with my parents when I was very small.

My flying had been limited to some flying lessons with Arthur Harjula, an old bush pilot from Thomaston, Maine, and some "lessons" from Bob Stenger of Down East Airlines. All he did was smoke cigarettes and scream at me. Between getting airsick from the smell of the smoke and being nervous from his hollering at me, the only thing I learned from him was that he was a lousy instructor. I used to work at the airport for one dollar an hour, which I would convert into flight time at the rate of fourteen dollars an hour. No deals, just straight across. But it was no deal. At least when I went flying with Arthur, I learned something.

Of course we were big men now, having joined the World's Largest Nuclear Navy! Some of the guys tried to get the flight attendants to serve them drinks. They had already been warned by the recruiters not to. I tried to be friendly with the girls, but they had seen too many like us, just meat to be shipped to some foreign country to the slaughter. I guess in their minds we didn't count. Funny how when you're eighteen you can't fathom a feeling like that someone might harbor, but when you get older it makes sense. You don't approve of it, but you know it's real. It's something that has to be lived through, kind of like racism and all the other politically incorrect tendencies of today.

The plane touched down at O'Hare some hours later. We walked off the plane and, as we had been told, found our way to baggage claim. Only a few of us had any checked baggage, as some of us didn't own anything but the clothes we were wearing. At the baggage claim we were met by men from the Naval Recruit Training Center, Great Lakes, a couple of petty officers and a few "service weeks," recruits who were partway through boot camp. During service week they had to work in the chow hall, work grounds detail, or help the drill instructors handle new recruits. Those guys had been in the Navy about seven weeks longer than we had, so I guess they thought they were old salts.

Immediately they began the usual boot camp harassment. I knew that was their mission and just did what I was told. Some of the boys took their insults personally and it cost them. They were down for push-ups and getting screamed at up close. I did not, and had no problems. Having taken flying lessons from Bob Stenger, I was quite familiar with being screamed at by someone with a limited vocabulary; I felt right at home.

It was late at night when we arrived at Camp Barry and the Recruit Training Center, where we encountered the usual intimidation. Everybody got off the bus, and we had to stand around while they messed with us and made us hurry up and wait. I could not tell if that was intentional or if they had just screwed up their scheduling. I thought it was probably the latter. Sometimes our handlers seemed as pissed off as I thought *we* should be. They managed to get us into a chow hall, where we were fed. We could not go back for seconds but I didn't need to as I ate some of the food the other guys wouldn't eat. I thought it was very good chow. At least it was free and plentiful.

The "service weeks" put us in a huge Quonset hut for the night. At about 0400 we were turned out to get haircuts, shots, and tests. There was a big building where the haircuts and shots were given. Some of us stood in line and got our haircuts. When we came out we went to the back of the line, where we stood to get our shots. It was extremely hot out there in the sun and a few of the boys passed out from heat exhaustion. The drill instructors warned us not to stand with our knees locked back. I didn't listen well. Finally, we started moving inside to get our blood drawn and our flu shots. When they drew our blood, the corpsman would have us walk along in a line and hang our right arm over a sloping board. Then another corpsman would shove a needle into a vein. We would then proceed to the next board, where the next medic would drain some blood into a test tube. At the board after that, another man would drain some more, pull out the needle, throw it into a trash can, and put a piece of gauze on the needle hole. We were supposed to double up our arms, trapping the gauze over the needle wound, and walk along in line. Then another corpsman jabbed a syringe full of some thick marshmallow-looking goo into your bicep and left the needle hanging. The next guy squeezed the stuff into the arm and pulled out the needle. Then we stepped up to a table and picked up a specimen cup. A left turn then led down a set of concrete steps into the coolness of the basement, where the "heads" ("toilets" to landlubbers) were located. It was nice and cool down there, but it smelled strongly of urine. I walked over to a urinal mounted on the wall, and the last thing I remember is looking down at my lower unit to make sure I was hitting the cup. Then I woke up with three people standing over me. One guy was looking into my eyes with a little flashlight and asking me if I was okay. He said I had passed out and hit my head on something. The back of my head felt sandy, as if I had been lying on the beach. The corpsmen took me to another room, where a doctor stitched me up. I spent the next week in sick bay in and out of bed because the doctors were worried about one of my pupils being larger than the other. I told them that it had always been that way; it had not, but I was afraid they would throw me out of the Navy if they thought I had suffered brain damage.

Most of the people in the ward with me were in for things like broken bones from jumping out of windows as they tried to run away from boot camp. Some were there for respiratory infections or had undergone appendectomies. One individual, who was sunburned very badly, worried that the Navy was going to take some sort of disciplinary action against him for getting sunburned, as if they considered it dereliction of duty and damaging government property or some such crap.

When I reported to boot camp I had been assigned to Company 242. When I got out of sick bay I was assigned to Company 303. It turned out to be a better deal; our company commander would not accept a company that had to do a service week, so we graduated two days after Company 242. In 303 there was a good cross section, everything from college graduates to barely literate hillbillies. I took the GCT (General Classification Test) and found I was right up there among the brain surgeons and rocket scientists. When I went to the classification team, where we would be assigned our schools, the counselor told me the Navy wanted me to be a sonar or missile technician on board a nuclear submarine. I told them I would have none of that; I wanted to be a photographer's mate. The career counselor scoffed at that and referred to men holding that rating as "titless Waves" and other derogatory terms. At the time I didn't know what he meant. But I was insistent and, with some disgust, they relented. I was assigned to Photographer's Mate "A" School, NAS (Naval Air Station) Pensacola, Florida, via nine months of "PSI (Programmed School Input) at Basic Naval Aviation Officers' School," whatever that was. Meanwhile, boot camp continued.

Each recruit company had a drill team and a swim team. I volunteered for the swim team as I could hardly walk and chew gum at the same time. I couldn't swim the crawl or the butterfly stroke, so I tried out for the backstroke. I got on the team, and we competed against other companies. I don't remember how well we did, but I do know it got me out of those damned barracks and away from the tedium of washing clothes and listening to the constant inane bullshit that was part of a recruit's daily life. We had to wash our clothes by hand and hang them out on the line behind the barracks to dry. My job, as sixth squad leader, was to ensure that the clothes stops—those little strings we hung the clothes from, were all straight. It was not a hard job, but it was nearly impossible to teach some of the men to line the knots up and get the clothes exactly the right distance from each other. I never had to resort to violence to get the point across, but I did give it some thought.

I remember one individual who was just very stupid. Once an instructor asked the kid what his GCT was. He said it was twenty-four. I couldn't believe it; the Navy had recruited a guy with an IQ just a few points above bread mold. What in the hell was this kid going to do? The Navy would train him and train him and he probably would never amount to a pisshole in a snowbank. I felt it was a gross misuse of money. Another guy, named Corwin, a Jewish kid from New York, got a lot of crap from the company commander, who asked the kid if he could call him "Abe."

The kid said, "No sir."

When asked, "Why not?" by the company commander, Corwin replied, "Because that's not my name, sir." I didn't know then about anti-Semitism. He was just another guy in my company. At that time company commanders also generally used a black guy for the "guide on," the man who marched in front of the company carrying the flag. The feeling was that the black kids had better rhythm and could keep in step. Robertson, one of my buddies, a black kid from Mississippi, said, "Those bastards better not put this nigger in front, or they're gonna find out just how bad my rhythm is." We all laughed and agreed that it would be pretty interesting if he happened to be picked as guide on. He wasn't.

The company commander was a chief damage controlman. He told the company that he was also an ordained minister in some church. I never asked which one, because I didn't care; any church that would have him as a minister was one I would never attend. He wouldn't allow any of the boys to use profanity, but he had to be the cruelest bastard I've ever met. If I had been stationed on a ship with him, I would have made sure he was given the "big swim." He always addressed the black kids as "boy," and one time when the dumb kid was standing in ranks for an inspection, the company commander kicked him in the legs until he fell down. The kid had laced up his leggings wrong. In fear, he got up crying and ran for the fence. A couple of the faster guys ran after him and grabbed him before he made it over the top of the perimeter's chain-link fence.

I felt sorry for the kid, to think anyone could be treated like that just because he had tied some knots wrong. After that inspection I showed him how to tie them correctly and made sure he did it right from then on. He disappeared before we graduated. That kind of thing happened a lot: guys would just not be there when we came back to the barracks. In most cases, I think, the instructors may have checked the records and found something about a recruit's medical condition. In the particular case of the dumb kid, I think they finally figured out that they were wasting everybody's time trying to train him. There were rumors that some men couldn't hack the regimentation and harassment and had jumped out of windows, hanged themselves, or cut their wrists. I even heard one story about a guy throwing himself down the stairs in the indoctrination building. They said he ended up in sick bay for about a week and they didn't know what became of him. I grinned, because I knew they were talking about me. They hadn't gotten the story straight, but I wasn't about to help them out.

The chow was good and we could go back for seconds once we got to Camp Porter. The place was newly constructed and quite nice. The barracks were well-lit and had new sidewalks and the lights all worked, things that most people take for granted. Once in a while we were allowed to go to the exchange and buy things like stationery, candy, soap, and the like. My mother sent me money once in a while, usually a five-dollar bill, and I received letters from Mary and my father. Mary's father also wrote me, as he was a great one for corresponding and put a lot of heart into his letters.

Boot camp turned out not to be difficult at all, either mentally or physically. I guess some of the city slickers might have thought so, but I didn't think it was much more than an indoctrination for us. Rumors sometimes added spice—we heard the standard one about a whole company dying of meningitis, and that we would have to stay an extra month in quarantine, that sort of thing.

Two weeks or so before we were to graduate from basic training, we were allowed to go on our first liberty. We had two choices, Chicago or Milwaukee. I chose Chicago. It was my first time on a train and I was excited. Ned Dentry, a fellow I had become friends with, and I went together. Ned had about seven years of college and a master's degree in something. One of the most intelligent men in the company, he was about twenty-seven years old and not the typical sailor type.

We had no desire to get drunk or chase down members of the local female population; we correctly assumed that the girls in Chicago would have had their fill of "boot camps" and not be the least bit interested in us. For some reason I did not want to drink. The company commander had told us that drinking was strictly taboo, and I believed it was a good warning as I did not need to get in trouble. I had respect for the uniform and figured if I got drunk, I might get robbed. They had paid each of us fifty dollars, but after taking out what our uniforms cost and the rest of it, there wasn't much left. It was commonly believed by us that uniforms were free. I understood that. The petty officers told us if we lost or destroyed any of our clothing, we would have to pay for it because it belonged to Uncle Sam, but I thought that was garbage since they had already taken the cost out of our pay.

Ned Dentry and I walked to the train station and rode to Chicago. We wandered around the streets for a while and finally went into a restaurant. I ordered fish, and he, a steak. After that we explored Chicago further. It wasn't like the locals had never seen sailors in town. The naval training command unleashed sailors on the town frequently, and we were just another batch going through the process. I had my two little green stripes[1] and Ned had his three. He went into the Navy as an E-3 because of his college degrees. They wanted him to be an officer, but he declined.

We finally tired of drifting in and out of stores and went back to the train station. The next time the company had liberty was a repeat of the same thing. I almost didn't go, but I figured it would be better than hanging around the barracks and getting assigned to shit details. It felt good to be a sailor. I wanted to be the sharpest guy around even though I knew I was probably one of the laziest bastards ever to don the uniform. I always kept a sharp appearance. And I was not bothered by asthma anymore, although one night I awoke in the middle of a thunderstorm with a fairly bad attack. By morning it was nearly gone and didn't have any effect on my performance that day.

---

1. Green stripes designated an aviation nonrated person, black was deck, red was engineering, and light blue was Seabees.

The word filtered down the grapevine that the North Vietnamese had attacked a couple of our destroyers using gunboats. I couldn't imagine a bunch of Vietnamese attacking a U.S. Navy destroyer with gunboats, and I thought that might be stretching things a little bit. But I figured if that was what was reported, then it must be true. Then rumors started flying that we would all be sent directly to Vietnam. Funny how things like that get started. I didn't think the Navy had anybody on the ground there in those days.

We carried old Springfield rifles around everywhere we went. The barrels were plugged and the bolts were missing. When we went to class we had to stack the rifles outside and one unlucky bastard would have to stand out there at parade rest in the stifling July and August heat to guard them. On occasion I would be standing outside in ranks waiting to go to class, and one of the service weeks who marched us around would go down the ranks asking our GCT scores. At first I proudly stated I had a 69 (out of a possible 75). After a while I figured out what they were doing: the training was not designed for rocket scientists, but you had to pass the tests. They picked the guys with high GCTs to guard the rifles, as they figured those guys could easily catch up later on. I smartened up real quick and started quoting my test scores as being in the forties. When I graduated, I was quite near the top of my company. The numerical grade escapes me, but I knew I was one of the best. It didn't matter; I don't remember anybody flunking out who made it to the end of training.

Graduation day at boot camp had no special meaning for me other than the fact that I was getting out of Great Lakes Naval Recruit Training Command. Maybe people would treat us more humanely somewhere else. I had orders to Pensacola, Florida, to a place called Basic NAO School at Sherman Field. Nobody had a clue what it was. Ned Dentry and Dave Duchene, another guy in my boot camp class, were also going to Pensacola and we would be in the same class in photo school. Dave, the lucky son of a bitch, was getting stationed at the NAS Pensacola Photo Lab until our class started. We both would be assigned to nine months of PSI, but we didn't know what that was. They had authorized me some leave between the time I left boot camp and when I was to report in at my new duty station. We all would be flying most of the way home. My flight would take me from O'Hare to Boston. From there I would take a cab to the bus station and then grab the Greyhound to Rockland. These events passed mostly without incident.

I remember the death-defying ride from Logan Airport in a cab driven by a foreign national. Two other sailors were also going to the bus station, so we shared a cab. When we arrived at the bus station, the driver tried to hustle us out of money for putting our sea bags in the trunk. But a Boston cop walked over and gave the cabbie a little talking to, then wished us luck. There always seemed to be people quick to rip off a military man. As life went on, I encountered more and more of his type and developed a dislike for them, unsurpassed even by my lack of love for men I fought in wars or bars.

The bus ride to Maine was a study in boredom and human nature. I could always strike up a conversation with somebody on "the many windows." In those days, riding the bus was not beneath the dignity of the common man. With the demise of passenger rail service up and down the coast of Maine, there were always a number of older people and a few college students riding the buses. I never got along very well with the college types. Most of them had no great desire to converse with military people. I guess they were afraid the calling might rub off and they might come down with a mad desire to join the service. At that time, the draft was in full swing and huge numbers of college students had deferments because of their student status. Guys I went to high school with went on to college to keep from being drafted, and if they flunked out, they immediately got married. I guess it's all right to kill off the poor and unfortunate and let the cream of the crop go on to run the country. But who's going to pick up the garbage and sweep the streets if they wipe out all the people whose daddies can't afford to send them to college?

I do have an attitude about the people who got draft deferments when I think of men like Joshua Chamberlain, of Maine, who gambled his life for his country in the Civil War, and earned the Medal of Honor while fighting with the 20th Maine. He was a professor at Bowdoin, and had to lie about wanting to go abroad and study. He then joined the Union Army and became a hero and later governor of the State of Maine. And the man who trained him, Adelbert Ames, was a man from Rockland, Maine, who himself had the Medal of Honor. During one ferocious battle, he was wounded so badly that he had his men tie him to a caisson and wheel him around the field so that he could direct artillery fire. He did so until he passed out from loss of blood. (Adelbert died in 1933 in Rockland, Maine, not far from where I graduated from high school.) Neither of those men had to go and fight, but they felt it was their duty to their country and to their fellow citizens. So maybe I was following in these men's footsteps; I didn't give it much thought. We were fighting a different kind of war by the time I got my chance.

The student deferment used to piss me off. In World War II, rich guys and movie actors volunteered to go and fight. I had an attitude about draft dodgers, and still do. Later on I found out that just about as many kids from wealthy families joined up as poor ones, but the antiwar people never publicized that. And twice as many Canadians came to the United States to join the service, compared to the number of American draft dodgers who ran off to Canada. I think there is a message here.

I was ready to do my duty for my country, whether or not the war was just or honorable. After they are over, wars are usually Monday-morning-quarterbacked to pieces, so no matter how honorable they seem going in, there are usually those who can find a reason to say they were a waste of lives and material. In all cases, they are; the results are sometimes worth it.

CHAPTER THREE

Boot Leave

Arriving by bus in Rockland is not a major event. When I arrived that early morning you could have fired a cannon loaded with grapeshot down Main Street and never touched a soul. The only person at the bus station was a cab driver from Rokes and Harvey Taxi Company, the transportation vulture who usually showed when a bus disgorged its load of sleepy passengers. For two bucks I caught a ride home to the hunting camp I had left twelve weeks before. My mother and sisters were glad to see me. Then I walked over to my father's chicken farm and visited with him and my stepmother for a while. He asked me about boot camp and where I would be stationed. My grandfather, Harry Waterman, lived next door, so I stopped by for a visit. He had served in World War I in the Navy but had never been in combat. Later he had contracted the flu and nearly died. When he got his medical discharge the doctor had told his mother, my great-grandmother Nellie, that if he was lucky he would live six months. Well, he made it to ninety-four, as she had. That fifteen-dollar-a-month pension he started drawing had zoomed up to several hundred dollars by the time he died.

I called Mary Ware, my high-school girlfriend, at her house in Rockland. When there was no answer, I tried the family's cottage on Lucia Beach in Owl's Head, a nearby town. Her mother answered the phone and I talked with her for a few minutes, then her father took the phone and asked me how things were going and when I was coming over to see them. Mary was somewhere else. I changed out of my uniform. As proud as I was of it, at first I still felt a little self-conscious running around Rockland in whites. Blues always had more appeal and made you look more like a real sailor instead of an ice cream man. You can get away with more wearing blues, and blues don't show the dirt as readily.

In about an hour Mary showed up at the camp in her Volkswagen. She had heard from somebody in Rockland that I was home. She had this old black VW "Bug" and had obtained her driver's license before I left for boot camp. We drove to her parents' place on the water at Lucia Beach. The house was a large one that had originally been built by some people from Rockland. Her father had purchased it for a small amount of money and had added on and fixed it up. From the front porch you could spit in the ocean at high tide. What a view. It was on a dead-end road and the envy of every summer person who ever set foot in the area. Mary was glad to see me, and I was quite happy to be home, but there was just something missing about my life. I didn't know what it was.

I wanted to walk the streets of Rockland at least one time dressed in my white uniform. Hell, I was a sailor, ready to do battle with any enemy on, above, or under the water. People should be proud of me. After all, I had just gone through nearly twelve weeks of hellish basic training. I had learned how to wash clothes by hand, salute senior people wearing gold braid, and I could tie knots almost as well as when I left home. Men before me wearing that uniform had died for the red, white, and blue. Songs had been written about sailors and the sea. So there I was, ready for the honors that I deserved now that I was one of the men of the sea. 'Course, that ain't how it works. My stepfather, Tint Drinkwater, was going to give me a ride to Rockland but I would not ride in his pickup truck because it might soil my pristine white uniform. So I started walking up the road and had gone about half a mile, when he and my mother came along and talked me into taking a ride. Aw, what the hell is a little dirt, anyway, compared to walking eight miles? I thought.

I made the rounds of the old poolroom where I hung out during my high school days, stopped by the drugstore and had a chocolate frappe (shake to the rest of the world), and generally meandered about the streets. Most of my former classmates had gone off to college by then or also joined the service, and a few had even quit school and preceded me into the military. Vietnam was cranking up and they didn't want to miss the action. I don't think patriotism was high on the list of reasons to serve; when you are living in a coastal community in Maine and your options for making a living are limited to about three things, all of them having something to do with lobstering, fishing, or working in a stuffy factory building, it ain't that hard to arrive at the decision to jump on the first opportunity to get the hell out of Dodge.

I was rapidly running out of things to do and getting eager to see what Florida held in store. I had never been to Florida, so I called the airline and scheduled an earlier flight to Pensacola. In those days a serviceman in uniform got to fly half price, if he didn't mind going standby. I found very little problem getting around and was almost never bumped from a flight. Military standbys also had the option of paying the full rate if they were going to get bumped. I never had to do that.

My flight would leave from Boston. Once again I rode the bus to catch the plane. Flights on Down East Airlines were leaving from Owl's Head Airport, but the additional cost was not worth it. On a pay of seventy-two dollars a month if you don't have rich parents, it is not always cost-effective to take the plane.

Whenever I was transferred to a new unit or place, I always had some apprehension that I would not like the billet or get along with the people there. In most all cases, the feeling abated quickly as I made new friends and learned new jobs.

CHAPTER FOUR

Pensacola

I was tired when I arrived in Pensacola and wanted to get some sleep, so I hoped that checking in would not be too tedious a process. The cab driver dropped me off at Naval Air Technical Training Unit (NATTU), at Mainside. After much questioning about why I had checked in two weeks early, it turned out to be the wrong place. I grabbed my gear, and the duty driver took me down the road to the administration building of Naval Air Station (NAS) Pensacola. It, too, was the wrong place. In fact, nobody seemed to know just where the hell "BNAO School" was or, for that matter, if the place even existed. I had not a clue, being a boot and all, so I left it up to those who I felt should know. Lesson one: assume you know more than everybody else until they prove differently, then follow the one who seems to know the most.

I finally caught a base shuttle out to Sherman Field. There, it turned out, they trained backseat drivers for F-4 Phantom fighter planes and bombardier-navigators for A-6A Intruder bombers. I had to sign in at a building on the east side of Sherman Field, checking in with a chief by the name of Butler. He was in charge of personnel. The CO's name was Cumbie and the executive officer (XO) was a Lieutenant Commander Bloom. Two Waves worked in the office, Pat Busby and Liz Lawson. Busby was, I believe, from Texas. Lawson was from some southern state like North Carolina or Tennessee. They were quite attractive. Busby had blond hair, was quite thin, and very nice looking by my standards.

I was assigned to the "Training Aids Division," which was in charge of cleaning blackboards, making coffee, taking care of projectors, and other support activities. My assignment there may be one reason why I never developed a taste for coffee until I had been out of the Navy almost twenty years; I made about fifteen pots of it a day. Coffee was what BNAO School ran on. While there I made friends with many of the officer candidates. They were called OCANs, for Officer Candidate Airman. While there they were paid the equivalent of an E-5, petty officer, second class. They had no rank as such, but we were told we had to treat them as though they were ensigns (paygrade O-1, the lowest grade of officer). I guess they needed the practice.

I figured I had it made here. The work was easy, and the people, for the most part, were not screamers and thrashers. I got over calling chiefs "sir" in about five minutes, and soon got to know most of the men I would be working with—Saas, a knife fighter; Valentine, a skinny chain smoker; Facemeyer, a pretty boy; and Young, a fairly sharp little guy who had his own Ford Mustang. There was also a pair of twins. They spent a lot of time looking longingly into each other's eyes and often were in the same bunk come reveille. We didn't think much of it as long as they stayed away from us. Another kid I got to know was Robert "Frenchie" LaPointe. Frenchie was from Maine and we got to know one another quite soon after I arrived at Pensacola.

BNAO School was about five miles from the barracks. We lived in the old, brick, two-story type built prior to World War II. The floors were concrete and they each had a long screened-in sunporch on the front. The showers were off to the end of each berthing area, and we had open berthing. Bunk beds. I had a bottom bunk in the corner—my favorite place. Most of the time the senior guys got the bottom bunk, but I happened to run across somebody who actually liked the top bunk, so I lucked out. Movies were twenty-five cents and the bus was free to anywhere on the base.

I was supposed to go to photography school there and always wondered why I wasn't assigned there right away when I left boot camp. For some reason I figured it was punishment for not going into the nuke program or becoming some other brain-intensive rating. My math was weak and I hated it on top of that, so I didn't think I would be able to hack anything that technical.

I would have to wait until May 1965 to start photo school. To pass the time I went to the education office and checked out all the books I would need to advance to petty officer, third class. I had not made airman (E-3) as yet.

The rate I was striking for was an aviation rating. Anyone "striking for" an aviation rating could be an airman recruit

(paygrade E-1), airman apprentice (E-2), or airman (E-3). From any of those paygrades (E-1 through E-3) one might become a designated striker, either by finishing the appropriate 'A' school, or by passing the test for petty officer, third class (paygrade E-4) but not making a high enough score to be advanced. While I was picking up the materials for the correspondence course for airman, I also grabbed the manual for photographer's mate. The rule was that you could take the test for airman (E-3) any time you thought you could pass it. If you passed, the command would keep your test scores on record and advance you automatically when you had enough time in grade. When I took the test I got a 90 percent, so I could then concentrate on studying for E-4, petty officer, third class. When I finished the courses for that paygrade, I went on and fulfilled the requirements for petty officer second (E-5) and petty officer, first class. By the time I put on my E-3 airman's stripes I had done all the courses up to and including photographer's mate first class, E-6. I guess that looked pretty good in my record. I really didn't have much else to do during the day when I wasn't busy. The senior people liked to see kids studying.

On weekends I would sometimes ride the bus into town. One of my friends was a quiet little guy named Brown, a hard guy to get into a conversation. For some reason he and I got along. Neither of us was a real woman-chaser although we would have relished the opportunity to snag one once in a while. We couldn't wear civilian clothes until we made E-4, and making seventy-two dollars a month didn't really allow us to demonstrate a high profile. Women seemed to like guys with cars and nice clothes. Good looks didn't go very far, except with the homosexuals who seemed to prey on young sailors. If you were hitchhiking back to the base after dark, it was about seven to one odds that the person offering you a ride would want something other than to help out a young seagoing pedestrian.

One of my duties was copying the OCANs' tests on the mimeograph machine for Evelyn, a civil service worker in charge of education and training. Evelyn made up the tests, then gave me the stencils. I would take her stencils, run off copies for her, and then staple them together. Any that I messed up went into the burn bag, which had to be taken out about once a week and burned in an incinerator down at Mainside because the tests were considered classified material. I gave some thought to enhancing my meager income by slipping the students copies of the tests, but figured one of them would be a snake and turn me in. That might have ended my naval career prematurely.

The command had inspections quite frequently. All of us had to look sharp in uniform and have neat haircuts. I was not old enough to grow a mustache, but if I had been, that was the only facial hair acceptable at the time.

We had to keep the buildings looking sharp. The administration building got a lot of foot traffic and the floors needed more work than the other building, which housed the break room and the Blue Angels' office. The team was gone most of the time putting on air shows throughout the world, but once in a while I got to meet some of them and they gave me posters, patches, and other souvenirs.

Although the buildings were old cement block and brick structures, both had linoleum-tile floors that took a tremendous shine if worked properly. We had large electric floor-buffers that required both hands to operate. One day I was busy buffing the floor. The machine I was using had a broken power switch and couldn't be turned off. You had to hang onto it with one hand, bend over and plug it in, and be ready to buff when it jumped to life. The things weighed about fifty pounds and were quite difficult to hang onto. On that particular morning I was working my way down the passageway in front of the administration office when I stretched the cord to the limit and the plug came out of the wall. Without a second thought, I moved it to the receptacle on the other side of the buffer. There was a horrible scream as I plugged it in. I turned and saw a young lieutenant doubled over on the floor. I had completely forgotten about the broken switch! When I plugged the machine in, the handle of the buffer had swung around and nailed the lieutenant right in the groin, and he was doubled over with the dry heaves. I got the hell out of there, and fast. When I came back the buffer was gone. By that afternoon we had a new one. When the incident happened I had been aghast, but as I related it to my buddies, the hilarity of the situation nearly overcame us.

On occasion some of us young enlisted guys had a chance to fly with the instructor pilots. They were old guys by our standards, and we welcomed the opportunity to go up in the old Beechcraft they used for training the OCANs. I even had a chance to fly with one of the last remaining enlisted pilots, Chief Johnson.

The Beechcrafts were affectionately known as Bug Smashers. I guess that was because they hated to fly very high. It took a lot of fuel to attain any altitude. One year, just about time for Christmas leaves to begin, a couple of pilots said that if enough of us were going to New York they would requisition a plane and fly us to some obscure naval air station there, where we could catch our connecting flights or buses. I took advantage of that and flew home. Nothing stands out in my mind about that flight except the fact that I almost froze my ass off in that old plane. I rode the Greyhound from New York City to home. One of the guys was from Jersey or some other densely populated place and made sure I didn't end up dead or lost in New York. We had to find our own way to get back to Florida, but the money the flight saved us was considerable. I had not planned on going home that Christmas. Once home, I looked Mary up and we spent some time together. As usual, her father was quite happy to see me. He treated me as though I were one of the family.

The rest of my time at BNAO School was quite bland. I avoided fights and got along with most of the people. I became friends with many of the instructors and students. Some nights I stood watch in the room where students were taught Morse code, running the machine that put out the coded messages at different rates. It was quite easy for me to learn code and I had nearly qualified for my amateur radio license before I went in the Navy. Those future backseat airplane drivers had to learn only five words per minute in order to qualify. I helped many a Naval and Marine Corps officer get up to speed and probably kept them in the program. For some reason, Morse code was a major stumbling block for some of them. One Marine captain could do anything except learn the code. I worked with him for several nights and even came in when I didn't have the duty. He finally learned his code. Although I never got any official thanks or recognition for it, I felt good, knowing I had helped somebody overcome an obstacle that didn't exist for me. I hoped that someday I would have the favor returned.

One of the men who worked at BNAO School was an EASCN, that is an Engineering Aide Surveyor, Constructionman. He was from Texas and a Seabee. He was proud of both, but I think he was afraid of water because I don't believe he ever took a shower. He had an armpit stink that would melt glass, and he was always rubbing himself. And he was crazy. One weekend I rode into town with him in his Ford convertible, and he drove like a wild man. He was around twenty-seven so we stopped and bought some beer. The next thing I knew we were heading across the Pensacola Bay Bridge at about 110 miles per hour. I was in the backseat and somebody else was riding shotgun. I was so goddamn scared I couldn't breathe. We made it to the other end of the bridge, slowed down, and immediately had a flat tire. As we rolled flop-flop into a nearby service station, we were stone cold sober. Never again. Anytime after that, if he offered me the chance to go to town with him, I found something better to do—like shine my shoes or make my rack.

I would have dribbled a basketball through a minefield blind-folded to get next to Pat Busby, the Wave in the CO's office, but she had a boyfriend who was a second class. She treated me like her little brother and I think she liked me as she would have a little brother. The other Wave in the office was accused of being a les-bian by someone who left a note to that effect in her typewriter. When she found it she broke down and cried. I thought that was cruel, and figured that whoever left the note did it because she wouldn't go out with him. I never asked her to go out because all I could do was take her to the club or go for a walk, and the next day I would have gotten the third degree about whether I had slept with her. In those days I was quite shy.

I used to go into town once a week, or less. Usually I walked around looking in store windows or listening to the sales pitch of one of those "all you need is your Navy ID card for credit here" types. I decided if I was going to be a photographer, then I needed a Nikon camera. So I found a camera store that would give credit to a serviceman and bought my first Nikon, a Pho-tomic FTN, and I took pictures of everything with it. I could get free film from guys at the base photo lab, but I paid for process-ing because I didn't know how easy it was to cumshaw[1] stuff.

One of the officers told me if I qualified in the ejection seat and high-altitude chamber I could possibly get a ride in a jet trainer and, when I got to my next duty station after school, those

1. A term that denotes trading stuff you don't own for something another per-son has but doesn't really own, like government property. The saying went: "What passes for cumshaw in the Navy would be considered grand larceny on the outside."

qualifications might help me get on aircrew status. The chief let me go one day. The chamber and ejection seat were at Mainside, across the street from the barracks. They strapped us into a real ejection seat mounted on a rail. Above us was some sort of pneumatic shock absorber. Under the seat was an explosive charge mounted inside a tube, which was inside another tube mounted to the seat. When you pulled the face curtain on the ejection seat, the explosive charge would fire and the outer tube would slide up the rails until holes in it let the gas escape. Then the shock absorber would quickly slow you down. All that took place in about one-tenth of a second. I could never remember going up the rail, only coming back down. After we successfully rode the rocket they gave us a card called the OMIAS card, pronounced "Oh, My Ass." In actuality, it was not my ass that suffered, it was my shoulders; I was quite tall for the seat and the headrest usually hit me between the shoulder blades.

The high-altitude chamber was a large steel compartment very much like a diving recompression chamber, except the door kept the pressure out, not in. Students sat along each side of the chamber. Hanging above each student's station was an oxygen mask. The purpose of this evolution was to show prospective air crewmen and pilots what happens when they are exposed to reduced levels of oxygen at high altitude.

We all filed into the chamber and sat down. The corpsman who ran the chamber told us to just breathe normally and he would take us up. We sat there looking at each other across the small distance between the two opposing benches and popped our ears by swallowing and yawning. The altimeter inside the chamber showed the altitude as we "climbed" toward the stratosphere. We stopped at fifteen thousand feet and sat for a few minutes. We noticed that we had to breathe faster to get the same results. The corpsman acting as the inside tender told us of the problems of hypoxia (lack of oxygen) and how it could affect the performance and even the lives of air crewmen. He told us to put on our masks and breathe normally, which we did. He put his own mask on and started reducing the pressure inside the chamber. A mist formed out of the air and coated us with a cold clammy layer of moisture. This was caused by the air being so thin that it would not hold water vapor any longer. As we reached something above twenty thousand feet, he told us to take off our masks two at a time, on opposite sides of the chamber, and play a game of patty-cake, slapping our hands on our knees, then slapping the hands of the person opposite, alternating back and forth in a particular pattern as he directed us. In a short time we were unable to perform the game and were on the verge of blacking out from hypoxia.

Then another couple would do it until we all had experienced the light-headedness brought on by lack of oxygen. Afterward we went higher, and pressure-breathing was demonstrated. This is used when you are so high in the atmosphere that you do not get enough oxygen even with a 100 percent flow so it has to be forced into your lungs, and that makes it difficult to exhale. By the time we were back "on the ground," we had a firm appreciation for what high altitude could do to us. The Navy demanded that oxygen be used in the daytime above fifteen thousand feet, and at night above ten thousand. The difference is based on the extra oxygen required for the vision cells of the eye to operate properly; the cones relied on during the day need less than the rods that supply night vision.

Dave Duchene and Ned Dentry, my boot camp buddies, were also stationed in Pensacola. However, I was out at Sherman Field, where we had our own chow hall, so sometimes I would see them on weekends when I ate at the Mainside chow hall near the barracks. Once in a while I would run across Ned at the club, though I did not go there very much.

I thought the food was better out at Sherman, so I sometimes took the base shuttle out there for something to do when I didn't have the duty. Pensacola Naval Air Station was a huge base and very beautiful, and I covered about every inch of it, either on foot or riding the base shuttles, which were like UPS delivery trucks with seats. One morning a few of us were standing in line to eat when a Marine drill sergeant walked up and asked us to stand aside. About that time a bus drove up and a group of Vietnamese troops got out and filed past us into the chow hall. I wondered, "What are those guys doing here?"

"They're being trained to fly here," somebody offered.

"I wonder how many of them are Viet Cong," I joked. Later on I heard they had found a couple who were just that.

I'd been told that you could get into the OCAN (Officer Candidate Airman) program with two years of college or the equivalent.

The equivalent was passing the college-level GED[2] test. I inquired about it and found I could sign up to take the test. Chief Butler let me have the time off to do it, so I went to the base education office and sat through it. I can't remember how well I did, but I know I passed it. I started the paperwork to become an OCAN, but about the time I got the paperwork done, the Navy issued a new directive that all NAVCADs (Naval Aviation Cadets) and OCANs were required to have at least a bachelor's degree. That took care of my first attempt to become an officer.

The time was drawing near when I would be transferred to NATTU (Naval Air Technical Training Unit) and attend photo school. I was eager to go. Cleaning blackboards and making coffee was getting pretty old. I was advanced to airman in March 1965, and the huge raise that went with it pushed my monthly pay to ninety-nine dollars. I'd made many short-term friends at BNAO School. The only one I have seen since then is Frenchie LaPointe, who lives somewhere in Maine and, last I heard, was working at a post office.

In May 1965, I checked out of BNAO School and signed in at the quarterdeck of NATTU, located about a half mile from the barracks where I had been living for nine months.

I was looking forward to finally being able to start what I considered to be my real Navy career. There was no doubt that I would enjoy being a Navy photographer, but I didn't have a clue what it would eventually involve.

---

2. The GED, or General Education Development test, was used in the military to give soldiers and sailors the equivalent of a high school diploma. The test I took was to give me the equivalent of two years of college.

CHAPTER FIVE

Photo School

I was assigned to a room on the second floor of barracks #698, a yellow, wooden, World War II barracks building directly across the street from a similar structure that housed NAVCADs. Every morning the cars would drive up one by one and sharply dressed Marine drill sergeants would get out. Most of them would walk around to the driver's side and kiss their wives good-bye, say a few words, and then walk briskly up the steps into the NAVCAD barracks. At that point each Marine became a screaming animal. We would hear them kicking trash cans over, upsetting lockers, and generally raising hell. At the end of the day it would be the reverse. The drill instructors would walk down the steps to the waiting cars, slide in on the passenger side, lean over, kiss their women, and the cars would drive off. I was amazed by the way they could make the personality shift so readily, but I could never imagine myself doing that type of work; I had too much of a sense of humor.

I shared my room in the barracks with three other guys. Dave Duchene was one of them. The other two were named Willis and Noyes. Noyes slept on the bottom rack on my side of the room and Willis had the bottom rack on the other side. They had checked in first, so had gotten first choice. I was the senior person after a skinny kid named Riley. But he flunked out of school in a matter of weeks and I became class leader.

Our lead instructor was PH1 (E-6) Art Giberson. His assistant was a PH2 (E-5) Berry. Both of them were very professional in their demeanor and the way they handled the class. There were twenty-one of us in the class, including five Waves or so, five Marines, and one Coast Guardsman. The rest of us were sailors.

Shortly after classes began I took the test for photographer's mate, third class (E-4). I ran through it in about one-third of the allotted time, but as I was walking back to school I was overcome with doubt about whether I had taken enough time and care answering the questions. I thought I had probably failed to make a high enough score to be advanced to PH3.

Photo school was not the most difficult in the aviation field, but the course of instruction was comparable to college courses in photography offered throughout the country. The main difference was, all we studied was photography.

The first piece of equipment we were issued was a four-by-five-inch view camera equipped with a fiberboard case that contained cut film holders and a lens shade. We were each issued a wooden tripod. The camera itself could not be used without the tripod. Our first project was to photograph a brick wall. The shot had to be properly exposed, in focus, and a certain number of bricks had to be in the frame. That required a great deal of manipulation of the camera back and forth; as you got closer, you had to refocus, and then the number of bricks would not be correct. The school issued us each one sheet of film on which to make that historic first photo. I managed to get mine done and not ruin the film, but many others got the shot, then screwed something up in processing their film. We "souped" our film in a tray instead of the stainless steel tanks we would use at photo labs after we left the school.

We were trained in portraiture, small parts photography, and photographing damaged equipment using painted light. This technique was very interesting. The camera was placed on a tripod and the aperture closed down nearly all the way, to about f/22 or f/32. Then the photographer would take a common household light bulb in a reflector-type fixture and "paint" the object with light, moving it around the whole while so there would be no "hot spots." The detail in the ensuing photograph was remarkable, and no shadows were visible. The technique was extremely useful in photographing cracks in turbine blades, defective electric motors, and items of that nature. The detail is incredible when properly done.

After a few weeks we were issued small-format cameras. In those days of roll film cameras, the Mamiya C-3 was the standard. Thirty-five millimeter film had not taken off as yet. The Mamiya took size 120 film and produced twelve shots per roll. That was almost like owning a machine gun compared with shooting the view camera's sheet film, which we had to load in the dark and then unload from the holders before processing. Our assignments with the 120 camera were more photojournalistic and we were assigned stories to illustrate. Photo students could be seen all over the base with their bulky Mamiya cameras, taking pictures of anything from men washing airplanes to mess cooks preparing meals.

The other two phases of the school were for motion pictures and aerial photography. During the motion picture phase—"mopic" we called it—we were issued the Bell and Howell 70 KRM camera, a spring-wound, turret lens, 16mm movie camera. Most of the American footage you see nowadays that was shot in World War II was taken with a B&H 70 KRM or the larger 35mm movie camera, the Bell and Howell Eyemo. The 70 KRM had a variable frame rate and took a standard hundred-foot roll of 16mm, double perforated film. It could also be fitted with an electric motor and a four-hundred-foot magazine, but we never used that setup in school. The lens was focused by looking through a tiny viewfinder on the side of the camera. To do this, the lens you wanted to focus was rotated to the position next to the viewfinder, then the lens focusing ring was turned until the view was sharp, then the turret was rotated back so the lens was in the shooting position. The procedure was quite awkward and, once we had some experience, except when using a wide aperture or telephoto lens, many of us guessed at the distance and that was usually close enough. The 70 KRM also came in a heavy case, and we still had the same bulky wooden tripods.

We were taught how to edit in the camera and how to tell a story using only a hundred feet of film, about three minutes' worth when shot at sound speed (twenty-four frames per second). There are forty frames in a foot of 16mm movie film, so the math wasn't hard to figure out. Even though we did not shoot sound, we shot the film at sound speed. The first couple of feet were devoted to "slating" the film. Each of us had a slate—a piece of cardboard with our name and class number and date on it. Most of us added the name of the production.

Surprisingly, many members of our class produced excellent little projects on that short length of black-and-white movie film.

During the aerial photography phase we were taught to lay out an aerial mosaic map from prints we made from negatives provided by the Photographer's Mate "B" School, whose students were petty officers advanced in their studies of naval photography.

They learned color photography, sound motion picture photography, and actually got to fly to take "aerials."

The trick in laying out a map of aerial photos is not to make any straight line cuts. Instead, you cut down the middle of winding roads, along the edges of fields, and so on. If you do it properly, when you stand back a little and look at the photo collage it is difficult to see the seams at all. The whole thing is stuck to a piece of Masonite with gum acacia.

Things went quite well in school for a while. Then we started having problems with one guy I'll call Smit. Always late to class, he didn't quite fall in with the rest of us, and some of the kids in the class started bitching about him. I had been riding Smit pretty hard to get him to straighten out, but he had been thrown out of school.

When studies weren't too difficult, many of us would go to the enlisted club and drink beer. We weren't old enough to drink real beer so we had "three-two" beer, 3.2 percent alcohol. Somehow we managed to get drunk even on that. One evening I was at the enlisted club and happened to go to the head. As I was finishing up, three men walked through the door—Smit, a black guy, and a Puerto Rican I didn't know.

"Is that the dude who's giving you all the shit?" one of them asked. Smit affirmed that it was.

"Why you giving my man Smit all the shit?" the black guy asked.

"I ain't giving anybody any shit," I answered.

He stepped a little closer and took a swing at me. I ducked it and hit him in the head with my right fist. I might as well have blown him a kiss. He launched a kick at my groin. I just twisted to one side, and the kick landed on the inside of my right thigh. I punched him in the inside of his thigh, on the leg he kicked me with. That hurt, and he dropped his guard a little. So I punched him hard in the throat, then I kicked him in the groin and he went down. During the scuffle my glasses got knocked off but I quickly retrieved them from behind one of the commodes. Smit and the Puerto Rican were helping the black guy up off the floor. He was still hanging onto his crotch and trying to get his breath.

I hauled ass out of the head and went out into an area of tables by the bar. The bar was outside the dance floor. I noticed Pat Busby, the Wave from BNAO School, sitting at a table with her boyfriend. She noticed my disheveled appearance and the footprint on my thigh and called out, "Steve, what happened to you?"

"I just got in a fight with a guy from the barracks. There's three of them and I imagine they will try to whip the dogshit out of me," I replied, nearly out of breath.

"Get out of here and go back to the barracks. Tell the other guys in your class and they'll help you. Just don't hang around here."

I headed out the door and ran back to the barracks. I had been running the obstacle course down by the Officers' Club and there was a cross-country course behind the barracks that the NAVCADs used. A couple of us ran that every night. It was mostly soft sand, so I was in shape. I doubted if any of those guys could have caught me.

I made it to the barracks in record time and woke up a few of the guys in the room next to mine. One of them, Jim Kerr, was a skinny guy from Pennsylvania. When he smoked, he tilted his head to the side and squinted one eye so the smoke wouldn't make his eye water. He told me that he and the boys would handle the situation. They told me to hit the rack and not to worry. Kerr slept that night with a Coke bottle under his pillow, as did the rest of us. Anybody coming into one of our rooms would get that in the head. Meanwhile some Marines in another room got wind of what was going on and offered their help. As it turned out, we all got a good night's sleep. Nothing happened at the barracks that night. Not so at the club.

After the black guy got his balls back down where they belonged, he had gone outside the club looking for me and started a fight with somebody of my description. But he screwed up royally: the guy he picked on was a street fighter from New York City who just leaned back, snapped an antenna off a car, and whipped the man's face into bloody hamburger. Then he drop-kicked him to his knees and left.

I was walking through the barracks the next morning, a Saturday, and as I passed by the black guy's room I looked in. He was lying in bed looking toward the door. He spotted me and said, "Hey man, sorry about last night." I said it was okay and to forget it. I don't think he ever found out who pounded him, but I wasn't going to tell. A few weeks later he was returning to the barracks when I had the duty and he came in without paying the cab driver. When the cabbie came to the master-at-arms shack to complain, I told him to pay the guy. He couldn't get his wallet out fast enough. So much for diplomacy. Sometimes fear works better.

Almost every afternoon some of us photo school students went to the outdoor pool located about one hundred yards from the barracks. We ran the confidence course through the sand and then came back and swam and dived off the board for two or three hours. After that, we'd go inside, change, and run to the chow hall. This was a distance of about three-quarters of a mile. I would have to say I was in pretty good shape at that time.

One of the instructors at photo school, E-8 Marine Sergeant Guzman, was a real hard-ass. He wanted his Marines to look boot camp all the time they were at school. Guzman had lived through the Bataan Death March during World War II and was 150 percent Marine. But I thought he was a bit on the chicken-shit side. If a Marine needed a haircut, he would give them a Sergeant Guzman "special," i.e., shave the offending Marine's head just as if he was at boot camp. I thought that was radical, so I suggested to my class that the next time he pulled this shit, we would take the bite out of it by all shaving our heads. Well, it was leadership. We did it, but it didn't go over well with the senior instructor. I was relieved as class leader and replaced by a Marine by the name of Kevin Dalrymple, a kid about six-feet-five.

Near the end of the school, recruiters came around from Underwater Demolition Team Replacement Training. Posters all over the base showed frogmen jumping out of helicopters into the water and being picked up by rope ladders, and things like that. I asked around to see if anybody besides me wanted to try out for UDT training. I managed to talk Frank Archuleta and Don Trimble into going with me. The rest all said we were crazy or had something else to do on Saturday morning, when the test was to be given. The three of us took our boondockers and swimming trunks and walked down to the Officers' Club near the beach, where we would meet the recruiters from UDT training.

We expected to find a lot of men there but we were the only ones trying out. We met a young, rugged-looking lieutenant, junior grade (O-2) by the name of Gerry Yocum and an old wizzled-up chief boatswain's mate named John Parrish. They explained the requirements. We had to run a mile-and-a-half in less than twelve minutes wearing long pants and boondockers, low-cut combat-type boots that all naval personnel wore with their work uniforms. The three of us started out. I came in second, just behind Trimble. I felt slow. Parrish, sucking on one of his two pipes, looked at his watch.

"Not bad," he remarked, looking at me through wrinkled, squinting eyes. "You been doing any running?"

"Mostly away from fights."

"Nothing wrong with that, son, you'll live longer that way."

I could tell he was serious. Later I learned he was one of the most decorated frogmen of World War II.

Then we had a three-hundred-yard swim using underwater recovery strokes, i.e., our hands couldn't break the surface. I knew I couldn't swim that well, but thought I could bull my way through it. I finished in just under the maximum time allowed. The PT (physical training) test nearly killed me. We had to do push-ups, sit-ups, squat thrusts, and pull-ups. I barely made the pull-ups and was so uncoordinated I had to stop and restart doing the squat thrusts. Frank and I passed the test. Trimble's swimming was a little slow, and the chief told him he could come back and take it again the next weekend. I figured we could work on that and get him up to speed. The guy could run and do PT, no problem.

The next weekend we went back to watch Don. He cranked through the test again from start to finish, and made it. Another sailor was there taking the test for the third time. His name was Dave Hyde. He couldn't even swim as well as Trimble. I asked him about his military background. He said he was a former Green Beret and had joined the Navy to get into underwater demolition. The next time I saw him was at SEAL Team Two several years later. Of those of us who tried out for UDT/R, Hyde was the only one who attended UDT/R training.

We still had to take a physical and oxygen-tolerance and pressure tests. The physical was no problem. We three went through that together and passed. Then the corpsman told us we had to take the pressure and oxygen-tolerance test. But Chief Parrish had told us that we would be given it when we got to Little Creek for training. I told that to the personnel officer, but he said that the requirement was right in the manual and that he was not going to submit our orders until we had taken the tests. The chief at the school called Panama City and talked to the master diver in charge of the recompression chamber. Then we got Chief Byrd, one of the few remaining enlisted pilots, to fly us to Panama City in a Beechcraft the school used to train aerial photographers.

But when we got there we found out we couldn't take the test without our medical records. Pretty discouraged, we flew back to NAS Pensacola.

A few days later I was called into the office and told there was a flight at 1300 if I could get our records. I went to class and told Frank Archuleta. At the time we were in the aerial phase of photography school and doing a performance test in which we had to process, dry, and print a roll of aerial film with a continuous paper contact printer. My film had been processed and I was waiting to dry it. Frank said he would dry my film if I would run down and get the records. I took off and ran the mile or so to medical to get our records. When I got back I was told that I had cheated on a performance test and the skipper wanted to see me in his office. I told him I was not cheating and thought somebody was out to screw me for something, that the charge was so stupid it was not worth his or my time. The skipper smiled and said that if he'd thought I was cheating I would not even have been called to his office. He just wanted to tell me that he understood my enthusiasm for UDT, but I had to pay attention to the business at hand. I asked him if we could still go to Panama City to take the test. "Under the conditions," he said, no. He said that I should try again when I got to my next duty station.

Photo school wasn't too rough. I was quite interested in the material I was being presented and photographer's mate is not one of the rates that require you to be a member of MENSA (even though I am) to be able to handle the studies. During the time I was there I spent some nights at the enlisted club or went to the movies. For the most part I didn't go into town; I didn't like going in uniform; I always felt like a clown wearing that uniform when I was trying to have a good time. It just labeled you as "queer bait" or an easy mark for any shop owner. We could keep civilian clothes off base, but most of us didn't bother to. I never did. The "locker clubs" were another way to rip off servicemen of money they could ill afford to spend.

A couple of weekends, Dave Duchene and I went out to Pensacola Beach. There was always somebody who had a car and we always offered to chip in for gas, so we usually didn't have to take the bus.

Dave was a pretty good guy. He was from El Paso, Texas, and used to tell me horror stories about going to Mexico and getting in awful fights with the Mexicans. He was half Indian and very rugged. I didn't need to find out how rugged.

One incident that left a bitter taste in my mouth and wallet comes to mind. I was class leader and we were taking up a collection to have a party. I had collected thirty-five dollars from people who would attend. The money was in my room, stashed in my locker. When I went to retrieve it to pay for the beer and food, it was gone. I thought I might have put it in my pants pocket or hidden it in the locker. No way. I couldn't find it. I knew Dave or Willis would not have taken it. Noyes on the other hand always seemed to have more money than the rest of us. I suspected he might have done it so I went to security. They checked Noyes out and he confessed to having taken it. He received brig time and a fine. Then I went to the yeoman who worked for the legal officer because I had read something in the UCMJ (Uniform Code of Military Justice) about reparations being made to people for damage and loss caused by servicemen. I felt that I should be able to recoup the money from Noyes through fines and loss of pay. The yeoman gave me a song and dance about that rule being for guys who went into town and tore up a bar or the like. I told him I didn't see a bit of difference; I'd been wronged and had suffered a loss. The fact that I was in the Navy should not make a bit of difference. But the yeoman got angry and told me that was how it was and not to bother him with the matter anymore. I think the lazy son of a bitch was afraid it would mean more work for him. I never got the money back. I also never again saw the guy who took it.

The night I discovered the loss of money, one of the Waves asked me to come to the Wave barracks (affectionately known as the Wave Cage) to help her with some of the more technical aspects of her studies. We were sitting in the lounge, where men were allowed to visit. She was across from me at the table. I was trying to help her with the homework. Every time I looked up at her she was not looking at the books, but at me. Then she started to rub my lower leg with her stockinged foot. What a dumb-ass I was. It was the first chance I'd had to get laid in almost a year, and with the best-looking Wave in the class, and I was so damned upset over losing thirty-five dollars that I couldn't even figure out what she was trying to tell me. Needless to say, I wore out more than one pair of shoes kicking myself in the ass for that. I think she probably told the other Waves I was a homosexual, which a lot of my class was. That took care of any future sexual activity at photo school.

One of the other Waves came up to me one day while I was eating lunch and asked me where I was from. I said Maine. "Don't they have any queers up there where you live?" she asked.

"I guess so. I didn't know any, though."

She looked around over her shoulder and back at me to make sure nobody was listening. "Well, about a third of the guys in this class are queer."

I must have looked surprised. "Really, who are they?" I asked. Then she started naming them. There was the class leader, who'd flunked out, a sailor, three of the Marines, the one Coast Guardsman, and a couple of others, including Smit.

I was amazed. I told her I didn't really care as long as they stayed away from me. She was always a good shit and never gave me any trouble about anything. We ended up being stationed in the same building some years later. She'd had a nose job and looked very good. She was half Italian and half Jewish and exhibited the best characteristics of both.

One of my "friends" in the class introduced me to a black ensign (O-1, equivalent of a second lieutenant) in the flight program. I went to his barracks with one of the guys at school, and we sat in his room and drank beer. He was a pretty nice guy and seemed squared away. I didn't realize it then, but they were checking me out to see if I was homosexual. I wasn't, but I was so goddamn naive I never figured out what it was they were doing. Later that ensign got the boot when they busted a lot of homosexuals. Too bad, I thought he was just another guy.

When we graduated, the top person in the class was Stephen Nichols, a graduate of Rochester Institute of Technology. I can't remember who two and three were, but I was number four in a class of about twenty. Considering how badly I had pissed off some of the instructors and officers, that wasn't bad.

When I got my orders they were to NAS Oceana, where I would be stationed in the photo lab. We were all buzzing about where we were going. Gary Sherman, Jim Kerr, and I would be stationed there together. They were good guys and I was glad to be stationed with them. One Wave I knew was going to NAS Norfolk, and the others were being spread out all over the place. I hoped I would see them again, but didn't know if I would. We had our tickets home and then to our new duty stations. We asked around to see if any of the instructors could tell us about Oceana. Everybody said it was a great place to be stationed, near Virginia Beach, Virginia. The summers there were outrageous and women were everywhere. That made at least two of us quite happy.

I went home for just a few days' leave. I wanted to save most of it for some special reason. I had no particular desire to go home; Mary was in college. It was September, and college was in full swing.

I flew to Boston, then took a Greyhound from there to Rockland. Then I hitched a ride home. My parents and sisters were glad to see me. My grandfather was happy that I had joined the Navy. I made the rounds to all my friends and had short visits to tell them about my ventures. I hadn't really done anything, but they wanted to hear about it anyway. Mary's parents, Roland and Iva, were probably the happiest of anybody to see me but, as I'd thought, Mary was away at Colby College and would not be coming home.

I didn't have a driver's license, but I could drive quite well, so I borrowed my father's station wagon and went there. Mary didn't know I was coming, so I just showed up and had her paged. Since she was going with somebody else, at first she acted like a real bitch, but we ended up playing kissy-face in the front seat of my father's Chevy wagon. On the way home from Colby, I fell asleep at the wheel and was about to run off the road when I ran over somebody's cat. The screech and *thud* snapped me wide awake and I had no problem remaining so the rest of the drive.

A few days later I was walking home from Rockland and a man I didn't know offered me a ride. He kept saying he had been drinking and didn't feel well and needed to pull over and puke. I told him to go ahead and pull over. He said he was worried about cops. I told him there weren't any cops around here. He insisted that he needed to pull off on some side road to puke. By that time I was not feeling very comfortable with him and was prepared to defend myself. Finally we were in South Thomaston when he made a left turn down Grierson Road, which led through a sparsely populated rural area. As he made the turn he asked me where it went. I said it just dead-ended back a little ways. He turned around and drove back almost to the beginning of the road. Then he pulled over, got out, and walked to the back of the car. I thought he was really going out to throw up. I glanced in the rearview mirror and could see him back there masturbating. He got back into the car with his dick in his hand. I told him I had to get home and would walk from here.

He reached across the seat after my crotch and said, "Ah, come on."

I grabbed his wrist, looked him in the eye, and said, "Buddy, I oughta rip your head off right here."

He said, "You want to try it?"

"You're damn right, right now!" I said and started to get out of the car.

He said, "Hey, I'm sorry. I'll give you a ride home, where do you live?"

I had him drive until we were about a quarter mile from where I lived, and I got out. He turned around and headed back toward Rockland. I walked the rest of the way home, getting madder and madder.

Here I was, a reasonably good-looking young guy of nineteen. I had all my teeth and wasn't fat or anything. There had to be something wrong with me. Maybe I was homosexual and didn't know it. Women wouldn't come near me, gays loved me. What the hell was the problem?

I was so damned mad that I was crying by the time I got home. My mother was awake when I walked through the door so I asked her why gay men always came after me, but I couldn't even get in a conversation with a good looking girl. She had no useful advice. I don't think she could relate to the problem. I will never know. When I left home to fly to Virginia that time, I had less than a good attitude about myself or anything else. Since I had no reason to hang around, I took a bus back to Boston and got on the first available plane to Norfolk.

CHAPTER SIX

Naval Air Station, Oceana

I arrived in Norfolk in the late evening. By the time I took a cab out to NAS Oceana it was around 2200. The Navy guard at the gate gave the cab driver directions to the quarterdeck and the cabbie found the right place the first time, so I didn't have to run all over hell's half acre to find the proper barracks. I was signed in at the OOD's office and the duty driver gave me and my gear a ride to the barracks. The master-at-arms assigned me a rack in one of the barracks bays and I went upstairs, padlocked the seabag to the leg of my rack, crawled in, and went to sleep.

The next morning I walked to the photo lab and checked in with Lt. (O-3) Fred Schmidt and Chief Photographer's Mate Montgomery. Both of them seemed quite glad to see me. Kerr and Sherman hadn't arrived yet. Apparently they were having more fun on leave than I was. A PH1 by the name of Donald Van Horn showed me around the lab. The place was immaculate. For the time being, I was assigned to the printing room. Each photographer had to be checked out in all aspects of naval photography. Some of the other guys there at the time were PH1 Hendricks, PH3 Butch Wendell, and PH3 Ed Gaulin. They welcomed me aboard and seemed to be decent fellows.

The individual crews were assigned to each task for a few weeks or months and then rotated. The print room was where our mistakes were the easiest to correct; we wouldn't ruin anything there. The worst we could do was scratch a negative or fog a box of paper. If a job wasn't up to snuff, we just reprinted it until it was right. Usually the print crew did other things to learn the whole operation. If there were no prints to make, I went out and dried prints, stamped them with the number of the negative they were made from, and put jobs away in big, brown, Navy-issue envelopes. Logging negatives was a job everybody hated. You sat there with a Rapidograph pen, writing numbers on negatives and then logging them in a green logbook by date and negative number. I guess that's where archives come from.

The aerial crew and the shooting crew had the best jobs but I was too new even to hope to get on the aerial crew. The crash crew was assigned from the day's duty roster. The crash phone was hooked directly from air operations to the photo lab. When it rang, it rang continuously until somebody answered it. When it was answered, the person on the other end described the crash situation. Usually the alert wasn't for a crash but for a plane with some in-flight emergency, such as stuck landing gear, an indicator light showing that the landing gear wasn't locked, or no hydraulic pressure in the brake system. One runway was equipped with midfield arresting gear. If a plane needed to stop quickly, the crash crew from the airfield fire station would go out and rig it for use. The midfield arresting gear was made up of a large steel cable, some old tires cut in half, and two great lengths of anchor chain.

The plane would come in with its tail hook down, catch the arresting cable sitting on the tire halves, and drag the chain down the runway. One man had to shoot this whole operation with a 16mm camera set at 128 frames per second while the other shot still photos in rapid succession with a small aerial camera that used a five-inch roll of film. It was pretty exciting to have a Phantom or Crusader blast by at over one hundred miles per hour. Sometimes a plane would blow a tire and lurch off the runway, or a wheel would break off and fly by, just missing the photographers. None of us ever got killed or hurt taking crash photos, but that wasn't our fault.

One day right after I returned from the chow hall, I heard a horrendous noise that sounded like a plane crash. It was. I looked out toward the field just as the crash phone started jangling. Somebody reached for the phone, and the crash crew, including me, even though I wasn't on the crew that day, headed for the truck with duty camera bags in hand. We raced out to the field to see the ambulance already ahead of us by a hundred yards. Debris was strewn all over the runway and pieces of an A-6A Intruder were lying off to the sides of the concrete strip. The corpsmen had already found the pilot, who had managed to eject at an angle as the plane was nearly on the ground. Apparently the pilot had passed his wing-check man, the man who made sure his wings are down and locked, but one of them wasn't. As he took off, the one that wasn't locked simply folded up and the plane rolled. He ejected and was driven along the runway, still in his ejection seat. He lived but was physically and administratively bound to a desk for the remainder of his Navy days. I was glad that we didn't have to shoot pictures of body parts. Sometimes others on the crew had had to shoot photos of heads in helmets and feet in boots.

Occasionally we would be called upon to photograph an auto wreck if Navy personnel were killed. In one case a guy had tried to blow up his wife and her boyfriend with dynamite. Seems this guy's wife had been having her boyfriend over while her husband had the duty. One day he told her he had the duty but sneaked back to the house, where he had laid up a pretty hefty charge of dynamite just under the bed in the crawl space below their bedroom. He waited until things got going, then cranked it off. Well, both of them were blown out of bed and toward the roof. The boyfriend, on top, had his head driven through the ceiling and broke his neck. The woman suffered only a broken leg and some bruises. A sheet of plywood under the mattress had shielded her from the blast as she nearly went into orbit. Her boyfriend absorbed the shock of her hitting the ceiling. I guess the husband went to prison for quite a while.

We had the duty every fourth day and every fourth weekend. If we caught the duty on one Friday night, that meant the following weekend we would have the duty all weekend. Sometimes we swapped so we would have it from Friday night right through Sunday. That way we got shafted all at once. I liked working at the lab at Oceana, one of my favorite duty stations the entire time I was in the Navy. The base was beautiful and clean and it was crawling with naval aviators who needed pictures of themselves and would take you flying in trade. I could get leather flight jackets and other cumshaw from the parachute loft. It's amazing what you can get for making a color portrait for somebody.

The Red Cross was always running blood drives, and the units offered us an afternoon off if we gave a pint of blood. I had never given blood before, so I thought maybe it would be a good thing for the Red Cross and for me. I went in and stuck out my arm. The nurse drew my blood and thanked me. As I walked through the door of the lab, one of the petty officers called my name.

"Waterman, grab a Leica and a couple rolls of film and go out to the field. Some asshole just ran a plane off into the weeds and we have to document it."

"What about my afternoon off?" I asked, already guessing the answer.

"Some other time."

I got into the truck and we drove out to the runway where the incident had occurred. Before I finished shooting, processing, and printing the film, it was late afternoon. On occasions I was so damned weak from giving blood, I thought I would have to take a little nap. I could imagine what it must be like to get wounded and lose more than a pint, and then have to run or try to get out of a bad situation.

While stationed at Oceana I had the chance to fly in various types of helicopters and propeller-driven planes. The only time I got to go up in a jet was when VF-11, The Red Rippers, had their fortieth reunion. They needed photographs taken from the backseat of a Phantom and I got the job. I took a Leica, two lenses, and a Kodak Ciné Special 16mm camera. The pilot I got to fly with was a lieutenant named, no kidding, Flack Logan. He was Lt. Carl Flack Logan, USN. He drove a Model T Ford pickup truck and flew F-4 Phantoms. He had flown in combat, was single, and the women loved him. The guys in the other plane were Charlie Iovino and Tom Brown. Tom, I think, was a former enlisted man who had graduated from the NAVCAD[1] program. He was the pilot while Charlie rode in the back as the RIO (Radar Intercept Officer). We took off side by side, and I wasn't wearing a G-harness. Flack told me I might black out a little when we rotated (left the runway) as he was going to do a maximum performance takeoff. Well, we rotated and he pointed that Phantom straight at the sky. I watched the ground fall away as we headed for the stratosphere. That was really something special. Then I looked out and saw Brown and Iovino go by us like we weren't moving. They had kicked in afterburners and zoomed past us like a rocket. So much for my high-performance takeoff. We flew around and Tom got in formation with an old FF-1 and an F6F Hellcat. It was very hard for them to get lined up in formation. The FF-1 was a World War I biplane and the F6F was a low-wing, high-performance fighter from World War II. The Phantom's stall speed was just about the FF-1's top end. He had his wheels down, his flaps

1. This was a program in which men of the necessary mental abilities who could pass the physical could apply to the flight program. If they had a college degree, they got their commissions upon graduation from preflight training; otherwise they got them when they earned their wings.

down, his speed brakes out, and everything except the canopy open so he could fly slowly. He was about falling out of the sky. Finally we had to get just ahead of them and to the side. Then Tom would fly by the two older aircraft as slowly as possible and I would shoot pictures. I shot some film of them with the movie camera and some stills with the Leica. Flack did a slow roll while I held the movie camera straight up. It would have been great footage except that when I took it back to the lab, Charlie Famuliner, a new guy from photo school, processed it for me while I did the still film. He didn't close the top of the developer tank properly in the processing machine and my film fogged. I was pretty angry, but there was nothing I could do about it. I didn't let him forget it for a long time. The stills came out fine and I got the cover shot on *Naval Aviation* magazine.

That same night I went to the Officers' Club and photographed the squadron party, during which some of the officers put on a skit about how the squadron insignia was conceived. Something about a gin-drinking, baloney-slinging, two-balled bastard—complete with visual aids. I guess by today's standards it would be considered sexist, but in those days everybody had a great time.

The pilots never seemed to treat enlisted men badly the way some of the "blackshoe" officers did. I guess it might have been because all their mechanics and parachute riggers were enlisted. Even the admiral was a nice guy. I got plenty to eat at the party and just enough to drink that I could still maintain some degree of professionalism as I shot dozens of photos. The next day I processed all the film, large-format four-by-five stuff. Before the day was over, I had made hundreds of prints for the aviators who were at the party. I did that on an unofficial basis, but Lt. Schmidt encouraged me to do it; he knew that down the road, somebody from the lab might need a favor.

I found out shortly after arriving at NAS Oceana that I would be advanced to PH3. That meant I could wear civilian clothes and live off base. By now Charlie Famuliner and I had become pretty good buddies. Charlie drove an old Triumph of some kind, a black-and-white convertible. When he was in high school and college, Charlie used to drive around Mr. Piper of Piper Aircraft as his chauffeur. He had about four years of college and was ready to go into the flight program. Charlie just about had his pilot's license, and he should have been a shoo-in for the NAVCAD program. He had passed the physical, the board, and all. A really intelligent guy who almost had his degree, Charlie was shut out by the Navy flight program when it stopped accepting all but college graduates.

Charlie and I were tired of living in the barracks so we moved off base into Al Schnoebelen's place. Al was a thirty-year-old surf bum who always had young girls hanging around. Al was a pretty decent guy. He'd never served in the military, but his father was a Navy dentist. Al had a surf shop, creatively named Al's Surf Shop, on the water at 19th and Atlantic in Virginia Beach. A lot of freaks and surf bums hung out there. Charlie and I rented the apartment above the surf shop in the off season.

I spent most of my time next door at Bill McLellan's dive shop, Maritime Explorations, Ltd. Bill was an ex-Army hardhat diver who had been through some special warfare training. The SEALs were relatively new back in 1965, having been commissioned in early 1962. Bill had been in what the Army had called the BRAT Team, Beach Reconnaissance Amphibious Team. They were hand-picked commando types, and were to be the Army's version of SEALs. Bill was a wiry, strong guy who could do fifty one-arm push-ups without any trouble. He had been stationed at Fort Eustis, near Newport News across the Hampton Bridge on the other side of Langley Air Force Base. He'd met his wife, Joyce, when he was in the Army. They had a girl named Julie, a cute little kid Bill really loved. Bill and Joyce eventually got divorced. A couple years later Bill found out he had MS. It didn't seem to affect him much, but he quit diving. He was a hell of a good guy and I enjoyed working with him. The first time I went off base to Virginia Beach, I discovered his shop about a block from the Trailways bus station. I was walking toward the beach on 19th Street and just ran right into it. Bill McLellan was about the only real friend I had in the Virginia Beach area. Charlie and I were friends, but I was really close to Bill. Bill was like the older brother I never had.

Charlie Famuliner and I had a real snake ranch up over Al's Surf Shop, except Charlie did most of the snake charming. Charlie could talk the skivvies off a nun. I couldn't have made out in a Chinese whorehouse with a truckload of rice. The place had two bedrooms and a bathroom. The kitchen and living room were separated by a bar, which got its share of use. Upon arising we might walk into the living room to find one of our friends, or even a total stranger, who had come by to attend one of our social functions and found themselves unable to navigate after an evening of too much fun.

I helped Bill train the first class of NOAA (National Oceanic and Atmospheric Administration) divers. SM1 (Signalman, First Class) Jack Kennedy, of UDT-21, worked with us that week. We both took some leave, and Bill paid us to help him run the course. Jack was from Miles City, Montana, and his father owned a major piece of Shell Oil. We asked him why he had joined the Navy and become a frogman. He didn't have a good answer, but I figured it had something to do with adventure.

We used to take the NOAA students out on the beach and run the hell out of them. Jack led the runs. Then we would do PT for a while. Out of eight guys who started the first class, five made it. The others just weren't cut out to be divers. They were either really out of shape, or claustrophobic ("clausty," as we called it). One member of the class, Joe Dropp, went on to become an admiral in NOAA. Not everyone was that successful; one of the others got killed in a bar by a jealous husband who hit him in the back of the head with a claw hammer.

Bill would take on diving jobs now and then and I always attempted to get time off from the Navy to help him. Money wasn't the driving force, it was the adventure and the chance to learn something. Until then I'd had no training of any kind in diving. I had dived with scuba before joining the Navy, but had no formal training, civilian or military. Bill had an old Mark V helmet and suit in his shop. He had hose and all the other necessary equipment. I think it was stuff he had "requisitioned" from the Army one dark night. Anyway, I used to take the helmet and breastplate down into the training tank out back of his shop. I'd shove a small air hose up under the thing so I would have a little trickle of air to keep the carbon dioxide down. When we had students in the tank, I could sit on the bottom of the tank and tell them what to do next. I would holler at them, and they heard me through the water. That was the extent of my experience with the Mark V. I really wanted to go to diving school.

Bill had a friend named Mike Ryan, who knew all sorts of people. Mike was an ex-Marine and he had a friend over on the YFNB-17, the Navy's diving school, where second class divers were trained in all aspects of air diving. They were also given some degree of training in salvage methods; second class divers do the bulk of the work in the diving Navy.

Mike set up an appointment for me to go over to YFNB-17 at the Destroyer & Submarine Piers (D&S Piers) in Norfolk and take an indoctrination dive and pressure and oxygen tolerance test. I took the bus over from Virginia Beach (YFNB-17 was later moved to Little Creek Naval Amphibious Base in Virginia). I found the hospital corpsman, Mike's friend. He and another diver suited me up. I walked down the ladder and they lowered me to the bottom of Norfolk Harbor. There was no visibility at all. Of course, by then I knew better than to expect any. They told me to look around and tell them what I saw. I felt around and told them I saw some mud and an old tire and some tin cans and cable and some other garbage. Then one of them asked me how far I could see. I said that I couldn't see anything I couldn't reach with my hands. He laughed over the communications box and asked me what the hell I meant by that. I told him I had my eyes closed and was just feeling around. If I opened them I just got confused. They hauled me up and I got back into my uniform. One of the men told me that I was the first guy they'd ever had go down and not complain about the low visibility. They also said I probably would make a good diver if I could ever get through the paperwork and get into school. Boy, did they call it right on that one! I thanked them and hitchhiked back to Oceana. The divers on the barge gave me a paper showing that I had passed the pressure and oxygen test and the indoctrination dive. I figured I had it made now, and would be able to get into UDT. Wrong! I got back to the base and told Lt. Schmidt that I had passed the indoctrination and oxygen tolerance test and wanted to go to UDT training. He started pacing back and forth, shouting.

"Waterman, I've had to suck just about a mile of cock to get some people into this lab, and they'd cut my balls off if I approved your chit."

I took that to mean "No."

Otherwise, things went along smoothly. Charlie and I went to take the test for second class photographer's mate (PH2) together. We blasted through it in record time. I had been advanced to PH3 on November 16, 1965. Charlie picked it up one month later. Now we wondered if we would make it at the same time. I had already done all my courses right up through chief, so all I had to do was study the manuals a little. At the time, about half the people who took the test failed it, and less than half of those who passed were advanced. It was spring of 1966 and we wouldn't know anything about advancements until late summer.

Of course, at that time the war in Vietnam was in full swing and Oceana was humming twenty-four hours a day. One of the many things we had to photograph was the return of fighter and bomber squadrons from deployment. It always sent a cold shudder through me when I heard the formations of jets coming over and looked up to see that they were flying the "missing man" formation. I knew then that one of the guys I had probably had a cold one with was not coming back. I thought about how I would never get to sit and listen to him tell flying stories and that his girlfriend or wife and kids would be missing him. It was a sad experience, but one that I became accustomed to. I didn't get over it, just got used to it. My old division officer from BNAO School, Lt. Dale Doss, ended up a guest of the North Vietnamese as a result of his incursion into their airspace. I saw him one day in the base gedunk (Naval Exchange snack bar) after he had come home and he looked like one of the people you see in pictures of Auschwitz.

Late in the summer, around August, word came down that both Charlie and I had made PH2. I would put it on October 16 and he, November 16. I guess I might have answered about one question correctly that he had missed. That was good news. I was still only twenty years old.

We never went to the clubs on base except to buy beer. The Acey-Deucy Club was on the other side of the base. To get there, you had to drive out the main gate, take a left, drive a mile or so, take another left, go another half mile, and turn left again. All that was there was the skydiving club, the package store, the Chief's Club, and the Acey-Deucy Club. The Acey-Deucy Club was for first and second class petty officers and their guests. As I always went in uniform, I was never carded; the clerks never imagined that I could be an E-5 and not be old enough to drink legally. Pabst Blue Ribbon was eighty-five cents a six-pack of sixteen-ouncers. We could afford that. The Navy gave us sixty-five dollars a month for BAQ (Basic Allowance for Quarters) and we drew nonaircrew flight pay once in a while if we got to fly. We also drew another thirty bucks or so for eating off base.

I loved to shoot aerial photos, but I had one bad experience. One Saturday morning when I had the duty, I asked Neil V.

"Mac" McDaniel if I could go flying. He told me to go ahead, no problem. So I went flying with a commander named Cumbie. While waiting for the plane to be cleared for use, I ate a fruit pie and drank a carton of milk. Later on the flight I got sick. It could have been airsickness, but I think the milk was bad. Anyway, I was lying on the floor of the Beechcraft vomiting out the doorway (the door was off so I could take aerials). When I was done throwing up, I just kept shooting pictures, construction-progress photos of the base where they were building a new hangar or some other structure. I didn't fly again for quite a while. Then, one day, I overheard Lt. Schmidt talking to one of the other photographers. He said something about not being able to send Waterman because he got sick and puked all over everything whenever he went up. I was furious and asked him where he had heard that. He said Commander Cumbie had told him, so I went over to air operations, where Cumbie was the air operations officer, and asked him about it. He kind of squirmed in his seat and admitted I was right. I was quite polite about it and asked him if he would please straighten out Lt. Schmidt. He said he would, and he did. I started flying again shortly after that.

On another occasion, before I had moved off base with Charlie, I caught the flu and started feeling really nauseous. I told the chief that I needed to go back to bed. He told me to go ahead and come back the next day. I started walking back to the barracks but as I was passing by the chow hall, I was overcome by extreme nausea. I was vomiting so hard I thought my eyeballs would come out. Tears streamed from my eyes and I was in a world of my own. I finally stopped to take another breath and wipe my mouth and eyes. As I slowly regained my vision I could see two sets of shoes, and pants leading to them, standing back on the roadway. I looked up. Two sailors were watching me.

"Holy shit buddy, what the hell did they have for chow?" one of them asked.

In spite of my extreme sickness, I had to laugh. I told them I had the flu and had just stopped there to throw up on my way back to the barracks.

One night when I had the duty, the regular phone rang. It was the duty officer at air operations. An F-8 had crashed in North Carolina that afternoon and they needed pictures. I asked the guy on duty with me if I could do the job. He told me to check with the chief and see if it was okay. I called Chief Montgomery at home and he said to do it. I called the operations duty officer back and got the details. They would be leaving by helicopter in about an hour and they wanted just black-and-white still coverage.

I grabbed a box of cut film and went into the film loading room and filled a couple dozen film holders. Then I picked out a few film packs as a backup. Film packs are a low-rent version of four-by-five film. They are composed of sixteen sheets of thin-cut film held together by tape and paper. As you shoot one, you pull the paper tab out of the cut film holder and the next one is pulled around in front. You tear the tab off and stuff it in your pocket or throw it away, depending on where you are. Processing them is a pain. You have to separate the paper from the film and be careful not to scratch the emulsion. It is not as easy to do as cut film.

I made sure the strobe battery was charged and the solenoid that fired the camera's shutter had a fresh battery. It was not far to the air operations building, so I walked. We loaded aboard a helicopter and flew to where the F-8 had crashed, near Murfreesboro. An old farmer had been standing on his porch smoking his pipe when all of a sudden a plane came straight at the ground. He said it hit so hard that full-grown trees were thrown end over end in the air.

We arrived on scene and walked to where the aircraft had drilled into the ground. The pilot (I think his name was Lt. Warner) had already been rescued by another helo. He had punched out at about twenty-five thousand feet and watched the plane go straight down through the cloud cover. He had been ferrying the plane to another base, just flying along, when he lost hydraulic pressure in the controls and the stick felt like it was mounted in concrete. The plane started a slow roll and he ejected. At twenty-five thousand feet the pilot does not come out of the ejection seat. The seat falls with the pilot still in it, and a small chute, called a drogue chute, is deployed. If the main canopy opened at that high speed and altitude, the canopy might be destroyed by the pilot's speed, or the pilot might die from oxygen deprivation, so the seat falls to about ten thousand feet under the small parachute and then the aneroid opening device shoots the seat away from the airman and deploys the main canopy. In the seat pack are some survival items, including a strobe light and emergency radio. The pilot had barely had time to Mayday before he bailed out, but a helicopter was on the way from Oceana almost before he had hit the ground. Once there, he called them on his survival radio and when they were close, he popped an MK-13 smoke flare. His only injury was a scratch on his face suffered when they pulled him up through the branches of a tree with the rescue sling.

It was much too dark to do any photography, so I crawled into the back of a truck that had come down with some of the ground crew and got some sleep. Next morning the old black farmer on whose land this thing had crashed served us up a big breakfast.

We walked into the woods where the plane had impacted and I saw a hole about the size of a two-thousand-gallon fuel tank. Pieces of aluminum were stuck in the trees all around and I found the pilot's knee board with his notepad still attached. The plane's impact had blown full-size trees out of the ground and upended them into the surrounding woods. There were actually pieces of the plane driven into the trees as far as twenty yards away. The investigators were probing the hole with long metal rods. The best estimate they had was that the plane was about seventy feet in the ground. The canopy was found in a field nearby and other items blown from the cockpit were found in the woods.

I shot photos of metal fragments stuck in the trees and other objects from the plane. The hole in the ground was so big I couldn't move back far enough to get it in one frame, so I shot a mosaic of it and pieced the shots together later on.

I don't believe they ever discovered what caused the crash, but they never got the plane out of the ground. It was this pilot's second ejection in a few months. When the other plane was recovered, it was found that the problem was entirely mechanical so they had no reason to believe the accident in North Carolina was pilot error. The pilot had a good flight record except for those two incidents. I loved this work.

When I got back and processed the photos, the chief got a phone call from the CO of the plane's squadron. He congratulated the chief on the quality of the work I had done. That did not hurt my reputation at all.

One day, out of boredom, I put in a chit to go to Vietnam. The chief looked at it and tore it up. "What the hell do you want to do something like that for? That place is a shithole. Sooner or later, you'll get to go if you just stay around long enough. Probably once you get over there, you'll wish you'd never seen the place."

I dropped the subject.

CHAPTER SEVEN

More Time at Oceana

As the summer of '66 drew on, Bill McLellan, from the dive shop, started working across the river in Portsmouth at Peck Iron and Metal, a huge scrap yard where old ships were cut up for scrap metal. Bill was working with Beldon Little. Beldon was famous in his own right as a book had been written about him, *Raising of the Queen,* by Jerry Korn. It told of how he and some others salvaged the stern section of the tanker *African Queen*, which had broken in two off the East Coast. With primitive equipment and almost no supplies, Beldon and the others managed to refloat the stern section of the vessel and tow it into Norfolk, where they sold the power plant to a foreign country. I checked out a copy of it from the base library and still have it today. I only wish I had had Beldon autograph it for me. At the time it didn't mean anything.

Bill asked me if I wanted to help try to raise a sunken dredge. It had been bought for scrap and, through neglect, sunk alongside the dock in a slip in the scrap yard. I said I would. Bill would let me use his gear and Beldon would pay me fifteen dollars a day. I didn't have any way to get to Peck, and no driver's license, but PH3 Don Marks at the lab had a Honda 310 motorcycle I could rent from him for three dollars a day. I didn't tell Don I had no license. So now I had a chance to clear twelve dollars a day as a salvage diver working under the famous Beldon Little.

The chief knew I had something going and let me off early because I would make it up some other way. I would have other guys cover for me and take their duty to pay them back. If it looked like we were going to get some work done and the weather was good, I took a couple of days' leave. It was a good arrangement and worked well for everybody. I never got stopped for driving without a license and Marks got his money when I got paid.

Irving Dennis was an uneducated black guy who worked for Beldon. He was right out of *Uncle Tom's Cabin*, but the nicest guy you'd ever want to meet. Since Dennis couldn't swim a stroke, Beldon trained him to be a tender. He was probably the best line tender I'd worked with then, or have worked with since. When diving "surface supplied," you could hardly tell he was on the other end of the hose. When you needed some slack or gave him a signal to hold a strain, he was right on the ball. Beldon always bought lunch: Beanie Weenies, Pepsi, sardines, and saltine crackers. Same thing every day. I liked the stuff. For entertainment Bill and I would get Dennis (we thought his first name was Dennis, so we always called him that) talking about his scars. He had one on his shoulder where he'd been knifed in a fight, and another on his calf, where his girlfriend shot him when she caught him fooling around on her. All in all he had some pretty wild stories. We enjoyed his company very much.

Initially we were working to find where the water was entering the sunken dredge; we had pumped with three or more big pumps but could never get ahead of the leakage. We worked all up and down the hull on the outside and found no leaks. Beldon got the idea that the water was probably coming in through the cutter head on the barge's dredging equipment. We could not get to that without going way down inside the dredge barge.

Diving on the dredge was just short of deadly. We were working inside the thing using Beldon's old compressor and a Jack Browne mask (open circuit, surface-supplied, free-flow mask). Sometimes we used scuba gear. We worked down two or three decks in total darkness with only a line to the surface. If anything had gone wrong we would still be there. One day when we were trying to move a large section of grating, we had no communications. Bill was on one end of it and I was on the other. We started to lift it and it got away from us. I jumped back and I guess Bill did, too. We heard the thing crash and bang as it fell into the pump room of the dredge. I was afraid Bill had gotten caught on it or something—that day he was diving the Jack Browne mask and I had the scuba, so he had a hose to worry about. I started to work over to where I knew he was when something grabbed me by the shoulder. It was Bill. We surfaced and laughed about the incident.

On and off we spent a couple of months working on that damned dredge. We pumped half of Hampton Roads through it and the most we ever lowered the water inside was about two feet. Finally Beldon gave up on it. But before that happened, I learned a lot about salvage work and how you can do about anything with almost nothing if you have ingenuity and common sense. Beldon was a master at jury-rigging. I would have worked for him free if I'd had to.

When I turned twenty, I had an insurance policy that came due. My grandfather had bought it for me when I was a baby. I had forgotten about it, but my mother wrote me and reminded me about it and said she needed money. She told me she wouldn't sign it off unless I gave her half of it. I figured that half of something was better than all of nothing, so I did. I had gone for my driver's license a little time before that. One of the guys let me take the test in his car and I passed.

I received four hundred dollars as my half of the insurance policy, borrowed another two hundred from my father, and headed to a local used-auto dealer to look for something I could afford. I found a Simca. I had never heard of Simca, but it looked like a good car and seemed to run okay. I bought it and insured it. Well, the day I bought the insurance, I was given a piece of paper stating that the coverage wouldn't go into effect until midnight that night. By nine that night I had rear-ended a lieutenant from New Jersey while driving up Atlantic Avenue. Bernie and Al from the surf shop were with me. I dented the chrome on his Ford Fairlane and totaled my Simca. The State of Virginia took my license for failure to have insurance (I could have fought it) and I was fined for following too closely. I was actually about half in the bag at the time, but the cop never bothered to push for that. I took the wrecked car to the dealer where I had bought it and he gave me two hundred dollars for it. I went down to Frank Ford Jewelers on Atlantic Avenue in Virginia Beach and bought a Rolex Submariner. That watch never got me into any trouble and I still have it.

Later that summer Bill had a diving job on the Catawba River in North Carolina. The C. S. Lenore Pipeline Company out of Texas needed somebody to put large concrete weights on a gas pipeline that ran across the river. Somebody had given them Bill's name. He didn't really want to do the job as he had recently learned that he had MS so he quoted them a high price. They asked when he could be there. He asked me if I could get time off to help him. I took some leave and we went down and did the job.

We took all the hardhat gear and I took my scuba gear with me. I made one dive in the Mark V and ended up doing the rest of the job in scuba. We made pretty good money and I got paid as soon as Bill did. Working with Bill McLellan was always fun.

Things were slack around the lab on occasion, so I would volunteer for things to do. One day somebody called and asked for a man to go down to the strafing range to help pick up spent 20mm shell casings. It was nice weather and the middle of the week, so I volunteered. We were loaded into the back of a couple of trucks full of fifty-five-gallon barrels with one end cut out. The ride to the range was about an hour long, and when we got there, all we had to do was walk around and pick up the brass from the strafing runs the fighter planes made over the targets. The only problem with that was the black widow spiders that liked to make their homes inside the empty shell casings. On occasion that made things kind of exciting, so we watched each other pretty closely in case one of the little shiny critters got on us. As we were riding back to the base, one crawled up the side of the face of the guy beside me. It didn't take him long to get rid of that.

Back at the beach, I used to drink at the Surf Rider near the easternmost end of Virginia Beach. Most of the people who hung out there were pilots, frogmen, schoolteachers who fooled around with the pilots and frogmen, and guys like me who had a little class and thought they might get some leftovers. Al, of the surf shop, had introduced Charlie and me to Jack Kennedy, a signalman, first class, who was stationed with Underwater Demolition Team Twenty-one. Jack was about the best-looking guy around. The women used to crawl all over him. I had seen him at parties where he could barely stand up and watched one of the hottest girls there walk up, grab him by the hand, and drag him upstairs to a bedroom. I felt (I hoped, I prayed) I might learn from him. I never did. On Saturday evenings a Dixieland jazz band played at the Surf Rider. The owner, Joe Weller, was an ex-Marine and treated the military patrons very well. He had to; in the winter that was all he had. The manager, Stu, was a good guy liked by everybody, but he ended up killing himself a few years later. They found him dead in his garage with the car running.

I had taken the test for PH2 in the early part of 1966. The results came back and I was advanced in the first increment. This would be October 16, 1966, eleven months after I had made

PH3. I was still not twenty-one and was over halfway up the rank structure. E-9 was as high as it went for enlisted. I had no illusions that it would be so easy all the way to E-9, but I didn't think it much of a challenge. I helped other sailors study for the tests, but some of them were just not cut out for taking tests. They would freeze up whenever a test was set in front of them. Charlie Famuliner and I made PH2 at the same time.

We could use Al's apartment only during the winter when Al was away somewhere. Al had married a woman called "Mouse." By my standards she was really nice. He had met her at the Surf Rider right after she had canned her husband.

I got tired of wearing glasses, so I went to an optometrist by the name of Kahn and told him I wanted contact lenses. Even though I wasn't twenty-one, he gave me credit. I did business with him until I left the area. Later, when I was in Vietnam, he mailed me a couple of spare pairs of lenses, which I had paid for with some of the traveler's checks I had left from my reenlistment bonus. Had I waited until I was in Vietnam to reenlist, I would have received ten thousand dollars tax-free. Missed again.

I had also decided I wanted to get into skydiving. The Navy had a club, Tidewater Navy Skydivers, that jumped over by the Acey-Deucy Club. It had been given an old building to use, where they packed parachutes. Most of the jumpers were from the UDT and SEAL teams. Lt. Cmdr. Joe Heinlein, the skipper of UDT-21, gave me my ground school, and Davy (Diamond Dave) Sutherland and Joe Hulse of Team-21 put me out on my first and second jumps. Some of the others there that I can remember were Tommy Sutherland (no relation to Davy), Dan "Mud" Zmuda, Dusty Rhodes, Bobby Stamey, Stan Janecka, Hershel Davis, Bud Thrift, and Ty Zellers. Cmdr. Norm "Stormin' Norman" Olson used to jump with us. He was quite a wild bastard, and a SEAL. He was one of the nicest guys there, always helping out the new guys and pulling strings to get us airplanes to jump from. But he had a bad temper and became enraged when little things didn't go right. I guess that's where he got his name. Ty Zellers had reenlisted in free fall. It had been fake because you really can't take an oath while you are falling at 120 miles per hour. They wrote him up in the base and local newspapers. Of course, he reenlisted for UDT training. Ty was an aviation electronics technician, third class. He ended up retiring from the Navy as an E-8 boatswain's mate. Quite a change for a techie type.

NAS Oceana was like home to me. I knew most everybody there and it was a friendly place. A new guy had checked in, Joe Leo, an Italian kid from New York. He was a good guy and we got along well. He and I would end up meeting again at other duty stations.

Another photographer, Neil V. "Mac" McDaniel, was from Clarksville, West Virginia. He was a tall, thin guy. I can't remember ever meeting his wife, but I am sure I did. He always said he had a bus ticket home in a picture frame on the wall of his house. If his wife didn't like it here, she could just take it and haul ass. I think he meant it. Mac had given me the nickname "Lurch" some time before, and there were people who actually thought it was my real last name.

One night when Mac and I had the duty, he brought in a fifth of bourbon. I hated bourbon, but I couldn't let that stop me from breaking the rules. It was Saturday night and nothing ever happened on Saturday night. On this particular night a civilian aircraft was making an approach to Norfolk Airport when the pilots realized their landing gear would not lock down. The tower routed them to NAS Oceana because we had the longest runways, the best crash crews, and could foam the runway. Well, the crash phone went off and we were both unconscious. When Mac finally woke up, the crash phone was ringing and men were pounding on the back door of the lab, the front door, and the window of the bunk room. I knew nothing of that until the next morning. Fortunately, nobody had realized we were drunk and we didn't get in any trouble over the incident, but we decided not to do it again. Mac's pictures actually came out. He had to take a few shots of the landing gear. The pilots had landed safely, or we might have had trouble on our hands. Mac eventually got out of the Navy and went to work for Eastman Kodak.

I don't remember if I went home for Christmas in 1966, but if I did, it doesn't stand out in my mind. I was still writing Mary once in a while, but she was in Colby College and on another planet.

In 1967 I moved into an apartment over a small garage in Virginia Beach across from the Trailways bus station. My roommate was a journalist from Dam Neck by the name of Adam Katala, a nerdy-looking character with thick glasses and a little mustache. We had a hell of a deal on rent. The place had two bed-rooms. You walked in the door, up the stairs, and the bathroom was dead ahead at the top of the stairs. To the left was his room and to the right was mine. The kitchen/living room was all one. We didn't have a television, as we didn't want one, nor could we afford one. We had a cheap stereo and a refrigerator and stove. It was not exactly a luxury operation, and the rent was about a hundred dollars a month. We didn't have to pay the utilities. The old woman who owned the place lived about a half block away. When I went to pay the rent I always made it a point to stay a few minutes and tell her how things were going. I wanted her to think we were really nice young men. Huh!

About February 1967 we got a new chief and a new photo of-ficer. The chief was a guy from New York who had spent a tour in England. He had a phony British accent. His name was McAffrey, and he drove a Deux Cheveaux, a tiny Citroen that looked like it was made from a tin roof. I think he paid about nine hundred dollars for it brand new. The photo officer was Warrant Officer Don "Bud" Sheehan. He was a pretty decent guy. He looked out for the enlisted man because he'd been one himself. Schmidt had retired. Before he did, though, he just about broke my arm taking advantage of the custom called "tacking on your crow." That in-volved punching the arm on the newly acquired arm insignia. I was sitting at the desk filling out the logbook with my left elbow resting on the desk. Schmidt came up and nailed me on the left arm. I nearly flew out of the chair. Talk about pain! I told him if it wasn't for the fact that he was an officer and probably could whip my ass anyway, I would have dropped him for that. He just laughed. He retired and went to work as the San Diego Zoo's photographer.

Those days I was hanging around with members of Under-water Demolition Teams Twenty-one and Twenty-two. A few of the guys were in SEAL Team Two, but they were usually de-ployed to Vietnam at that time. Virginia UDTs were sent to the Mediterranean, Puerto Rico, and St. Thomas. My buddy Jack Kennedy spent quite a lot of time hanging around the envi-ronment of 19th and Atlantic and we consumed a lot of beer together.

During the summers the Virginia Beach Police augmented their forces with college kids who worked as part-time cops. Some of them were law students and many of them visualized themselves as something more than just part-timers. Al always tried to get on their good side and many of them hung out at the shop when they were off duty. We knew we would be having parties, drinking on the sidewalk, and shooting off M-80 firecrackers and the like, so we wanted all the friends we could get. One afternoon Al and another couple of guys were standing out in front of the shop drinking beer when a summer cop came up and told them they would have to stop drinking on the sidewalk. Al just looked at him and grinned. The cop stepped a little closer to Al and then the other two guys grabbed the cop. Al pulled out the cop's handcuffs and they handcuffed him to a sign pole and hauled his pants and skivvies down around his ankles and left him there. Al got his ass chewed out for that and had to do some fast talking to keep from going to jail, but the story got a good laugh for quite a while around Virginia Beach.

The surf shop crowd used to cross Atlantic Avenue, the beach's main drag, to a coffeehouse where black singer Donald Leace performed. The backup was John Cyr, who was from Old Town, Maine. Leace was really good. Al, Charlie, Bernie, and the rest of us would go over there, but the place didn't stay open very long. Their not selling liquor might have had some role in their lack of success. There was not much room for war protesters in a town that depended greatly on the military for its economy.

On routine training flight operations one weekend, an A-6A crashed in the ocean off the Outer Banks and the Navy was going to send a diving vessel to salvage it. They needed to know what had caused it to crash. I got the job. I took a Super Speed Graphic, a strobe, and a whole case full of cut film and Grafmatic film holders. I had a total of fifty sheets of four-by-five film with me. We went aboard an ASR (Auxiliary, Submarine Rescue). They had a barge and tug along. This was my first exposure to Navy diving. I was just an Airedale puke photographer to those guys, but I felt like I was one of them. One guy went down in a Mark V but couldn't get anything accomplished. The tenders had to pull him up and send somebody else down who could do the job. The divers had to rig slings on the lift points of the aircraft, which was intact except for the engines. They had broken loose as the plane impacted the ocean. Apparently the A-6A ran out of fuel, the crew ejected, and the plane glided into the water, skipped along, and sank.

The divers got the A-6A Intruder rigged to be picked up. Before they moved it an underwater photographer from combat camera group had to go down and photograph all the switches in the cockpit. They wanted to see the position of the switches that controlled the fuel transfer pumps. The photographer, PH1 Frank Stitt, came up with the Nikonos he was using and told me to unload it and process the film. He trusted me. I put it in my bag where I was sure I would not lose it. When they brought the plane up, I took forty-nine pictures of it with my Speed Graphic. I went home with forty-nine perfect shots and one spare sheet of film. I processed Frank's film and gave it an extra 20 percent in the developer as he recommended. The shots came out quite good. As a result of the photographs Frank took, the pilot was canned; he had not transferred fuel from the wing tanks to the centerline tanks and therefore had starved the engines. By the time the problem was discovered and the engines were dying, fuel could not be transferred quickly enough. The plane had ten total hours on it since arriving brand new from Grumman Aircraft. The pilot would fly a desk for the remainder of his career.

It turned out that I knew Norm Zuchra, the bombardier navigator who had been flying with him that day. Norm was Polish, but we called him Zorba the Greek. He told us over beers that they were flying along a few hundred feet above the surf when it got real quiet. The pilot looked down at the panel and couldn't figure out what had happened. The engines had just died. Norm said he pointed up at the canopy with his hand and looked at the pilot. The pilot nodded his head. Norm ejected. The pilot punched out a few seconds later. Norm said he was preparing for a water landing with harness unhooked and his hand through his "G" harness and all that stuff they train you to do. He hit the water and it was about up to his knees. He disentangled himself from his parachute and walked up the beach, where a few kids were standing. One of them asked him where his plane was. He pointed at the water. He got out of his gear and walked over to help the pilot, who had hurt his hip when he landed on the beach. When he looked up, all the kids were gone. Norm walked over the sand dunes and didn't see a sign of them. After a while a helicopter from Oceana came and picked up the two downed aviators and flew them back to sick bay at Oceana for evaluation. The pilot suffered an injury to his hip, but it didn't matter; he wouldn't be flying again for the Navy. Bad for him, good for me: the event gave me a taste of Navy diving and renewed my interest in underwater photography.

A few weeks after that incident, I received surprise orders to Dam Neck, a base near Oceana. I would be assigned there as the public affairs photographer for the guided missile school. I would have preferred to go almost anywhere else in the whole Navy. To some it would be choice duty, but to me it was a shit detail. The photographer who held the billet at the time, PH1 Steve Rock, was getting transferred to an aircraft carrier photo lab and I was his replacement. He started to rub it in, as he knew how I hated public affairs photography.

I wanted to know how I had been selected. I thought somebody had put my name in the hat but that was not the case. I just happened to be up for transfer and the bases were very close to each other. A few days later Comdr. Jerry Pulley was visiting our photo lab. The commanding officer of Combat Camera Group, Pulley, had served in the Pacific as a combat photographer during World War II. He had been an enlisted man and still acted like one. Word was he always looked out for the troops. Everybody I ever met liked him. I asked him if they needed another underwater photographer at Combat Camera Group. He looked me up and down and asked me if I could swim. I told him I could. He looked over at Don Sheehan, the photo officer, and asked him, "Is this guy any good?" Sheehan smiled and winked at Commander Pulley and told him he had to kick me in the ass every once in a while, but I was good. Commander Pulley looked me in the eye and said, "Go ahead and put in for it, run it through me, and I'll put a little note with it."

I thought that would be the end of it. I had tried to go to UDT a couple of times while I was at NAS Oceana and they wouldn't hear of it. I figured this would be the same. If I could get into underwater photography, that would be a better deal. I could go anywhere with that and wouldn't have to bust my ass to go through the extremely rigorous UDT/R training. What a deal! I wrote up my request. Don Sheehan approved it. He said it didn't matter as I was going to be leaving for Dam Neck in a few weeks anyway. I ran it through my department head and the CO of the base, and then to Commander Pulley. They all approved it. Then it went to the Bureau of Personnel. After it went to Commander Pulley, I lost track of it. Meanwhile, I went to sick bay and traded some film for a diving physical. I wanted it in my record. I needed a waiver for my uncorrected eyesight in order to get into school. The requirements were "correctable to 20/30." I had 20/100 or worse, but it was correctable to 20/15, which was even better. The doctor passed me with no trouble and they filled out the paperwork to request the waiver.

My orders to Dam Neck arrived. I was allowed up to thirty days' leave between duty stations, but I chose just to go over and check in as I wanted to save my leave. The guided missile school at Dam Neck is part of the submarine Navy. And submariners are a different breed. They are just too damned serious all the time, and most of them have IQs so high they can't even hold a conversation with normal people.

I worked for a couple of old mustang (former enlisted) lieutenants and a Wave ensign. She was a short redheaded bitch who clearly felt superior to enlisted people.

One Saturday night I was in the Officers' Club at Fort Story, a local Army base, as the guest of an Army major who worked in intelligence and was one of the beach crowd. He was about thirty years old and liked to drink beer and chase women like the rest of us. I noticed the Wave ensign there that night. When I came back to work on Monday morning my division officer asked me why I had been at the Officers' Club. I explained that I had been the guest of an Army major who was a friend of mine. Even so he told me to stay out of the Officers' Club. I told him I didn't understand why a civilian could go to the club as the guest of an officer, but an enlisted person couldn't. He said that was just the way it was. I agreed that I wouldn't go there again, at least when I knew the redheaded bitch was there. He mumbled something else and I walked away. The incident really angered me and I began to realize how strong the military caste system is. But no bitch ensign was going to mess up my social life. I went there a few more times, but was careful to make sure she was not around.

I was stuck at Dam Neck and hated the place. It was where missile technicians were trained to fire Polaris missiles. Missile technicians and fire control technicians were crawling all over. The skipper, a captain named Gagliano, or something like that, ran the place. My job was to shoot pictures of "grips and grins," reenlistments, promotions, and attaboys as we called them. There was no lab at Dam Neck, so I had to do my processing at Oceana. I spent as much time there as I could.

I now had a second roommate at my apartment on the beach. Tom Hummer was a lieutenant in UDT-21 who had been "transferred" from the West Coast for riding his motorcycle around the porch of the BOQ (bachelor officers' quarters). He did some other stuff, too, but I guess that was what got him his transfer. Tom and the captain of the team, Bob Condon, didn't get along (Bob Condon was killed in Vietnam). I gave Tom my bedroom when he was not deployed and I slept on the couch. He needed the place only to store his stuff when he went on Mediterranean cruises and he was willing to pay the rent for that. He was gone most of the time and still paid a third of the rent, which was a pretty good deal for us.

The summer of 1967 I finally started figuring out what girls were for. I remember one instance when I was down at Tom's Donut Shop, which was really a restaurant. It had booths in the back and served the coldest beer in town. A barmaid there was about thirty. She seemed pretty friendly, so I asked her if she would like to come over to the house for a beer. She said she would. I didn't have any beer, so I told her I would go to the convenience store and meet her at my apartment. I ran about half a block, bought a six-pack of PBR, then walked the two blocks back to my place. She was already there. I opened a beer and offered her one. She said she really didn't want a beer and started taking her clothes off. It didn't take me too long to figure out what was going on.

Usually at parties, as soon as the schoolteachers and nurses found out I was an enlisted man, they turned their attention elsewhere. But one night Tom Hummer and I pulled a trick. He told them he was a boatswain's mate, third class and I told them I was a lieutenant. It worked. I seemed to get much more attention than he did, even though he looked like Ryan O'Neal and was in much better shape than I. After a while we told them the truth and neither of us made out that night. They were embarrassed to have fallen for that.

Finally my orders came. They read: Combat Camera via underwater swimmers school, Key West, Florida. There was only one catch: I had to wait for a replacement, which I guess was only fair. In a couple of weeks my replacement's orders arrived at GMS (guided missile school). He would arrive in mid-September, which meant I would be able to leave soon after that, depending on when the class at UWSS would begin. As soon as I knew I had orders to underwater swimmers school, I moved out of the apartment by the bus station and moved in with Chuck Conklin and Gene Gluhareff up on 86th Street at the beach. I needed the rent money I'd save. It was a two-bedroom place, but Gene's room had two beds. When he had his girlfriend over for the night I slept on the couch. Chuck had been in the teams, and was selling cars for Checkered Flag Motors; Gene was in UDT-21. Chuck was from Maine, but had stayed in the Tidewater area when he got out of the Navy. He was one of the guys who had dived on the SS *Lusitania* with John Light. I always thought he had been bullshitting about that until I saw it on television—there was Chuck.

We lived on 86th Street almost at the front gate of Fort Story so I had to catch rides or buses to get to work each morning. I didn't bother to get my license back; in my financial state, I had no use for one anyway. I couldn't afford a car.

I didn't have a girlfriend. In fact, the only one I ever had that I considered a girlfriend was Mary from Maine. The rest of them were just temporary. It wasn't that I didn't want one, I just wasn't able to find anybody to hang out with for more than a few hours.

Bill McLellan still owned the dive shop, but had moved his family out of the small apartment over the shop to a house out in one of the new housing developments. Bill gave me a key to his old apartment. He told me I could use it if I needed a place to sleep if I was stuck down at the beach. I had made friends with a girl whose mother owned the motel next door to the shop. She told me that the song "Jennifer Juniper" by Donovan was written about her friend Jennifer Juniper. I believed her. Her mother and I got along pretty well. Monica and I used to sneak upstairs into Bill's old apartment for evening entertainment, but I never saw her again after that summer. She wrote me a couple of times and once, when I was passing through D.C., on the way to Maine, with a buddy, I stopped to see her. She wasn't home, but I talked with her mother for a few minutes.

She was kind of a hippie type, although we never discussed her politics. I wasn't paying any attention to Vietnam yet. The only thing I saw of it was the guys returning from there at Oceana. Charlie and I used to go to the welcome-home parties in the hangars and shoot pictures of the aviators coming home and hugging their wives and so forth. We just gave them away or traded them for whatever we could get. I spent as much time as possible at the Oceana photo lab. There was some loose record-keeping of the materials I used, but they didn't really care. That's how it was in those days.

Once I found out I was going to swim school, I began to be extremely careful about my parachute landings. I certainly did not want to get injured and not be able to attend school. Especially after I had imposed on so many people who had helped me to get to Combat Camera Group.

The rule allows thirty days of leave between permanent changes of duty stations. Thirty-three days before I was due to check into swim school at Key West, I checked out of GMS, Dam Neck. I went back to the apartment on 86th Street, packed away the gear that I wouldn't need, and got everything ready that I would need in Key West. Then I went down to the beach and said good-bye to my friends. I took about two days' of leave, caught a ride to the airport, and flew to Key West. I would go home some other time. Chuck said I could keep my stuff at the apartment until I came back from underwater swimmers school. He and Gene had been through UWSS as part of their training with UDT/R. They called it underwater track school. They told me that all they did was run, swim, and do PT. Before it was over I would agree with them fully. I hoped I would be able to hack it. I hadn't been to any physically demanding schools as yet, and wondered about my endurance.

I had never been to Key West and seen only picture postcards of it that my great-grandmother had shown me when I was little. She had made the trip there when the railroad still ran down the Keys.

CHAPTER EIGHT

Underwater Swimmers School

I caught a cab from the Key West airport and the driver took me to the old sub base, where I signed in at the quarterdeck of U.S. Naval School, Underwater Swimmers. It was in the first week of October 1967, but my class wasn't due to start until November 4. When I handed my orders to the chief in personnel, he asked me why I was there so early. I told him I wanted to get in shape so I wouldn't have any trouble making it through. He looked me over and told me I would get in shape all right; I'd be a hell of a painter by the time class started. I said that where I came from I would consider painting outhouse walls a joyful change of pace. He glanced back down at my orders to see where I had come from, then grinned.

"I see what you mean," he said.

I guess I wasn't the only one to have an attitude about guided missile school. He told me to grab a rack in the east wing and put my stuff in a locker. The uniform at UWSS was swimming trunks, fatigue shirt, Marine Corps fatigue hat with rank insignia, and white tennis shoes. I liked it.

My bunk was on the bottom of a set of two-layer bunk beds in the east end of the bottom deck. Most of the guys there were UDT trainees or swim school staff. I remember Jimmy Glasscock slept in the top bunk of the next row. Another guy, Slator Blackiston III, had a reputation of being a wild man. He could do the dance of the flaming asshole[1] better than anybody.

One of the staff was John Kirby, an ENFA (Engineman Fireman Apprentice) who used to work out with the UDT trainees and then run on his own before and after work. He planned to go

---

1. A large handful of toilet paper is crammed between the cheeks of one's buttocks and then set on fire. The gyrations one has to perform to prevent burns is "The Dance of the Flaming Asshole."

to UDT training. Well, he did and eventually became command master chief petty officer of SEAL Team 2.

The first few days at UWSS were devoted to getting to know my way around. I met many of the instructors: Al Hale, Bill Wright, Steve Nash, and Joe Kaczmar, all West Coast frogmen. Most of the instructors were members of UDT teams or SEAL teams who were serving at UWSS for shore duty. In the Navy there are several different types of duty. The teams were considered sea duty because the men were always being deployed somewhere and subject to long periods away from home. Shore duty would be somewhere like Key West, where they had a nine-to-five job much like a civilian. Some of the instructors had pretty interesting backgrounds. One of them, Everett Owl, was a large American Indian who had a tattoo of an Indian chief on his arm. If all the Indians had been like this guy, there wouldn't be many white men living today. Chief Owl was a great guy and an outstanding instructor. We had a few little talks now and then, and he told me how he would do things if he could start over. I always liked to get the perspective from people who had been everywhere and done everything. You know, "BTDT," been there, done that. He advised me that explosive ordnance disposal (EOD) would be his choice if he were my age and had my mental makeup. I told him I was a photographer's mate being assigned as an underwater photographer to a combat camera group. He told me I probably wouldn't be able to do any better than that. If I wanted to serve with any outfit like SEAL team, UDT, or EOD, all I had to do was ask; they would love to have their activities documented by a Navy photographer. They got sick of civilians making films and doing stories about them when they didn't really know the full story or have a grip on the "big picture." Some of these civilians wanted to play the big bad role but didn't have a clue what the missions really were. They would get in the way and ask stupid questions. There really *are* stupid questions, no matter what anybody says.

One of the other instructors, Bruce Lisle, a first class diver, was a seventh degree black belt in karate. He had won the Japanese championships in karate a few years prior, and the Japanese were pretty upset when an American from the Navy beat up their best guy. He was bad. He used to train students at night in the school, including some of the UDT trainees and men from around the base. He beat on them harder after school than anything they had to put up with during the day. All of them had the utmost respect for Chief Lisle.

The commanding officer of the school, a redheaded lieutenant commander named Peter Willits, used to wander around the school holding his cat. Neither Willits nor his cat was liked very much. So some of the trainees captured his cat and put it in a clothes dryer with a cormorant they had captured. Needless to say, the cat suffered a lot of pain and Willits was out to can anybody who presented the slightest disciplinary problem. The members of that UDT class had to watch their asses very closely.

About a week or so after reporting for duty at UWSS, I went to a party with Ensign Rich Kuhn and Seaman Harry Hinckley. Hinckley was from Maine and I think he had dropped out of medical school to join the Navy. There was probably a draft board breathing down his neck, had I known the full story. Anyway, we three ended up at a party at somebody's house in Key West. We were the "clean-cut American boy" type and the girls liked us. I ended up going home with one. I told her I didn't want to go back to the base as it was late and I was pretty drunk. She said I could stay at her house and sleep on the couch. Of course, as soon as I got over to her house she dragged me into the bedroom, and I wasn't too reluctant. I got the impression she thought I was an officer. Except for Hinckley and me, all the other guys at the party were officers. Hinckley had about six years of college and used big words all the time, so they could have easily mistaken him for one. I had been hanging out with officers and people of superior intellect most of the time I had been in the Navy. My use of proper English was a dead giveaway that I might have some education.

In the morning before I left, she asked me how I liked the BOQ. I told her I lived in the barracks. She lost me on that, but at least she still had a real-live frogman on her hands—or so she thought. She asked me how I liked UDT training. Was it hard? I informed her I thought it was, but didn't know firsthand as I was not part of it. I was training to be an underwater photographer. That took care of future dates. She would never go out with me again. The secretary at the UWSS, Marlene, had a list of young available women for the officers to date. My date was on that list. So was a girl who had been with Harry that night. I don't think she ever went out with Harry again, either. Those honeys were just like the ones in Virginia Beach and the rest of the Navy towns throughout America, looking to marry an officer who would help them climb in social status and live happily ever after.

One of the guys in the UDT class, Rodney Wilkerson, had been kicked out of his training class for oversleeping. Apparently he had been out late and had a few too many drinks. When they weren't able to wake him in the morning, he missed muster. He and I were assigned to work together while the school decided whether to drop him from UDT training permanently. Wilkie and I did a lot of painting. One day we had to paint the buoyant escape tank in the school. There was a mermaid painted on one wall and seahorses and other underwater scenes on the other. We took turns painting because the fumes from the paint were very strong, but before the day was out we were both stoned out of our minds on the fumes. I don't know why we didn't die from that. We already knew we had brain damage or we wouldn't be at the school, so that was not a problem. After a while Wilkie got back with his class and eventually made it to the teams. He was later assigned to help train astronauts underwater in the space simulation tank in Huntsville, Alabama.

Wilkie claims he is the only man who has pissed on a man who has walked on the moon. He took a leak on Deke Slayton's leg while they were showering together after a training session. Slayton, who has the requisite sense of humor to be an astronaut, thought it was quite a riot.

After a month or so of painting and shit details, I started the course. The UDT class was about to graduate. One day there was a commotion in the recreation room on the first floor of the school. Somebody had been stealing chocolate milk out of the vending machine and the XO of the school, an old mustang[2] lieutenant we called Shaky Jake, was determined to find the thief and have him thrown out of school. He took fluorescent powder and dusted parts of the machine with it. Sure enough, the next time somebody stole milk, he brought out the black light to catch him. The first two guys he shined the light on were a couple of young kids, Bill Barth and Wellington (Duke) Leonard. They had to be the culprits. Their careers in naval special warfare were going to be abruptly halted by a vending machine theft. The black light clearly showed that they had been handling a fluores-

2. In the Navy, a mustang officer is one with prior enlisted service who came up through the ranks.

cent material. Their platoon officer, Kuhn, talked to the two men and they swore they were innocent. Rich believed them. He went in the back room and got a handful of baralyme dust, the barium hydroxide compound used to scrub carbon dioxide from the breathing gas in a mixed-gas (closed circuit) diving rig. He walked out into the recreation room and asked Shaky Jake to shine the ultraviolet light on the dust. It glowed brightly. Rich told Jake that all the men had been handling the stuff and that is why it showed up under the light. Jake didn't like that and threatened to throw the two sailors out anyway. Rich replied that if he did, the whole UDT training class would quit in protest. It would not look good if seventy-three of the Navy's finest young frogmen candidates quit a few days before graduating. Jake backed off and never did find out who had been stealing. That was my first taste of how frogmen and SEALs stick together in a bad situation.

My class finally started. It was made up of Marines going to Force Recon and men starting EOD school. There were only five enlisted in a class of more than twenty students. We were paired up according to our swimming ability. I had been practicing with fins and had bought a pair of Scubapro Jet Fins from HM1 Martin, a corpsman who ran a small dive shop out of sick bay. It turned out I was the fastest swimmer in the class. I could also hold my breath over two-and-a-half minutes underwater if I wasn't swimming. That impressed the instructors. My swim buddy was First Lieutenant Jones of the Marine Corps. He was a pretty good guy—for a Marine. Jones was a former enlisted man, so he was pretty sharp, all in all, and understood how things were supposed to work.

Of all the things we did in training, I liked the underwater relay races and the "town runs" the best. In the underwater relay races they would break us into two teams. One man from each team was given a Jack Browne[3] weight belt weighing about forty pounds, each man would jump into the water and run underwater to the other end of the pool, then hand the belt to the next guy in line, who jumped into the water and ran along the bottom of the pool to the other end. This continued until all the men had swapped ends. The winning team got to sit down and rest; the losing team was split in two and the halves had to compete with

3. The Jack Browne weight belt is about forty pounds and made of leather with lead ingots bolted to the belt. It has shoulder straps, also made of leather.

each other. Once again, the winning team could sit down and rest. Pretty soon it was down to two guys competing with each other. As soon as they finished, the rest of us had to get up and continue with whatever training evolution came next. That practice was called *"It pays to be a winner."* Nobody argued with that. Sometimes we swam with a fin in each hand and none on our feet. Other times we had a towel in each hand and it had to be slapped on the water each stroke when we swam the crawl. One day the instructors had us swim with a bucket in our hands. Lying on our backs on the edge of the pool with a face mask full of water, singing, and doing flutter kicks was always a lot of fun, too. It was hard to sing without having the water run up your nose and down your throat and start you coughing.

There was a Marine major in the class. Old, by our standards, and pretty hard-core, he wore a skinhead haircut and was always chewing tobacco or smoking a cigar. If he wasn't smoking it, he chewed it, even on the runs. I liked the guy, even though we all thought he was a bullshitter. He was about thirty-three and looked about fifty. His swim buddy was a little Marine private. They got along great.

On our final compass swim, which was the longest one and at night, the major, who had never had any trouble with his compass before, ended up swimming slightly off course and landed on the beach right in front of the Officers' Club. Another strange coincidence was that he just happened to have a twenty dollar bill stashed in his trunks. When the rest of us landed on the beach guided by the headlights of a truck, the major was nowhere to be found. After a few minutes he and his enlisted-Marine swim buddy came walking down the road with their tanks on their backs. Each had a beer in his hand and a shit-eating grin on his face. The instructors didn't get too upset over it, as I am sure most of them, being frogmen, had done the same or worse.

We practiced hull inspections and made free ascents from thirty feet in the harbor near the old submarine piers. This last maneuver was a safety thing in case we ran out of air. For our final qualifying deep dive we were taken offshore to a depth of 130 feet, where we would dive to the bottom, staying on a descending line, swim around for about ten minutes, and then surface. The instructors had us stop at ten feet for a safety decompression stop. Ray Gladding, an EOD man who was an instructor, was in charge of that evolution. He told us the story of a master diver, Chief Garlick, at the school who had saved the people inside a decompression chamber when a fire had started. Somehow he had vented the chamber quickly enough to keep the occupants from being incinerated. I believe he got an award for that. In all the other chamber fires I ever heard of, everybody was burned to a crisp in the high-oxygen-content atmosphere.

Less than half the members of our class were enlisted. Most of the officers were okay; they didn't pull any rank. All the instructors were enlisted so if they saw any student officers treating the enlisted trainees badly, they would cram it to them hard. One instructor, Pappy Hewitt, was about fifty years old. I was lying on my back doing flutter kicks one day, but not particularly enthusiastically, when Pappy Hewitt happened to run by. He stopped and looked down at me.

"How old are you, kid?" he asked.

"Twenty-one," I answered.

"How old is your father?" he asked.

"Forty-two."

"Shit, I'm over twice your age and older than your old man, and I can still run your ass off. Now put some ass behind it."

That made me a little humble. I was wearing tennis shoes, a T-shirt, and a pair of trunks. I was in good shape and that old chief could run me into the ground wearing combat boots. Pappy Hewitt was a legend in Key West.

One day a huge, fat hospital corpsman checked in. He said he was there to attend the school because he wanted to become a special operations technician (SOT). SOTs were corpsmen who operated with special-warfare types. They had to be well trained in diving medicine, field surgery, and other specialties conducive to performing emergency medicine in the field under combat conditions. The instructors took one look at the guy, Dick Wolf, and told him he didn't have a snowball's chance in hell of getting through the school in the shape he was in. He would have to lose over fifty pounds and get in better condition. Wolf told them he would do it if they would give him a chance. They wouldn't let him start the class he had been assigned to, but told him he could start the next one and just work out with the one he was supposed to be in. He agreed. He melted that weight off and got into excellent physical shape. When he had arrived at swim school he had had a bad attitude and was kind of a prick. As he got thinner his attitude improved until he was a pretty nice guy. He no longer started fights in town or bad-mouthed people. He finally graduated from the school and went to one of the teams. He was killed in Vietnam a few years later when hit in the head by a helicopter blade. At the time he was working with SEAL Team One.

We lost only two guys from our class. One of them was an enlisted guy who couldn't handle the academic part of the course and the other was a chief[4] who just couldn't keep up physically. The rest of us graduated in the first week of December 1967. I was the only photographer's mate. All the others went to their respective duty stations. The only ones I ever saw again were Lieutenants Dichiachio and Lashutka, who eventually were stationed at Fort Story, Virginia, when the Navy started stationing EOD teams there.

I graduated number four in the class. We left right after we received our diplomas. Some of us buddied up on cabs and headed out to the airport through the driving rain, typical for a fall day in Key West.

I boarded a plane to Norfolk and reported in at Combat Camera Group. I was really proud of that little black scuba diver patch on the right sleeve of my uniform. Anybody qualified as a diver was designated by a "(DV)" after their rank, so I was now PH2 (DV) Steve Waterman. Also, I was now a really special kind of guy, one of the elite, even more so than a frogman. I was a Navy underwater photographer, even though I had never taken a single underwater photograph in my life.

---

4. Chiefs (E-7) are also enlisted men. But they are also minor gods.

CHAPTER NINE

Combat Camera Group

I signed in at Atlantic Fleet Combat Camera Group (AFCCG). When I went to see the skipper, Commander Jerry Pulley, he gave me the usual greeting. He quickly walked out from behind his desk, reached out and grasped my hand, and shook it warmly while slapping me on the right shoulder. He kept shaking my hand for a few seconds and told me how glad he was to have me aboard. He was as enthusiastic about meeting me as anybody I have ever met. Jerry Pulley was the kind of guy I would never let down. He made you feel he was genuinely glad to see you, because he really was.

After I met the XO, Lt. Dick Wade, I went down and met the guys in the diving locker. PHC (Chief Photographers Mate) Dick Johnson was a rugged man about thirty-two years old. Six-foot-one with brown hair and a slight stoop to his shoulders, which I later found out was the result of milking cows at a very young age, he was a native of California and had recently been promoted to chief.

PH1 Ron Hamilton was a thin guy with a blond crew cut and glasses. He was not the typical robust swashbuckling sailor type, although he was one hell of a cameraman and I liked working with him. He had attended the naval cinematographer course at USC, as had Dick Johnson. One of the training films they'd worked on was with George Lucas when he was a student at USC. The production was called *THX-1138*, and it featured Dick as a character called Perfectbody. A number of other Navy photographers in it were attending the USC motion picture director's course. One of them, Dan Nachtsheim, worked in the editing section of Combat Camera Group. He had been the star of the film. All he did was run through the airport with a fearful look on his face as though trying to escape from a pursuer. From that first film, Lucas got a contract and made a release version of the film. It bombed, but he has come to the front since then and is now well-known in the moviemaking industry.

PH1 Dave Graver was more the typical sailor type, the kind of guy who was seriously under the impression that every woman wanted him, and badly. Dave was a pretty good underwater cameraman, and an all-around good hand with boats. We always got along well and went on many jobs together.

PH1 Art Cutter was getting ready to be transferred. He was a good man with a movie camera and had served on the DOD (Department of Defense) photo team in Vietnam. That made him popular with the old Korea and World War II veterans.

PH2 Howard Trotter was a fanatic for neatness and doing the job right. He was married to a younger woman and we used to kid him about that all the time.

PH2 Gus Kennedy was from out West and wore a belt buckle showing a bucking horse. He claimed he used to ride broncos. Gus gave me a belt buckle with a Mark V diver's helmet on it, as he didn't wear it. He was a good shipmate and would do anything for his friends. We got along well.

PH3 Bill Curtsinger was waiting to go to underwater swimmers school. Bill was a fairly skinny, blond, serious type. He was one of Jerry Pulley's favorites. The skipper saw a lot of potential in him. Bill could handle a Nikon. He could also hustle his rejects to magazines and photo agencies. In the Navy, when a photographer shoots pictures and sends Kodachrome off to the Naval Photographic Center for processing, NPC sends back the rejects. If he shoots enough film, which we all did, he gets a lot of great stuff that he can unload wherever. It wasn't exactly ethical, but we all did it when we could. Curtsinger was the king.

PH1 Frank Stitt, the underwater photographer I'd met on the A-6A job, was still in the diving locker, but he was due to transfer to some better deal on the West Coast that he had hustled. Frank was about six-foot-four and as "gaumy"[1] as they come. The rest of the crew started telling "Stitt stories" shortly after I arrived. There was the one about him trying to change lenses on a Nikonos camera while underwater. I couldn't believe anybody would do that, but I was convinced by them that it was true. One day he was sitting on a stool in the diving locker and had his feet

---

1. This is a Maine term that denotes one who is extremely uncoordinated. It has been used to describe me in my younger years.

stuck through the rungs. When he went to get up, his feet were trapped and he fell flat on his face on the tile floor. He was a damn good cinematographer and director. I think he went on to some civilian job and made good.

PH2 Harry Kulu, a native Hawaiian, was an excellent diver and photographer in and out of the water. Harry and I had the same measurements except for height. He was one rugged son of a bitch, broad of beam and not an ounce of fat. He had dropped out of school at a young age and that was a disadvantage to him when it came to getting promoted. His wife, Debbie, had a Ph.D. and taught college at Old Dominion University in Norfolk.

One night we were at the Stag Lounge in the Acey-Deucy Club at Norfolk Naval Air Station. Harry and I were indulging in some social beverages. After a while we rode out to his house on his Harley hog. Later on he went out for more beer and got a ticket for drunk driving. Harry would come up to a stoplight and forget to put his feet down. After two repetitions of this with a Virginia Beach cop following him, he got pulled over. The cop, who had a bike himself, told him he perfectly understood having a Hog fall over at a stoplight, but after the third time he just had to check him out.

Combat Camera Group was heaven for a photographer. We could sign out an Arriflex 16S motion picture camera and shoot "training film" on weekends. If you wanted to go diving for fun, you could take your gear and fill your tanks with the Navy compressor. To get film, you just went to the supply office and signed it out. There was a certain budget for training and plenty of film for it. We had a big responsibility to the archives, and the Navy wanted to insure that we were as good at our trade as possible.

After I had been at AFCCG a couple of days, Chief Johnson drove me down to the local dive shop and I was measured for my first custom-made quarter-inch wet suit. I also picked up my fins, mask, regulator, weight belt, life jacket, and other gear. The owner of the dive shop was Hyrum Mulliken, a retired Navy master diver. He had all the open-purchase Navy business in the area. The men from the teams got most of their open-purchase equipment there, too. Open-purchase items were things not in the Navy supply system, like wet suits, specialized clothing, and other products not purchased in large quantities. Our wet suits were all custom-made, so they could not be stock items. There was a list of Navy "approved" regulators, so we had to choose one on the list. I got what everybody else had so we could stock fewer spare parts.

Back at the unit, I was assigned a locker to keep all my gear in. The chief issued me my PT gear. He was a big one on physical fitness, and we had PT three days a week. Most of the time we went over to the gym, changed, went for a couple-mile run and then did PT for about a half hour. Sometimes we swam in the pool if it wasn't being used for training. There was a Dilbert Dunker at the pool, the device used to train pilots to escape from a downed aircraft that has landed in the water. The instructors strap a man into a device that looks like the cockpit of a plane. Then a brake is released and the Dunker runs down a track, crashes into the water, flips over, and sinks. When the safety diver taps the victim on the top of his helmet, he unstraps and pushes out of the cockpit to swim away and surface. We were surprised at how many flyers have a lot of trouble with that simple procedure. Marine pilots were the absolute worst; they tended to panic almost every time. We worked as safety divers a few times on the Dilbert Dunker, and when the Marines were training you could count on getting the regulator kicked out of your mouth at least a couple of times.

The first job I went on with AFCCG was back in Key West. The chief had finagled a job to train with the Naval Ordnance Unit at the naval station in Key West. An old mustang photo officer named Matson was going with us. He hadn't been a diver for years, but he was going along anyway. It was just a vacation for him and a chance to get back into the water, illegally.

The crew to Key West was Ron Hamilton, Dick Johnson, Dave Graver, Harry Kulu, Bill Curtsinger, and me. Bill would be staying behind at Key West, as his class at underwater swimmers school started before the job was over. Part of the assignment was to shoot film of some aquanauts from Canada, England, and Australia who were part of the SEALAB program. There was some sort of exchange program and Combat Camera Group had to document it. Although 90 percent of the filming would be done topside, we carried along all of our underwater gear so we could get in some training while there. Ron Hamilton and Dick Johnson were the guys with formal training in filmmaking. The rest of us just knew how to operate cameras and ended up being grips.[2]

2. The people who carry things around for the "real" cameramen.

The Navy graciously supplied a plane for our trip and we loaded all our gear on board. We had just taken delivery of some new 16mm Milliken DBM-5 and DBM-123 underwater motion picture cameras and were eager to try them out. They had a "water corrected" lens. That meant the front element of the lens was not in contact with the water, but the front port had a slight minus correction that made up for the magnification factor of the water. All it did was correct a little for the fact that water has a greater optical density than air. Topside, they did not shoot clear and sharp footage, but underwater they were good. The cameras were powered by rechargeable batteries and they had to be treated with care to prevent ruining them by overcharging. The DBM-5s would take a four-hundred-foot spool load and the DBM-123s took a two-hundred-foot spool load. The 5s had a Milliken movement, a movie camera mechanism that was all ball bearing or roller bearing movement. The things could be driven up to four hundred frames per second by changing the drive motor and the cam on the drive sprocket. We thought the 123s were mostly garbage, as they were nothing more than Bell & Howell Filmo mechanisms in a Rebikoff housing. Still, these 123s were better than what we had been using because they had internal rechargeable batteries and would shoot a whole load of film without having to be rewound or messed with in some other way. We also had a couple of Pegasus vehicles to test. They were also made by Dmitri Rebikoff. The Pegasus looked like a stainless steel torpedo with aircraft controls. The theory behind it was to mount a camera on one and use it for underwater mapping or some other purpose. The only thing I can think of that we did with them that actually benefited anybody was when we sold the old Yardney Silvercells back to Yardney for scrap silver and put the money into our slush fund. We used it to buy new swim trunks and have a party or two now and then. The Pegasus was a lot of fun to fly but I didn't think it had a practical use. Some UDT teams had them and I think they arrived at the same conclusion. It was a bitch to hang onto them as they flew through the water, and that alone wore you out. You could go about three knots, but if the water was cold, you cooled off too much with the movement through it. If you turned your head and your face mask was not on tight, it would be ripped off.

While in Key West we thought it would be nice if we could get some photos of hardhat divers at work. The divers at the Naval Ordnance Unit had some Mark V gear, the old standard Navy hardhat stuff, and agreed that it would be good to give them an excuse to dive it. They took us out and anchored their dive boat in about thirty feet of water. We took turns going down and shooting photos and film of them picking up rocks and putting them in a tool bag. This was just for effect, but the people at the Naval Photo Center in DC didn't care.[3]

Some divers at the Naval Ordnance Unit were avid spear fishermen. I never was much for shooting fish, except an occasional few for food, but I liked to tag along and shoot movies. One of the men, a first class petty officer named Nielsen, was a very good spear fisherman. So several of us took one of the larger boats out to where the good fishing was to spend the day shooting fish for the freezer. I was following Nielsen around as he dived down over a hundred feet to shoot grouper and snapper. I used up two sets of double-scuba air bottles. After I had used the last set and we were starting back to shore, I started figuring out how much bottom time I had against me and how little time I had spent on the surface between dives. Then it hit me that I had certainly gone way over the tables and most probably would get hit with decompression sickness. I started getting nervous and was expecting to experience numbness or some kind of paralysis in part of my body. The other divers were also concerned about me. I sat up on the foredeck and tried not to think about it. Pretty soon my right hip started aching like I had pulled a muscle. "This is it," I thought, "my first case of the bends."

By the time we got back to the dock it had gotten a little worse. It felt like a pulled muscle, or a sprain, but with no sign of relief no matter what position I moved into. It was a dull throbbing ache.

The divers drove me over to a submarine tender, the USS *Bushnell*, at the wharf near underwater swimmers school and we went aboard. Of course it was Friday, and payday to boot. How-

---

3. Twenty years later, when I was working as a commercial diver, one of the divers in the company showed me a picture of his uncle, who had been a Navy warrant officer and diver in EOD. It was a photograph I had taken back in 1968 at the Naval Ordnance Unit in Key West. Small world.

ever, the dive gang stayed around to treat this dumb bastard on a Table One A.[4] Their oxygen system was out of commission so the whole treatment was done on air alone. That meant my treatment took several hours before I was allowed out of the chamber. Then I had to sleep aboard the ship in sick bay for the night. I swore if I did something stupid like that again, at least I would have the decency to do it on a Monday morning and not on a Friday evening on payday. The crew had a pretty good sense of humor about it.

When we returned to Norfolk, I got word that I would be going to Little Creek to attend SERE School. SERE stands for survival, evasion, resistance, and escape. The school was designed to provide basic survival skills to those who might find themselves out in the boonies as a result of an aircraft accident or being shot down. It also included a mock prisoner of war camp.

Our first course was firearms training. We were loaded onto stake trucks and driven over to Dam Neck, right past guided missile school. I shuddered at the thought of being stationed there again. At the firing range, Marine firearms instructors with the help of our Navy instructors took us through the use of the M-16, M-60 machine gun, and the .50-caliber machine gun. We all got to fire the weapons and, for me, it was the first time I had fired any of them. Although I had been around guns all my life, I had never fired a machine gun. It was quite an experience.

After that phase, we had one day of booby-trap orientation. As we filed back into the classroom from lunch on this particular day, one of the instructors, standing outside the classroom door and sucking on a cigarette, said, "Be careful in there, fellas." He had a grin that went along with his warning. I knew what was next.

The class moved into the room, carefully looking around to see if they could detect any booby traps. Then someone threw an empty soda can into the trash and there was an explosion. It had been booby-trapped and a loud *bang* was the result. The booby traps were very small noisemakers, but they were effective in getting the point across.

For the survival and "camp" phase of the training we were bused to Camp A. P. Hill, some distance from Little Creek. After

4. The Table One A was the shortest treatment schedule for simple decompression sickness without supplemental oxygen. It lasted much longer than the oxygen tables, due to the effective partial pressure of oxygen in the breathing gas used during treatment.

the survival phase, came the "camp." A member of the staff, who called himself the "friendly partisan," was supposed to help us avoid being captured by the "bad guys," but he turned out to be one of the bad guys. During the "green," or survival phase, we had to build shelters. The friendly partisan came into our area where my group was camped and looked over the shelter we had built.

"I think you boys have built yourselves an 'Aw, shit,' " he said while spitting tobacco juice at his feet.

One of the guys asked him what that meant.

"You'll know when the time comes."

That night the shelter was so crowded that I slept on the ground in my sleeping bag a short distance away. About midnight I heard a crash as the sleeping platform collapsed.

"Aw, shit!" was the next thing I heard; after that we all fully understood what the friendly partisan had meant.

When we made our next move in the morning we had to cover some territory to get to a "safe" place. Of course the "bad guys" were waiting for us along the way.

We were all captured and interrogated. There was no food, only water, and you just about had to beg for that. The instructors (bad guys) had a mattress glued to the wall and they would bounce us off that until our teeth rattled while they were screaming at us and telling us we would be shot if we did not cooperate. The object was to get us to tell them certain things that we were not supposed to divulge. Hardly any of us talked. One of the men just wandering around the camp acting sort of neutral was a lieutenant by the name of José Taylor. He wore Navy jump wings on his uniform. At that time the SEAL insignia had not been developed so we all thought he was a SEAL. He just as well could have been a parachute rigger that had become jump qualified.

None of us died or got seriously injured in SERE School, and we were all happy to be going to Little Creek to graduate. I thought I had learned a lot in the school. The main thing I learned was that I would not eat rabbits and could go a long time, by my standards, without food. The instructors gave us one rabbit to kill and share, but I did not eat any of it. I could eat a snake, any kind of bird, frog, or rat, but, for some reason, not a rabbit.

The next goody waiting for me was a set of orders back to Little Creek for a two-week course in small craft operation. Harry Kulu and I were selected to attend. I was looking forward to it and thought it would be fun. We were trying to get some boats for the underwater photo team; often we had to operate boats on some jobs, so it followed that we should be checked out in them. I had already had some boat-handling experience before I joined the Navy, and Harry was from Hawaii and had spent a lot of time in and on the water before he enlisted so I guess we were the right ones to pick.

I moved to the barracks at Little Creek and walked back and forth to the school for that course. We were in the class with a lot of bosun's mates, enginemen, and other blackshoe[5] ratings. We were trained in the operation of small landing craft—LCVPs that were left over from World War II—the wooden type with a bow ramp that dropped to let personnel and small machinery off. Harry and I finished the class with a standing of number one and number two. Not bad for aviation types, especially considering that one of us did not even *start* high school let alone finish it. We got our diplomas and Harry gave me a ride (his wife rode his motorcycle to work) back to NAS Norfolk.

I was still living in the barracks, only about a hundred yards from Combat Camera Group, so it was convenient. I would be gone a lot but I wouldn't have to pay any rent while I was gone, as I would have if I lived off base. There are advantages to living on base, but damn few. One evening Gus Kennedy and I were at the petty officers' club on the base. We made friends with a couple of married women who were there without their husbands. Neither Gus nor I had a car, so we caught a ride with them to one of their apartments. The one I was after was black; she was much better looking than the white one Kennedy escorted. Both women's kids were home, asleep, and had been left alone while the women went out partying. I didn't think too much of that. Here we were, two horny sailors out looking for some strange at an E-8 chief's house with his wife and kids. It was the middle of the night and the weather was colder than a witch's tit. Gus and I started to sober up. Before very long, I looked over at Gus and he was looking back at me with that "You've got to be shitting me" look. He got the message. We said we had to get back and thanks for a great evening. We stumbled out and started walking toward the base.

There we were, two white boys in the heart of the black section of Norfolk. We'd heard stories about white guys being

5. Deck.

beaten up there just because of their color. But it was so damned cold that we were the only ones crazy enough to be outside that night. Finally we caught a cab and returned to the base.

Gus went straight to bed but I was hungry after all that exertion. I walked to the hall where they kept the gedunk[6] machines, and two white guys and a black guy were beating on one of them. I walked up and asked what the hell they were doing. One of them looked at me and said the goddamn machine had taken his money and he was going to fix it. I informed him in my quiet, subtle way that he was not going about it in an approved manner. He should write his name on a piece of paper and take it to the master-at-arms'[7] office. When the vendor came to fill the machine he would insure that he got his money back. In so many words, he told me to mind my own business. I reiterated my position and informed them that I ate most of my meals out of those machines and considered them almost like my mother, and that I would not take kindly to them beating on my mother. I then advised that I would kick the hell out of all three of them if they didn't leave the machines alone. At that, one of them pulled a knife. Not a large knife, but a knife. I looked at it and told him he would soon have it shoved up his ass unless he was either very good with it or threw it away. He threw it away and jumped me. I grabbed him and sunk my teeth into his throat in an attempt to rip out his jugular vein. Mind you, I was still pretty drunk and did not have the necessary force in my jaws to complete the task but he screamed anyway and jerked away from me. About that time the black guy jumped on my back and tried to choke me from behind. I reached back, grabbed him by the hair, shoved a thumb in his eye, twisted him, and got him in a headlock so that his body was behind me. I then ran his head into the brick wall of the barracks. That served its purpose and he was out of the fight. The other white guy chose to be a bystander and merely stepped on my glasses, which had fallen to the floor. He actually won the fight. Until then I had suffered no injury. But after his cowardly act, I was

6. A Navy term referring to any type of junk food or a place where hamburgers or quick food can be purchased.

7. The master-at-arms is the man in charge of the barracks. This job usually was rotated among people in the commands. We never had to do it as we were on sea duty. I don't know why that made a difference, except that we were subject to deployment.

nearly blind. The fighting was over and we all left.The gedunk machines were intact, and I got something to eat and went to bed.

The next morning Dave Graver took me aside and asked me what had happened in the barracks. He had heard that I tried to kill somebody. I told him that had been the general idea. There were three of them and only one of me. What else was I supposed to do? He told me that if I put in a chit, they would approve it and I could live off base and draw sixty-five dollars a month in BAQ (basic allowance for quarters). I thought it over for almost as long as it took me to find a pad of special request chits. I put the request in and it was approved. Chief Dick Johnson said I could move into his place and we'd split the rent. I could sleep in the living room. There was a couch, but it wasn't long enough for a person of my height, so I found a cot and a mattress somewhere. I took an old parachute and used that for a blanket.

The place was certainly not a palace. The rent was only forty dollars a month total, but in the winter the heat cost more than that; the wind blew right through it. The apartment was a small house over on Chesapeake Street in Ocean View. It was not very far outside the gate nearest the petty officers' club and it was about a half mile from the beach in Ocean View. At that time Ocean View was mostly a low-rent area. Dick had an old blue Buick he drove back and forth to work. At the time I didn't have a car or a driver's license so I had to depend on the goodwill and friendship of others.

Just before daylight one morning I was awakened by a loud crash when a drunk drove around the corner and slammed into Dick's car. The impact shoved it up on the sidewalk and nearly onto our front porch. The car was a total loss. After that we had to walk to work or to the base and catch the base shuttle, a pretty unreliable method of transportation. A week or so later Dick bought a big orange Harley motorcycle. It didn't have "buddy pegs" on it and he had only one helmet so I would ride it to the gate that was closer to combat camera, then get off and walk the rest of the way. That worked for a while until the Navy made a rule that motorcyclists in uniform had to wear a helmet. Then I'd catch rides with other guys who lived nearby, or start early and walk.

When I was in the Navy—before it became politically incorrect—there was a tendency for military personnel to drink maybe a little more than they do now. The men of Combat Camera Group were no exception. PH3 Jim Kerr, who I had been stationed with at Oceana, was now stationed at the NAS Norfolk photo lab, so we saw each other about every day when I was in town. The NAS photo lab shared the same building as combat camera, and we had use of its facilities for black-and-white and Ektachrome processing.

Dick and I decided that his place was no place for civilized people to live. We had two plates, two forks, one big spoon, a frying pan, and a saucepan. Dick had a stereo and a reel-to-reel tape deck. All I had were my clothes and my parachute. Neither of us owned a camera. We started to look for another place to live and finally found a brand-new upstairs apartment with two bedrooms, a kitchen, and a bathroom with a shower. And it was furnished. The rent was only $140 a month. The manager didn't mind renting to sailors, even single ones. It was within easy walking distance of the supermarket and not far from the main gate to the naval air station. With the assistance of a friend with a pickup truck, we moved our gear in.

While parachute-jumping in Suffolk, I made friends with Electronics Technician Wesley Boles. He was a tall, skinny, squirrel-faced kind of guy, very smart and from Texas, with the drawl to match. We had common interests in skydiving and women. He had a car, and we used to drive to Suffolk Airport on weekends and jump. I had started jumping again when I got back from underwater swimmers school and had bought a new parachute rig with a loan from the Navy federal credit union. It was a Paracommander in all the colors they made except olive drab. The pattern was called the Clown. There were only two of us around with that pattern. The other guy was from West Point, Virginia. His name was Acey Bryan and he used to come down to Suffolk on weekends once in a while to jump with us.

I also had a new type of reserve chute, a twenty-three-foot triconical in a Crossbow piggyback pack so that the entire affair could be worn on my back. With the piggyback arrangement the main ripcord was on your right (if you are right-handed) and the reserve ripcord was a little "panic handle" more like a triangular knob on the left. If there was a malfunction, you had to release your main chute using the Capewell quick-release buckles on the risers. The piggyback was rigged so that, as you fell away from your cutaway main parachute, one of the riser straps pulled the ripcord housing off the reserve chute, thus opening the reserve.

Before I had gone to UWSS I had made one last jump. Denny Morse, a chief machinery repairman and a Navy master diver, had jumpmastered on my third jump. I leaned over just before we reached jump altitude and told him I was scared shitless. He just gave me a shit-eating grin and said, "Fuck it."

I made the jump with no mishaps. Denny was a short, rugged guy in his early thirties. We became friends. He was stationed on board an ASR at the D&S Piers in Norfolk and, at the time, was one of the youngest master divers in the Navy. Back in 1964 he and three other divers had successfully salvaged the statue of Admiral Andrea Doria from the inside of the sunken vessel *Andrea Doria*. That was quite an accomplishment, given that the water was over two hundred feet deep and the entire operation, including blasting through the hull and hacksawing the statue out, was done on scuba gear with air as the breathing medium.

Wes Boles and I spent a lot of time drinking beer and chasing women. We also jumped out of airplanes a lot, nearly every weekend. Most of the time we went out to the DZ (drop zone) at the airport in Suffolk, Virginia. Once in a while we drove to somewhere like West Point, Virginia, or Roanoke Rapids, North Carolina, where a jump meet was taking place. One of the guys I met as a result of my parachute-jumping was supposedly the nephew of Vito Genovese of the New York Mafia. A great guy, he was nuts for military weapons and parachuting and had a hell of a sense of humor. He had never served in the military, but he had an ID card that said he was a lieutenant on active duty. I didn't ask him where he got it.

When Wes had the duty or was at sea, I rode out to the DZ with Frank. Frank kept a pet boa constrictor in his house and would go to the pet shop and order "two white mice to go" when it was time to feed the thing. Frank had a pilot's license and used to fly us when the other pilots didn't show up. The club owned a Cessna 180 taildragger, and it logged a lot of hours on weekends. Sometimes we would even go out during the week to make jumps if we could get enough people together who could get the time off.

Dick Johnson also had his pilot's license and he flew us now and then. He made a couple of parachute jumps, but preferred to fly. Later on he acquired his flight instructor's license and I took flying lessons from him.

Off and on we had underwater photo jobs at Andros in the Bahamas, where the Navy had a contract facility operated by RCA. At AUTEC (Atlantic Underseas Task and Evaluation Center) the torpedoes were tested by firing them from nuclear submarines. The water there was a thousand fathoms deep so the club on the base was the Thousand Fathom Club.

That particular job required us to do underwater motion picture photography of a Naval vessel as it passed overhead. Dick Johnson threw a crew together consisting of Harry Kulu, Bill Curtsinger, and me, and we flew to Andros for three days. The weather was nice and we had no mechanical problems with our gear.

Later that summer, Dick Johnson and I and a few topside photographers went aboard a small ship and headed up Chesapeake Bay to cover the testing of a fiberglass-hulled minesweeper. The idea was to fire a one-thousand-pound charge of HBX[8] at it sixty feet from the hull and sixty feet underwater. Dick and I were on-site to shoot photos and motion pictures of the exterior of the hull in the event a lot of damage was incurred. As the helicopter carrying the motion picture crew hovered over the scene, the shot was fired. The ensuing geyser of water came very close to knocking the chopper out of the sky. We thought it was pretty funny afterward, but the helo crew didn't appreciate our humor.

8. A very stable high explosive used by the military.

CHAPTER TEN

Panama City

When we got back from the Bahamas, Graver, Trotter, and I were sent to Panama City, Florida, to work with the SEALAB program doing underwater photography of the habitat and the aquanauts. Unfortunately, the weather became very windy so the work was canceled and the trip ended up becoming a drinking binge. We stayed at a small motel near Panama City and drove out to a large hotel on Panama Beach. Trotter and Graver started having the bartender slip 151-proof rum into my standard-issue rum and cokes. Before long I was pretty near out of it . . .

Sunken Barge "Salvage"

A week or so after we returned from Panama City, Dick arranged for us to go to Roosevelt Roads, Puerto Rico, for a few days' diving there. We could train and get some time in the water where it was clear. We loaded our gear in a pile, checked out some film, and made arrangements with squadron VRC-40 to fly us down. Usually there were a lot of cargo flights going back and forth to Puerto Rico, so it was not difficult to get a ride to and from the island.

When we got there we were settled into the barracks and had arranged to have a vehicle and some boat support. The chief got the word that a Navy fuel barge had sunk while being towed to San Juan. He asked me if I wanted to get some pictures of the salvage operation. I told him I'd love to, so I got my gear ready, grabbed a topside and an underwater still camera, and caught a boat to the salvage scene.

When I got there, two Navy ships, an ASR and an ARS, were rafted together. The ASR (auxiliary submarine rescue) had more qualified divers, mostly first class divers, and the ARS (auxiliary rescue & salvage ship) had a few, but they were mostly second class divers. Between the two ships over two dozen divers were capable of diving to the depth necessary to work on the barge. The water was warm and it was not the worst place to dive. The barge had been partially loaded with diesel oil and a tug was towing it up the coast to dock in San Juan. But a piece of plate had been missing in the hull above the waterline and the workers had replaced it with canvas and just painted it gray, so when they got under way, the canvas fell out, the water came in, and the barge sank. Now it was on the bottom in about seventy-five feet of water halfway between Roosevelt Roads and San Juan.

There was a Navy master diver on the scene, one of the cigarette-smoking, hard looking kind of Navy diver that I was familiar with. He didn't say much, but you better damn well listen when he did talk. Because of the "environmental considerations" of the salvage job, oil leaking out and all, there must have been a dozen commanders and above running around the ships who acted as if they knew something about salvage diving.

I asked the master diver if I could make a dive on the barge to get some photos. He told me to talk to the chief in the diving locker. I did, and soon I was all rigged up in my brown UDT swimming trunks, life vest, and a set of scuba gear. I had a Nikonos underwater camera and a dozen #5 flashbulbs stuck in a strip of rubber we used for carrying them. The chief told me just to follow the hose of one of the Jack Browne[1] divers working on the barge. I did that and arrived at the barge a few minutes later. The water was clear and the men were rigging salvage balloons[2] on the barge, chaining them to the bollards, then rigging air hoses to them. The barge was lying on edge. The plan also included putting air into the barge internally to float it to the surface. Theoretically, that would allow the crew to find and patch the holes before it sank again.

I shot up what film I could and used up all my flashbulbs. Then I returned to the surface and climbed the ladder. After I had

1. The Jack Browne rig is a full face mask that covers the mouth, eyes, and nose. It is fed by a hose from the surface and air freeflows into it. It apparently is named for its developer.
2. A salvage balloon is a large cylindrical, rubberized fabric bladder with a steel padeye in each end and fittings so that air can be injected into it. I believe the ones we had were rated for ten tons.

washed off the saltwater in the shower and dressed, I went out on deck. The master diver was standing with one foot up on a chock along the side of the ship, staring off into space with a cigarette in one hand and the other in his pocket.

"Hey, Chief," I said, "what's the plan?"

He looked me up and down a little before he spoke.

"Well, they are hooking lift balloons onto the thing and then they are gonna pump air into the hull and lift it to the surface. Why?"

"I don't want to piss you off or hurt your feelings, Chief, but I sure hope you ain't the one who came up with that scheme."

He looked around at me with one eye a little squinted.

"Why's that?"

"Well, it ain't gonna work, that's why."

"How come it ain't?" I was beginning to think I had strayed into forbidden territory.

"Well, they oughta be putting enough balloons on to almost lift the whole thing when they are full, and then winch it to the surface and let them blow off the excess air. That way it won't get away from them. They can put extra ones on to blow on the surface to keep it up here. The way they're doing it, it'll come up to the surface all right, but the air they blow inside the barge will rupture the internal bulkheads and the damn thing is just gonna go right back down and be harder to raise next try."

I thought I had pissed him off. He just looked at me for a few seconds. Then he took hold of my right arm and moved me a little so he could see the scuba patch sewn onto the right sleeve of my tropical white uniform.

"Okay, now let me get this straight. You're a scuba diver, I am a master diver, and we are the only two sons of bitches on this whole damned operation who know what the hell is going on. Why do you think that is?"

"Well, Chief, for one thing," I joked, "I don't own a slide rule and don't know how to use one. I just know what air does when it expands three times and it ain't got any place to go."

He smiled, "You're right, kid, but you ain't a commander and neither am I. I don't think either one of us has to worry about making admiral or pissing one off."

We stood watching the operation for a while. I didn't say anything more. It was a good feeling to be around somebody who had proved they had their act together. The master knew that no matter what he said or did, one of those hotshot diving salvage officers would come up with a better idea. He had committed himself to the fact they were going to shit and then fall back in it. It wouldn't make the difference of a piss hole in the snow to him or his diving career.

By late afternoon they had all the air hoses rigged and were ready to blow the thing up. Then somebody decided not to blow it until the next morning so they would have plenty of daylight to work in if they had any problems. We ate chow, watched a movie on the mess decks, then went to sleep. Due to the large number of people on board, they were out of racks, so I slept in the diving locker on some duffel bags with a blanket over me.

During the night I was awakened a couple of times by salvage balloons blasting to the surface. Apparently the divers had not secured them well and they had worked their way loose. Then they came rocketing upward as the air in them expanded and filled them to overflowing. Once they arrived at the surface, the balloons kept hissing out pressurized air like angry, round, black sea monsters.

We arose around 0600 the next morning, and everybody was eager to see how the thing would float. First the divers had to go down and reattach the balloons that had come loose. There had been no wind that night and it was easy for one of the ship's crew to go out in a boat and tie off the salvage balloons as they floated on the surface near the ship.

The first set of divers was able to get the balloons back in place. Apparently they had worked back and forth off the bitts where they'd been attached. That loosened the lashing that held the chains, allowing the chains to unwrap. Next time they used wire to secure the ends of the chains so they wouldn't come loose.

Then it was show time. All the men topside had cameras. I was standing beside the master at the rail. As they started the compressors to blow air into the balloons and the barge, he turned and winked at me. I just grinned back.

Before long there was some roiling of the water and then air bubbles appeared on the surface. That was a sign that the balloons were full and blowing off. Then a large mass of air bubbles and oil appeared. The barge was coming up. I hoped the corner of it did not hit the bottom of the ship, but I thought we were far enough away. One corner of the barge appeared on the surface and then another, then the flat surface of the bottom came up—it was upside down—then one balloon came off, and then another, then the barge lost upward momentum, hung there a few moments, and started to fill with water. One by one the tops of the salvage balloons disappeared as the barge dropped back to the bottom. The master just turned around and rolled his eyes.

A diver went back down to confirm that the barge had, in fact, landed on the bottom. Now it was flat on the bottom and that meant deeper water for the divers to work in, which cut down each diver's bottom time. Additionally, all the internal bulkheads had indeed been ruptured as a result of the trapped air expanding rapidly upon ascent.

I left that afternoon. I later learned that they finally sent some men down with explosives to blow the barge up and make it into a "fish sanctuary." The reason they gave for blowing it up was to insure that no fuel was trapped that would come leaking to the surface over time.

In the Azores

In late 1968 I had an underwater photo job in the Azores with PH1 Howard Trotter, PH1 Dave Graver, of Combat Camera Group, and Joe Gordon and Denny McLenny, both civilians from the Underwater Sound Lab out of Groton, Connecticut. Denny was the former PHC in charge of the diving locker at Atlantic Fleet Combat Camera Group. He was a gruff type of guy who really had a soft heart. Joe was a GS-13 civil servant. Originally from New York, he was all professional. We were going to be working with a black Navy master diver named Brown.[3]

The three of us caught a commercial flight out of Norfolk. After an uneventful, nearly empty flight to Lisbon, Portugal, we flew on an old DC-3 to Ponta Delgada in the Azores. It was one of those flights you occasionally hear about with chickens and goats on the plane. We touched down on a grass strip and caught a cab into town. We were supposed to catch the USS *Spiegel Grove*, an LSD (landing ship, dock) out of the Atlantic Gator Navy. It would not be in for a few days, so we had time to kill.

---

3. Master Diver "Bubba" Brown died a couple of years ago. He was a good man and will be missed by his friends and men who knew him in the diving Navy.

I spent some money on a couple of sweaters, and a local guy took me to one of the riding academies, where I was introduced to some Azorian honey about eighteen years old who was quite interested in my escudos (Portuguese money).

One morning the three of us were walking down the dock on the other side of the harbor when we saw a large sailing yacht flying an American flag. We walked closer to check it out. As we moved nearer we saw a man sitting in the cockpit reading a magazine. One of us called out that that was quite a boat and asked him if he was the owner. He replied he was the skipper and that the owner was ashore on business. We walked closer and struck up a conversation. His name was Walt Pikula, from Newport Beach, California. The boat, *Blackfin,* was brand new and had just been built in Bremerhaven, Germany. It was a sixty-five-foot aluminum ocean racing yacht, and the crew was taking it across the Atlantic and through the Panama Canal to California. Walt invited us aboard. It turned out that he was an ex-Navy diver and we had something in common. The owner, Ken Dumeuse, was an ex-Marine who had fought in Korea.

Walt offered us drinks and we started slamming down Beck's beer. Before long, Ken, the owner, came back and we met him. He turned out to be a genuinely nice guy and was not at all caught up in the fact that he was a multimillionaire. We drank some more beer and then he offered to take us to supper.

In that area of the Azores, dining out was not a great social event. If you could find a place to buy a roasted chicken and a gallon of cheap wine, you were in. That is exactly what happened to us. Ken, Dave, Howard, Walt, and the other two crew members, Germans from the shipyard where the boat was built, all made our way to a small outdoor restaurant and started eating chicken. Before long the drinking caught up with us. Dave Graver asked Ken if he had learned to eat glass while in the Marine Corps. Ken replied that he had not, but would be a most willing pupil if we would teach him. Well, Dave grabbed a wine glass and bit a chunk out of it and chewed it up. Ken asked to see it again, so Howard did it, then I. Before long Ken tried it. You would have thought he was the caveman who invented fire. I have never seen anyone so impressed by something he had learned. Especially something that cannot possibly have any socially redeeming value. At best you might not cut the hell out of your mouth or gums. Ken told us he was going to demonstrate this procedure at one of his wife's "stuffy social functions." We thought that to be about the most appropriate use for the skill and advised him to practice so as not to appear the least nervous. He should act as if eating glass was something he did every day.

We said good-bye at the restaurant and thanked him for the evening and the day's beer-drinking. When we got up the next day the *Blackfin* was gone.[4] They had offered to take us on as extra crew if we wanted to go. Before our job was over I wished I had gone with them.

In a few days the *Spiegel Grove* showed up at the pier, and we got out our uniforms and went aboard. Chief Bubba Brown was there. There were very few black divers and only two black master divers that we knew of. The other one, Carl Brashear, had lost one leg and was allowed to stay on active duty because of his good physical condition and determination. I personally knew that Carl Brashear was as sharp and knowledgeable as they come, as did many others.

I really made an impression on Bubba the first day I met him. Bubba and I were standing at the rail of the USS *Spiegel Grove*, and I hawked a lunger downwind toward the water but a vortex grabbed it, lifted it up, and hurled it on the front of Chief Brown's khaki shirt. He just looked at me and asked, "Been at sea long, Waterman?" as he wiped it off with his handkerchief.

"About an hour, Chief," was my only reply.

Our job in the Azores was to map out a section of the bottom off the island of Santa Maria in water shallower than one hundred feet. Beyond that, the submersible *Alvin* would chart the depths. Then the Navy would be installing a hydrophone system so it could hear Russian subs as they passed down the Atlantic. I had been told that my part of the job was not classified, but I got my ass chewed for talking about it in a bar one night. McLenny said I shouldn't tell people what we were doing. I let him know I was told it was unclassified. He said that they couldn't give it a classification as most of the people couldn't be cleared that high, so they just called it unclassified and "don't talk about it."

---

4. A couple of years later I was in the Beachcomber Bar in South Mission Beach, San Diego, and happened to be talking to a man wearing a T-shirt with a sailmaker's name on it. I asked him if he had heard of the *Blackfin*. He said he had and that Ken had been killed in a plane crash.

I never figured out his explanation, but I understood I was not to talk about our work.

Boatswain's Mate Seaman (BMSN) Bill Hooten was the coxswain who ran our dive boat. He was a high school dropout, but very intelligent. His brother was a doctor. Bill and I became buddies and one night we decided to go into town and drink some wine. Well, what we really wanted to do was get laid, but our second choice, due to the high percentage of Catholics and widows on Santa Maria, was get drunk. We ended up in a bar drinking with some EOD (explosive ordnance disposal) divers from the Portuguese minesweeper *St. Jorge*. They spoke minimal English and we spoke even less Portuguese, but as the night wore on we became unilingual. We were speaking Igboo, the universal language of drunks. It is a kind of mental telepathy accentuated with guttural sounds and much drooling. One who is not intoxicated cannot hope to enter into the conversation.

After consuming several bottles of Mateuse Rosé wine we thought it might be most appropriate to go to the airport bar, where we were sure we could hear a band and probably pick up some women. In our drunken state we imagined ourselves to be the very epitome of what any young Azorian woman would want to take home.

We caught a cab and headed for the airport. Expecting to be welcomed with open arms by all sorts of Portuguese sweeties, we sauntered into the lounge. Well, that's not at all what happened. The skipper of the ship was there with his all-purpose "follow him around from port to port" girlfriend from the States. He was a naval aviator serving as skipper of a Gator freighter to get his ticket punched for bigger and better things. I have forgotten his name, but he was a decent kind of guy.

I asked his woman to dance with me, which she did quite readily, as I was very cute and had a nice ass in those days. We danced a few times and I felt I might be getting out of line a little. The executive officer was also there. He took himself a mite on the serious side and, by my standards, tried to be too military.

Bill and I made up our fogged minds that it was time to leave. We had to get back to the ship. During our time at the airport lounge we didn't let the fact that we were already almost ossified deter us in the least from consuming more wine. Before we left, I was determined to have a souvenir of our trip to the airport lounge. Each table had a beautiful embroidered tablecloth on it, which had to be the work of one of the many old, bent, black-clad widows who occupied the island. They probably just sat around all day missing their dead husbands and embroidering. I casually wadded one up and shoved it down the front of my pants.

When we went out the door we didn't have a clue as to how we were going to get back to the pier. It was about midnight and we knew that the last boat left at 0100. We thought it would be appropriate if we stole the XO's VW bus and we looked in it, but the keys were gone.

"What the hell," we thought, "we can just push it and coast down to the dock. It's only four or five miles."

Wrong. Bill jumped into the driver's seat and I opened the passenger door and started pushing against the door frame. This way I would be able to jump into the seat as soon as the bus started rolling. We made it down the first hill and had enough momentum to get over the one that followed. But when we arrived at the bottom of the valley between the second and the third, we lost momentum and found ourselves trapped between two hills. We got out and pushed the van to the side of the road and started walking toward the pier. By then we were so drunk that I walked on one side of the road and Bill walked on the other. We had trouble just tracking straight down the sides of the road.

It took us until nearly 0200 to get back to the dock. We had missed the last liberty boat and were officially AWOL, or "over the hill" as it was called. I had never had that happen to me before and expected to be shot, or worse.

"Aw, the hell with it," I said. "Let's swim back to the ship. It's only about a mile or so."

Bill wasn't too excited about the prospect and advised me that he was not a great swimmer. I told him I would make sure he made it and swim right alongside him in case he got into trouble. We took off our hats and shoes, tied our shoes to the back of our belts, and stuck our whitehats inside the waistband of our trousers. Then we waded down the stone steps of the dock and into the warm water of the midatlantic.

We had gone about two hundred feet when Bill told me he didn't think he could swim that far. I didn't encourage him to try as I felt he would probably not make it if I pushed him. Even in my drunken state I had a little sense left. I escorted him back to the stone wharf and he climbed out and sat on a bollard. I turned back toward the small well-lit shape of the *Spiegel Grove*. She was the ship farthest out in the harbor. Later I would estimate it to be nearly two miles from the dock.

I started swimming and things were going well. The water was comfortably warm and the seas were calm. I breaststroked for a while, then sidestroked. Every so often I would lie on my back and float for a little breather. Finally I started getting tired. Not dead-dog tired, but just a little tired. I thought it would be nice to have a place to lie down and take a nap for a few minutes before continuing the swim. The only thing nearby was a large yellow buoy used for off-loading tankers in the harbor. I attempted to scale the side of it to no avail. It was not designed to be climbed onto from the water. I gave up this idea in short fashion and continued toward the ship. About a half mile farther I discerned the outline of the *St. Jorge*, the Portuguese minesweeper.

"Aha!" I thought to myself. "I'll sneak aboard and steal one of their life rings with the name of the ship on it and keep it as a souvenir."

Brilliant idea. I quietly swam around the ship looking for a place to climb aboard. My only chance would be to climb the anchor chain and slip up over the foredeck. I started climbing the chain and had reached the hawse pipe where the chain goes through the forward bulwarks. I was about to reach over the bulwarks for a handhold to climb onto the deck when I heard voices.

"What the hell is going on?" I thought. "Shit, these guys are getting under way." Then I realized the chain was slowly being drawn up into the hawse pipe. I did a back flip off the chain and dived headfirst into the water. I breaststroked underwater as far as I could to get out of pistol range of these guys. I imagined that they were armed with .45s at the very least and were not especially good shots. They never fired and all I heard was a bunch of Portuguese shouting and some commotion on deck. I repeated my evasive swimming maneuvers until I was well away from the vessel. I lay on my back with just my face above water to catch my breath. In a couple of minutes I started swimming for the *Spiegel Grove* again.

Suddenly somebody called out "Waterman!" I didn't recognize the voice, but I figured it had to be one of the good guys. I looked back toward the shore and saw the liberty boat coming toward me. I could just make out the green glow of the starboard running light reflecting in the water. By then the wind had started to pick up and there was a slight chop forming in the harbor. I raised an arm and they easily spotted the white sleeve against the blackness of the water.

The boat approached, and two sailors grabbed me by the arms and dragged me headfirst out of the water and onto the boat. Bill Hooten was standing there grinning. He had gone out looking for us and found Bill standing there soaking wet. The crew asked Bill where I was and he told them I had started swimming for the ship. It had been a fairly simple matter to track me down. They had seen me hanging from the chain of the *St. Jorge* and were heading in that direction when I dived off.

We got back to the ship and I walked up the brow. The warrant boatswain who was officer of the deck asked me in a most serious voice how I got wet. I told him I had dropped my hat overboard and reached to retrieve it and somehow lost my footing. He gave me one of those "You've got to be shitting me!" looks and said, "You've got until tomorrow morning to come up with a better one than that. Now hit the rack and get some sleep."

I awoke somewhat hung over. I had the top bunk. What a strange dream that had been! At least until I looked over the edge of the bunk. There on the floor were my whites, except they really weren't white anymore. The front was covered with rust stains.

"Oh shit," I thought, "now I am screwed. They'll probably court-martial me and ship me home for violating some international law or something."

About that time Denny McLenny, one of the civilians we were working for, came into the compartment.

"You little shit! What the hell did you think you were doing last night?"

He was trying to act pissed off, but I could tell he was amused by my actions. I got up, threw on a set of fatigues, and went to the mess decks; we had to go to work and, regardless of my condition, I would have to dive and shoot more underwater film. When I got up to the mess decks, I noticed some sailors pointing at me and whispering. Nobody got in my way and there were signs of newly gained respect from the crew. Guys would walk by and nod to me and say, "Good morning" or "How's it going?"

"What the hell is going on?" I wondered.

The senior civilian on the *Alvin* crew walked up to me and slapped me on the shoulder. "Helluva swim, kid," he said with a broad grin.

That was it! Everybody thought I was really cool for getting drunk, missing the liberty boat, nearly drowning a shipmate, attempting to board a foreign warship in the middle of the night, and leading a boat crew on a wild goose chase. Not to mention stealing the XO's van and running it off the road, and stealing an embroidered tablecloth from the airport lounge.

The other guys showed up and joined me at the table for breakfast. I ate the usual amount of eggs, bacon, sausage, biscuits, grits, milk, fried potatoes, and orange juice. I knew I'd probably puke it all up later, but at least I might get some use out of it before that happened.

We all climbed aboard the LCM-8 (landing craft, mechanized), our dive boat, and, with a hung-over BMSN Bill Hooten at the helm, steamed for the work area around the other side of the island. It took about an hour to run to the area where we were doing the survey. The job was to lay out a piece of rope from one hundred feet of depth to the shore and then swim along it with our 16mm underwater movie cameras and document the type of bottom and the amounts and types of obstacles that would have to be blown up or circumvented by a cable. We had to do that in something like five locations so they could pick the best route. The day was overcast and the wind was coming up a little so it wasn't long before I was down on my knees puking my guts out. That Mateuse wine has a tendency to do that even to hard-core drinkers like myself. Joe Gordon and Denny McLenny were just laughing at me, as were Dave Graver and Howard Trotter. Bill was trying to hang onto his breakfast, too, and Bubba Brown, the master diver, kept looking at me and shaking his head.

We got to the site and put the first two guys in the water. They shot their film and came back to reload. By then the wind had come up some more so Joe said we might as well pack it in. That was good news to me; I could go back to the ship and crawl in the rack and recover.

When we got back to the ship, we drove the boat into the well deck inside the ship and the crew pumped the deck down so the boats inside were high and dry. That way they wouldn't bang around as they would if tied off to the boat booms beside the vessel. LSDs are designed with an open well deck. They can carry many small craft inside, and when they arrive at the area of operation the well deck is flooded, the stern ramp lowered, and the boats are simply driven out.

I dragged myself off the boat. After going to the galley for a little chow to replace what I had sprayed overboard, I went down to the compartment and started to get out of my wet gear. A messenger came and told me the XO wanted to see me in uniform in his office in a half hour.

Shit! This is it, I thought. They're gonna send me off to Leavenworth or something terrible like that.

I dug out another set of whites, took a quick shower, shaved, and put on my still-wet black shoes. Fortunately, being the squared away sailor that I was, I had brought two white hats with me.

Dave Graver went to the XO's office with me, probably more for his own amusement than anything. I walked up to the XO's door and knocked. A gruff voice told me to come in. I walked inside, uncovered, and stood at some version of attention. I still was not feeling up to speed. The XO just sat there looking at some papers on his desk. Then he looked up.

"PH2 Waterman, are you in the habit of boarding foreign warships in the middle of the night?"

"No, sir, not usually."

"Well then, why did you decide to do it last night?"

"I don't know, sir, I guess it just seemed like the thing to do at the time."

"Ever been shot at?" he asked.

"Yes, sir." I lied. "But they missed."

He looked back down at the same mysterious papers on his desk and things got really quiet for a minute, then he looked up again.

"Well, sailor, fortunately for you I am in a good mood and Petty Officer Graver here speaks highly of you. The captain of the *St. Jorge* was quite impressed with your dedication to return to the ship in spite of having missed the last boat and said for me to congratulate you on the long swim. Now get out of here and don't ever do anything like that again while you're aboard my ship."

I was a free man. Jesus, that was luck. I'll never do anything like that again, I thought.

We finished the project and the ship left Santa Maria, then steamed over to Lajes, another island in the Azores, and our team left the ship. From there we were supposed to catch a flight back to the States.

We managed to spend a couple of days at the Lajes air force base, where I went to the exchange and ordered my first three-piece suit. It was made by Alexander's of London and cost me almost a hundred dollars. In the States it would have been around three hundred dollars or more. It was of wool worsted and a dark green. I figured I would never see the damn thing, but a few weeks later a package arrived from England and there it was. It fit perfectly and I got good mileage out of it for many years.

Graver, Trotter, and I went to the airport at Lajes and got a room while we waited for our flight. That night a British Overseas Airways plane came in and the crew stayed at the hotel. I met one of the flight attendants and we seemed to hit it off. She was extremely attractive and lived in Sussex, England. We wrote back and forth a few times and at one point I even planned to go visit her, but nothing ever materialized.

Our flight back to Norfolk via New York City was a few days later and we left the Azores behind.

CHAPTER ELEVEN

Back Home from the Azores

When my crew returned to Norfolk, I got together with Wes Boles and we decided to take some leave in Maine via Orange, Massachusetts, one of the primo skydiving places on the East Coast. We loaded his Ford Mustang with our jump gear and my cameras and headed up the coast. When we arrived at Orange we got a "room" at the Inn at Orange. It was a bunk room over the bar in an old house located at the DZ. We made some jumps, tried some relative work, and I made a relative work jump with Lew Sanborn, who was a legend among skydivers. Also Nate Pond jumped with us. Lew had United States Parachute Association license number D-1. Nate had D-69. He got it by special request. There is some sense of pride in having a low license number. Lew had been injured seriously in a plane crash some time back and had had plastic surgery done to his face. The surgeons did the best they could but he still looked a little screwed up. He was extremely lucky to live through the crash. Wes and I hung around Orange a few days and then drove for Maine. Wes met my mother, father, stepfather, and everybody else around. Mary was gone somewhere, so we didn't see her. I had planned on making a jump while home, but that didn't work out. I showed Wes around the area, and a few days later we drove back to Norfolk and continued our boring lives as sailors in the world's largest nuclear navy.

Sometimes Wes and I would frequent the 56 Club (E-5 and E-6 only) at Little Creek. On one occasion we happened to be "introduced" to a couple of fairly decent looking women who seemed interested in our minds and our bodies. We left with them and went to the Duck Inn, a restaurant that was famous for cold beer and good seafood. After a few cold ones there, we took them back to their car. They invited us out to their places a couple of days later. It so happened that the one I was with turned out to be the wife of a SEAL officer. I did not feel that there was a strong future in our relationship and did not pursue it.

Some days later I was out in the little lawn area between the apartment buildings where we lived. I had my parachute stretched out on the ground and was packing it to get ready to jump that weekend. This extremely attractive girl came out with a bucket of hot water and some car-washing gear. She stopped and introduced herself to me as my new neighbor. She lived with her sailor husband across the hall from the apartment Dick and I shared. Her husband was on board a carrier at sea, and she worked an ice cream shop in Norfolk. She told me she was new in the area and had met only one person. I told her I loved black raspberry ice cream.

A few days later there was a knock at the door and she had some black raspberry ice cream for me. I thanked her and put it in the freezer.

Wow, this is great, I thought, free ice cream! This kind of stuff just doesn't happen.

I never thought for a minute that she might be interested in something else. A few nights later when Dick was out, there was a knock at the door. It was she. She asked if I knew anything about televisions. I said I didn't own one but would see what I could do. She said hers wasn't coming in clearly. I walked the six feet to her apartment and went over to the TV. She asked me if I would like a drink.

Another freebie! "Sure, rum and coke if you have it."

While she mixed the drink, I frigged with the knobs on the TV set. She had turned all the adjustments around so the TV wouldn't work properly. All I did was readjust them so that the picture came in perfectly. Then it hit me: She was on the make! What a dumb bastard I was, twenty-one years old and still couldn't tell when a woman was interested in me.

I walked up to the counter, where she was standing with her back to me still mixing the drinks. I just brushed up against her back and started to put my arms around her to lean on the counter. She spun around and threw her arms around me and kissed me.

Christ, another freebie, I thought.

We managed to get to the couch and turn off the TV and some of the lights. It became a regular thing until her husband came home. Apparently she had never had sex with anybody other than her husband, and from what she had heard and read, he seemed to be a dud. One of her friends had told her to go try out somebody else and see if it was her or her husband, so I guess that's where I came in. Well, it must have been her husband because she told me she loved me and wanted to leave him. That scared me. Had I to do it over, I might have said "Go for it!"

When her husband came back from the cruise, I invited him over to have a drink and meet him. He was a pretty decent guy. Not too bad looking and fairly intelligent. The conversation came around to sex and I asked him if he had managed to gather any strange while in Puerto Rico. He went into detail about a couple of schoolteachers he and a buddy had supposedly turned every way but loose.

Hell, I thought, the best woman you'll ever have is right across the hall.

I don't know what was wrong with that guy. He must have thought his wife didn't have any sex drive. The first night he had the duty she came over and molested me heavily in my room. She was crying and didn't know what she would do, as she just wasn't enjoying his technique. I told her to try to change his habits. I told her to pick up some books on sex and leave a couple lying around the house. He would be sure to ask about them, and maybe she could drop the hint that he could use a little work on his technique.

"If that doesn't work, dump him before you ruin your life and start having kids," I told her. After that I decided to hang it up as a marriage counselor.

A few days later the phone rang again. It was Beldon Little, my salvage diving friend. He wanted me to see if I could get some "powder" and blow a propeller off an old Menhaden fishing boat in Elizabeth City, North Carolina. I told him I'd see what I could come up with. He had only blasting caps and no primacord, which I much preferred to use instead of putting caps in the water. I called some friends and finally located a guy who had about three pounds of C-4. Of course, that was illegally obtained from somebody in the teams. After procuring it from the guy, I called to see if some of my other buddies wanted to go to to Carolina and help me do this job. I didn't really need any help, but I thought they would have an interesting time.

We drove to where the boat was and met Beldon along with

professional scavenger Skinny Travis. He was into salvaging almost anything that could be sold for scrap. I asked Beldon again if he had located any det cord (primacord); he had not. I was going to have to get the C-4 to do the job that about four feet of primacord would have done. In the back of Beldon's pickup truck was a length of radiator hose. I asked him if he had any motor oil. He reached behind the truck seat and came out with a quart. I took the C-4, put it in an empty can, and worked it with motor oil until I had a thick goo that I could stuff down the radiator hose. Before I put the stuff in the hose, I ran a piece of thin line through the hose. I jammed the C-4 oil mix into the hose with a small piece of tree branch until it was full, then taped up one end of the hose. In the other end I stuck an electric cap. Then I taped up that end. Now I had a charge I could tie around the shaft to force the propeller off.

I climbed into my scuba gear and went down with a four-foot-long pipe wrench in my hand. I put the wrench to the nut that keeps the propeller on the shaft. It took about 110 percent of my strength to loosen the nut. I then removed it the rest of the way by hand. One of the topside people handed down my special charge and I tied it around the shaft forward and against the hub of the propeller. Then I got out of the water and climbed onto the old boat, which was just aground in the mud, not submerged all the way. I made sure all was clear around us and gave Beldon the signal to fire the shot. He raised the hood of his old truck and snapped the firing circuit wires, which ran to those coming from the cap on to the terminals of his battery. There was a WHUMP! from under the boat and the stern raised up an inch and dropped back. Fish started trying to walk on water, flipping around on the surface and then disappearing. I went back down, and the propeller had been blown about six feet off the end of the shaft. It was then a simple matter to put a piece of chain through the hole in the prop and drag it ashore. It weighed about 350 pounds and was solid bronze.

It was late 1968, and again I didn't go home for Christmas. A few days after Christmas, Fred Yelinek, a skydiving friend from Richmond, his girlfriend, and I headed for Florida to go skydiving at Paul Poppenhager's place near Indiantown. It was a famous DZ in Florida. All the heavies would be there, including Steve Snyder, coinventor of the square canopy, and several others I had known when traveling around the jumping circuit. We traveled in Fred's van and I drove some, even though I still had not gotten my driver's license back since I lost it in 1966.

We made it to Pop's place and jumped and drank for several days. I was starting to lose interest in jumping, but I managed to get in one on a new type of square canopy. Steve Snyder let me jump it. Due to the fact it was an experimental chute, when jumping that rig I was required to wear two reserves. I hopped out of the plane and popped the chute at about thirty-five hundred feet and flew the thing into a cow pasture by the Okee-chobee Canal. What a thrill! The damn thing had about a twenty-mile-per-hour forward speed. I really had to brake hard to keep from slamming into the ground. I braked it down to the minimum speed just off the ground and still went headfirst into the pasture grass. Even so, I managed to miss all the cow shit.

The next day was hot and nearly windless. I'd made my last jump of the day and was nursing a Pabst Blue Ribbon. We were watching some jumpers guiding their parachutes over to the canal and landing either on the bank or in the water. Some of them dropped out of their rigs just above the water. Then some-body shouted that someone had dropped out of his rig about a hundred feet above the canal. I heard somebody loudly moan "Aw, shit!" I looked over quickly and saw a canopy with nobody under it falling slowly to the ground. I took off running for the canal, a distance of about three hundred yards. By the time I got there I was about out of breath. The people by the canal were standing around in shock. I asked where the guy landed and it took a couple of seconds for me to get a straight answer. One of them pointed to the water and said he had landed there in a hands and knees position and immediately gone down. I jumped on a nearby raft and they quickly guided me to the spot. I was still about out of wind from the run. The hot weather and cold beer were taking their toll and I was pissed that I was not stone-cold sober. I jumped into the water and dived to the bottom repeat-edly. The water was around twenty feet deep and cold near the bottom. There was no visibility and I didn't have a face mask. I kept making surface dives and sweeping along the bottom with my hands until I was so exhausted I could barely climb onto the raft with help. I couldn't find the guy. The sheriff's people came after a while and dragged him up with one of those rigs with all the fishhooks on it. Kind of gruesome. I felt he could have been saved if we had found him quickly enough. There was no excuse for his death.

That night there was a dance in the hangar at the drop zone. I danced once with a girl who was really quiet. One of the jumpers told me that she was the guy's girlfriend. I guess she was still in shock.

After a couple of more days of parachuting, Fred, his girlfriend, and I headed up the coast and back to Norfolk. The neighbor couple was not home when I got there—apparently they were on leave, as I never saw them again.

When I got back to Norfolk, I decided that I should probably stay in the Navy forever, so I talked it over with some senior people and they told me to go for six more years. That way I wouldn't have to make any decisions for a long time. I thought it over a little while and put in my papers to ship over, as it's called. A few days later I raised my right hand and swore, once again, to uphold the Constitution and to defend the country from all enemies, foreign and domestic—at least for another six years. I got about eleven hundred dollars for reenlisting for six years. I went to the bank and purchased traveler's checks with it and stashed them in my locker.

A few more days passed before the word came down from Chief Dick Johnson that Graver, Trotter, and I were going on another operation. It was to be Project Tektite, and would take place in Lameshur Bay, St. John, the Virgin Islands. We would work with civilians and be there at least a few months.

Most people would have jumped at the chance to dive in the Virgin Islands doing underwater cinematography—and get paid, too. I was really looking forward to the trip, and Dave and Howard were not bad to work with, as long as there was no booze or women around. The trip down would be a joyride as we would not have to stand duty on board the ship because we were passengers.

This sounded like the ideal opportunity for anybody who liked to dive and take pictures in warm, clear water. We could drink cheap beer and rum, and might even run across a girl or two to make friends with. I looked forward to it.

CHAPTER TWELVE

Heading for the West Coast

Graver and Trotter were, of course, the same two guys who had messed me up with a beautiful woman in Panama City. They were not bad guys to hang out with but, socially, they were kind of messed up. Besides, I was junior man in the crew and thought that might result in me getting the shit end of the stick on this detail.

We took a commercial flight to Philadelphia, then at the Philadelphia Naval Shipyard boarded the USS *Hermitage*, an LSD. On that job we would be involved with a civilian/military experiment in air saturation diving at a shallow depth. Civilian scientists would spend about sixty days in a two-part habitat (Tektite) in the beautiful waters of the U.S. Virgin Islands in Lameshur Bay, St. John. Most people would kill for an assignment like this. I had to kill to get out of it.

My unplanned adventure started while I was still on the USS *Hermitage*, headed for St. John to help install the Tektite habitat. We had been out of Philadelphia a few days when a message came in requesting a volunteer of my particular skill (PH-8136 Underwater Photographer) to go to Underwater Demolition Team-13 on a WESPAC (Western Pacific, i.e., Asia! I knew what that meant) cruise and serve in their intelligence department. Most people thought I was crazy to give up a soft assignment in the Virgin Islands to go off to a war nobody wanted to fight. But I was the adventurous type and thought it might be interesting to do some of the things that others would not do.

I decided I would take my chances with the Viet Cong instead of a couple of guys who would probably make sure that I got all the shit details.

As it turned out, I was the only one in the entire Navy to volunteer for that billet. The ship pulled into Puerto Rico and I got off with my gear. One of the men from the combat camera detachment at Roosevelt Roads picked me up at the ship and took me to the unit, where I was cut a set of orders. The next day I was issued a TR (transportation request) for a ticket back to Norfolk. One of the photographers gave me a ride to the San Juan airport and I got out and checked my baggage. Then, in true Navy tradition, I headed for the bar. I got to shooting the shit with a German who most likely thought I had a cute ass, so he started buying me Heinekens. I happened to glance down the bar and noticed a righteous-looking honey looking me over. Pretty soon it became quite obvious and I motioned for her to join me. The German left to catch a plane.

The girl introduced herself and told me she lived in New Jersey and had been injured in a car wreck. She showed me the scar on her back where she had had surgery. She was a nurse, had rich parents, and her father had paid for her to come to Puerto Rico for a vacation to recover and have a little fun after finishing physical therapy. I guess she thought I should become part of that therapy. I was all for it, but my gear was checked and I didn't even have my shaving kit. She wanted me to stay and I wanted to stay, but finally they called my plane. I kissed her good-bye.

I had a few days to move out of my apartment and pack my stuff. I gave some things away and ended up with about two duffel bags and a suitcase full of clothes.

I went back to the unit on the last day and shook hands with all my friends. They wished me luck, told me to keep my head down, and all that. I went by the skipper's office and told him I was sorry to bail out on him, but I was ripe for adventure and my idea of adventure was not exactly being stuck in some tropical paradise getting shit duty (of course I put it a little more politely). He smiled and wished me luck as he shook my hand. I guess he knew the story.

Dick Johnson gave me a ride to the airport in his newly acquired beat-up station wagon. I climbed aboard the plane and was soon pointed for San Diego. I had planned it so that I would have time to catch a standby flight. That way I could cash in my full-fare ticket and pay half price. Of course, if the plane was full, I would have to wait for the next flight. In my case the plane *was* full, but not first class! The flight attendant put me up front with two Marines and "the rich people." I think she took great pleasure in bringing us free drinks and all the chow we wanted, a slap in the face to the sometimes smug types who ride first class and still complain. They don't want to get dirty sitting next to lowlife servicemen. Either that or they are so damned fat they can't fit into a regular airplane seat. In this case, had I used my regular ticket I would have been in the back of the cattle car. By going half price I got to ride first class. You gotta love it.

The two Marines and I had a very pleasant conversation during the flight. They worked in technical fields, so we talked about electronics.

CHAPTER THIRTEEN

Reporting for Duty with UDT-13

The plane landed in San Diego and I caught a cab for Coronado. Back then the ferry still ran across the bay as they hadn't finished the San Diego Bay Bridge.

Tom Hummer, my former roommate, now lived in South Mission Beach. He had left the Navy and become a stockbroker with Merrill Lynch. It was too late to call him and I was tired, so I stayed at a cheap motel in Coronado. The next day I caught a cab down the Silver Strand and checked in at the quarterdeck of UDT-13. As soon as I did, the guys I knew from Little Creek who were there as part of a "fleshing out" of UDT-13 came around to greet me. There were not enough bodies on the Left Coast to make up the full complement for Team-13, so they "borrowed" some guys from UDT-21. I had parachuted with some of those guys at Suffolk back on the East Coast. By virtue of the fact that I was greeted warmly by "real frogmen," the stigma of being an "admin puke" was not as great. The frogmen of UDT-13 were for the most part veterans of Vietnam drawn from all areas of the special warfare community. Some of them had had several tours and a few had even been there before we officially were over there.

After my arrival things were hectic. Everybody was getting ready to go to WESPAC, and all the gear not already shipped with the advance party had to be packed and put on pallets for the flight over.

HMC (Chief Hospital Corpsman) Robert Leroy "Doc" Worthington, of UDT-13, and Doc Myers, from UDT-21, finished giving us shots. The chief in the supply room issued me combat uniforms and other gear. "Chicken" McNair in UDT-11 sold me a Browning 9mm pistol for fifty dollars, as I thought I might need a handgun for the upcoming trip. I stuffed it in my gear but never used it except for target practice off the ship and when I went on liberty in Vietnam. When I carried it, I had it in a shoulder holster under my cammie shirt. You see, in a war zone we were not supposed to carry personal weapons, as we might get in a firefight and hurt somebody.

Out of boredom we went over to the rifle range at North Island Naval Air Station and burned through a few cases of ammunition. I got to fire an M-16 for the first time since attending SERE School. It was an easy weapon to learn and it had almost no recoil, so your aim was not messed up by anticipating the recoil. In later life I would fire Expert with the M-16 rifle on several occasions. We were ready for shipment to Vietnam.

We did not go directly to Vietnam, as UDT's headquarters were in Subic Bay, Philippines. From there we would go to whatever detachment we were assigned to, and then to Vietnam. Some of the platoons were in Vietnam, some were stationed aboard submarines, and some were assigned aboard surface ships as part of the Amphibious Ready Group, or ARG. We would relieve those platoons as we made our move overseas.

Tom Hummer, my friend from the East Coast, let me use his spare bedroom in South Mission Beach until I headed to Vietnam. I had a couple of weeks to hang out in some of the bars where the teams went drinking and met some of the people I would be working with. For the most part they were pretty sharp. Some had good stories about their former trips with SEAL Team One or one of the other UDT teams.

I remember drinking a few beers with Frank Bomar at the Tradewinds in Coronado. He was about my height but with a sizable beer gut. I asked him about that. He said they told him he could keep it as long as he could carry it around. He carried it right through training and up until he died[1] two years later in Vietnam.

A few nights after I arrived in California, I was at a party and met a girl named Chris. She was standing in a doorway as I squeezed past to get another beer out of the kitchen. She gave me "the look" and introduced herself. I told her I was Steve and she said I ought to look her up sometime. I said I would. I didn't get her last name. A few nights later I was again in the Beachcomber and asked the bartender (and owner) about her. It turned out she

---

1. Frank was a great guy. He was killed in Vietnam while with SEAL Team One along with a kid they "recruited" from UDT-13, Jim Riter.

was a schoolteacher who lived almost across the street from the bar.

I walked over and knocked on her door and a woman opened it. I asked her if Chris was there. She said, "I'm Chris."

Jesus, she was wearing glasses and I didn't recognize her.

"I'm Steve, we met the other night. I thought you might like to have a beer."

"Sure, let me get a sweater."

We walked the three blocks to my place and went upstairs to the apartment. Needless to say, it was a good night. We hung around together a while. She was very nice, quite intelligent, had a good disposition, and was not one of the standard barflies.

One night I was at her apartment and we were both naked and about to perform some unspeakable acts when there was a knock at the door. It was a guy named Charlie, a medically retired Marine captain. I told her not to go to the door but she was half drunk and opened it. I grabbed my clothes and ran to the bathroom to get dressed. Charlie came in, grabbed her, threw her naked over his shoulder, and lugged her down the street to his place. By the time I got my clothes on and ran out of the bathroom they were gone. I ran to his place and he was gone, but Chris was in there lying on the rug naked. All the doors and windows were locked so I couldn't "rescue" her. I guess he was just saving her from me. Later I asked around and learned that he was not too stable. He had taken some shrapnel in the brain housing and had not been the same old Charlie after he got back. I backed off a little and sort of faded out of her life. I didn't need to die for some stupid thing like that. He wasn't in love with her or anything, he just had some fixation about being her guardian. I would be leaving in a week or so and thought I would save myself for the Viet Cong. Charlie wasn't too bad a guy when he wasn't drinking, but that wasn't very often.

I never saw Chris again after that night. But she had given me one of her college graduation pictures. I kept it in my wallet with the only other picture I had, one of Mary, my girlfriend back home.

We hung around the team area doing PT and keeping the place clean. Some of us tied up loose ends and bought extra gear we thought we might need. I went over to the exchange and purchased a large buck folding knife with a leather belt case.

One of the frogmen in Team-13 "borrowed" forty dollars from me and promised to pay it back before we deployed. Well, I didn't know it, but he was about to get shitcanned out of the teams because he was a thief and lazy bastard. What a waste of good training, I thought. I never saw him or my forty bucks again, and thought it might have been worth it.

In a few days we would head for Subic Bay and, sometime after that, to Vietnam. But first we had several false starts, typical in those days. The airplane had a mechanical problem or the pilot was sick or something. I think we lugged several trucks full of gear over to North Island Naval Air Station about three times before we finally left the ground.

CHAPTER FOURTEEN

Overseas with Team-13

It was very cold at altitude and very few good things happened on the flight over. Except that our first stop on the way was NAS Barber's Point, Hawaii, and Lt. Chris Lomas, one of the officers, had a friend there who lent him a car, so a few of us got a good tour around the island. In true Navy fashion we managed to get drunk a few times sitting under the trees or in a club while waiting for the plane to be repaired, as they *always* broke down in Hawaii. All the people who flew back and forth to Vietnam via naval air got "stuck" in Hawaii because the crews' families lived there. It was the only way for the air crewmen to get a break from the hectic wartime schedule.

We stopped several other times, for fuel, at Guam, Wake, Midway or some of those other islands we took away from the Japs in World War II. We also fueled up our own tanks. Regulations forbade drinking on military aircraft, so we had to drink before we got back on board the plane. That made for a very heightened level of intoxication. And it was so damn cold in the plane, I thought we would freeze to death before we got to the Philippines.

Then the plane landed at Cubi Point Naval Air Station, Philippines, and we all thought we were stepping into a steam bath. Jesus, it was hot. Our clothes stuck to us like wet, gooey washcloths. The starch in our utilities turned to glue. Being from the East Coast and having grown up in Maine, I was used to cooler temperatures. However, I could get used to most anything. I stepped off the plane and walked into the terminal. A set of scales there was used for weighing baggage, so I assumed it was accurate. I stepped on it, and with my boots, hat, and wallet I weighed exactly 225 pounds. Oh, for those days again. A bus and some other vehicles were waiting for us with men from UDT-12, who were there to haul us down to the team area and help us get settled into the barracks. Some of UDT-13's men were already at Subic because they had gone over with the advance party to sign for weapons and things of that nature. The trucks dropped us off at the barracks and one of the officers told us to come down to the team area after we got racks and lockers and stashed our gear.

YN1 (Yeoman, First Class) DeLorme took me in to introduce me to the XO, Lt. Bob Peterson. He had served with SEAL Team 2 and been awarded the Silver Star on the same hairy-ass operation that Bob Gallagher had received the Navy Cross for. That earned Peterson respect among the boys in the team. Sometimes the award is more awesome than the deed, but in his case, those who knew felt he had earned it. I walked into his office, and he stood and shook hands with me.

"Well, Waterman, are you all ready to take pictures on enemy beaches?"

"Sure am, sir. Whatever it takes to keep me off the streets."

He didn't quite know how to respond to that and gave me an odd look. I guess he thought I was some sort of macho asshole, and afterward I thought it was kind of a dumb thing to say. However, he got over it.

One of the first things I did there, of course, was go to Olongapo on liberty. ST2 (Sonar Technician, Second Class) Steve Nash, one of the guys in UDT-13 who had been an instructor at underwater swimmers school in Key West when I was a student there, was going to show me the town. The first place we stopped was the U & I Bar, where he introduced me to Crazy Amy. Now Crazy Amy was one of those Filipinos who would have been a millionaire in the States. She owned the bar and still did a little hooking on the side. She liked frogmen and was my introduction to the Philippines. Not too impressed, but it was better than nothing—barely. I think she charged something like six dollars. A lot of money in those days, I guess.

I was first assigned to the USS *Cook*, LPR-130 (landing personnel reconnaissance), and there were fourteen of us on it from the team. The *Cook* was a small ship about 125 feet long upon which Detachment Bravo of UDT-13 would live for about a month until we rotated to another detachment. The skipper, a lieutenant commander, had been a gunner's mate before being commissioned. All of us liked him as he was extremely intelligent and had an excellent sense of humor. The job of the UDTs

on the *Cook* was to make hydrographic maps of the coastline of
Vietnam. I was issued a Nikonos amphibious camera, and PH1
Chip Maury, from UDT-12, had signed over his Leica M-2 for me
to use. It was a standard military-issue Leica with 50mm,
35mm, and 90mm lenses all contained in an olive-drab leather
gadget bag. By the time my tour was over, that Leica had been
destroyed by the humidity and the dirt. I had a lot of Kodak
Tri-X[1] film and some Kodachrome[2] and Ektachrome I had
scrounged from my old unit in Norfolk, Combat Camera Group.
I bought a number of Kodak mailers at the Navy exchange, as I
planned to shoot the color film and mail it to Kodak. I used my
father's address as a return address. That way I wouldn't have to
worry about losing the film for security or any other reasons. As
it turned out, it was a good thing I did it that way.

We went aboard the USS *Cook* at Subic Bay and got our racks
(bunks) assigned. We just threw our gear onto the one we
wanted. I had ST2 Arles "Steve" Nash's M-16. Nash had his own
CAR-16 carbine, so he let me use his issue M-16. I slept with my
rifle under the mattress to keep it from getting exposed too much
to the salt air, although during the day sometimes we would
wade through saltwater to get to the beach. I fired it from the
deck of the ship as much as I wanted to keep in practice. The famous Marine Corps general Lewis B. "Chesty" Puller always
said, "If you don't hit 'em, you don't hurt 'em." I subscribed to
that doctrine and wanted to be as good a shot as I could be. I
never carried more than a couple of hundred rounds of ammo, so
I felt I had to make them count. We were not expected to get into
prolonged firefights, just keep the bad guys' heads down while
the beach party and swimmers extracted.

On board the *Cook* we awoke around 0500, got our gear together, loaded it onto the boats, and then we'd go in to recon a
beach. That involved putting a number of the frogmen in the water on what is called the swimmer line. A number of us were on
the beach party, and we would be the only ones armed. There
were two men on forward security, two on rear. When I was in

1. Tri-X is a Kodak black-and-white film rated at a speed of 400. It was a favorite
of news photographers, and I used it almost exclusively for black-and-white work.
2. Kodachrome has to be sent to Kodak for processing, but Ektachrome can be
processed by the user in special chemistry kits available from Kodak. Both films
yield color slides of high quality. Kodachrome is more permanent because of the
type of process and dyes used.

the beach party, I was always on rear security with MR1 (Machinery Repairman, First Class) Charlie "Tobacco" Lewis. There would also be an officer in charge and the cartographer, who would note on his clipboard the terrain features. The two men with the cartographer would man the range poles. These were two poles, each with a different color flag on top, and one flagpole was longer than the other. The cartographers would lay out a baseline on the beach, then line up the range poles ninety degrees to that, and when the swimmers could see they were lined up, would take a sounding with a lead weight on a length of nylon string. Then the range pole guys would yell *"Mark!"* and move to the next line, usually twenty-five yards farther down the beach. The swimmers always arrived on line just before the beach crew hollered *"Mark!"* so nobody got to take a breather when we swam the beaches.

These numbers were recorded on a Plexiglas slate with a lead pencil. I swam about six miles of beach one day, and by the time it was over I had no trouble sleeping. I had not gone through UDT training and it was my first experience swimming a beach. Needless to say, it kept me in shape. I think they had me swim those beaches just to see if I could hack it. I did, but every time the guys on the beach yelled *"Mark!,"* I had just gotten on line and had a hell of a job getting the depths recorded while swimming to the next sounding. I asked if I was the only one who had this problem. The guys just grinned and said it was standard procedure.

On several occasions we met with unfriendly persons intent on killing us. The first time, I was with Lewis. We had two men named Lewis; the other one was a member of UDT-21 from the East Coast. This one was nicknamed "Tobacco," a ruddy-complexioned guy who had a previous tour in Vietnam with SEAL Team One. Lew always had a chew of tobacco stuffed in his cheek. He would take out his chew, lay it on his tray, eat chow, and then stuff it back in after he finished dessert.

The team would go in to the beach in an LCPR, a small plywood boat with a small ramp at the front. On the way in, we knew which direction the swimmers would be working in, so when the boat hit the beach, I always knew which way to run as soon as the ramp dropped. Lew and I were always the first out of the boat. We would go to the rear, which would mean either right or left of the rest. That was the worst part. I would be crouched behind that little wooden ramp, damned near out of breath. The first landing, I asked Lew how come I was all out of breath and hadn't even run or anything yet. He just grinned and told me I'd get over it after a few trips.

We got out of the LCPR and onto the beach. Lew and I headed up over a large sandy berm toward some vegetation. We crawled up into the bushes and Lewis eased up and looked inland. The next thing I knew, he was standing up and shooting. He shouted for me to run back down and tell the rest of the men to get the fuck out of there. I made it down the berm in about five steps, as it was almost a forty-five-degree downslope. We all ran into the water, put our fins on, and swam out to where the boats could pick us up. Steve Nash had left his fins on the ship that day and had to ditch his ammunition in order to keep afloat. We were all wearing gray UDT life jackets, but it is quite a job to swim with sneakers or coral booties on and no fins. Needless to say, we harassed him about it. To the best of my knowledge nobody shot at us that morning, although there were some near-misses as our boat's .50-caliber machine guns shot over our heads at the shoreline.

That same day we were to recon another beach some distance from the first. When we went ashore a little guy wearing beads and with long hair, for a military man, came up to talk to us. He was a Marine stationed near the village. His equipment didn't look too squared away to me. We told him we would be working down the beach and past a point of land that stuck out into the ocean. He told us we were crazy to go down there. Then a chief hospital corpsman came out of the village. He said he would walk down the beach with us for a ways. I talked to him for some time. He had fought in the tail end of World War II and been awarded the Purple Heart. Then he had fought in the Korean War and been wounded twice. So far he had been hit twice in Vietnam. I think he had a couple of Silver Stars. He also told us we were crazy to go past the point. I started to think that maybe the chief had something there.

By then I was walking in water up to my ankles and scanning the tree line quite intensely. The Doc left us and wished us luck. I was walking rear security with Tobacco Lew. Lewis was about six yards ahead of me and slightly up the beach from the water's edge. All of a sudden the bullets started flying. I could hear them zinging off the sand and splashing in the water around me. The VC had opened up on us with a machine gun. I started laying in semiautomatic fire along the berm and tried to see if the other guys were getting off the beach and into the water. We felt pretty safe in the water. All of us had shot at targets the size of a human head in the water and knew how hard it was to hit them. We imagined it was even more difficult if the heads are shooting back at you.

What happened was, Nash, the same guy who had not brought his fins that morning, spotted Viet Cong setting up a machine gun in the bushes and made the VC start shooting before they'd had a chance to set up. He probably saved a few of us from being hit. He shot two VC, and the rest of us ran to the water, firing into the berm as we did. Then the rest of them swam out to sea as the gunners on the boats poured fire into the bushes on the beach. This time I could hear the rounds zinging by and see little puffs of sand as the bullets hit near me. Nash burned up all of his ammo retreating to the water as the rest of the beach party extracted.

I waded out into the water and kept firing at the berm. Then a large wave upended me and I was rolled over in the surf. As soon as I regained my feet, I stood up, hauled back the charging handle on my M-16, and blew the water out of the breech. I then chambered a round, took aim at the berm again, and pulled the trigger. The rifle blew up in my face. At the time I guessed I hadn't cleared the gas tube completely of water.[3] That was the end of Steve Nash's M-16. I took some harassment for that. Fortunately I had been wearing contact lenses and didn't get any powder flecks in my eyes. I borrowed another rifle for the remainder of my time in Vietnam.

The boat crewmen offshore started firing machine guns at the beach and some of the rounds were hitting the water around us. It was bad enough to have the VC shooting at us, but we were not impressed by our own guys walking their guns through us swimmers.

The LCPR boat picked us up and as we were counting heads, a woman ran out of the bushes with a stick across her shoulders and a parcel hanging from each end. Nash wanted to fire on her and asked for a magazine, but Lieutenant Hollow, the assistant platoon officer, wouldn't give him one. Nash called him a

3. I later figured out it was more likely that the buffer spring housing was full of water. When the bolt moved back, it was stopped by the water and the force caused the rifle to split under the rear sight and the bolt jammed in the action. The extractor was blown off and the magazine was jammed in the rifle.

cocksucker or something like that, and Hollow told him he couldn't talk to him that way. Nash told him that after the shit he had pulled—having the .50s walk fire through the water while we were swimming out—he could talk to him any fucking way he wanted to. The woman escaped down the beach and the Marines took care of her later that day. She was a reloader for the Viet Cong. I don't think the rest of her day was very pleasant.

When we returned to the ship I remarked to Tobacco Lew that rounds did zing and snap when they went by, just like in the movies. He looked at me with one eye squinted and a slight hint of tobacco juice running from one corner of his mouth and said, "No shit!"

The rest of our trip with Detachment Bravo on the USS *Cook* was uneventful, except for getting thrown overboard fully clothed on my birthday and having to swim around the ship twice before they let me back aboard. It was all in great fun. Near the end of our trip on the USS *Cook*, the ship pulled into Hong Kong for ten days of R and R. Three of us, ETN3 Kent Larsen, BM3 Dan Sager, and I, got a room at the President Hotel in Kowloon and went to see the sights. I bought some handmade monogrammed shirts, a three-piece suit, and some other stuff. I never spent my money like a drunken sailor, even though on occasion I was one.

One pleasant thing that stands out in my mind about Hong Kong was one night when the three of us were eating in a restaurant. An older couple, obviously American, was at the next table over. The man asked if we were in the military. We told him we were and that we were taking a few days off from the war in Vietnam. He told us if we gave him our parents' phone numbers, they would call them when they got back to the States and let them know we were in good health and so forth. We figured we didn't have anything to lose by trusting them, so we did. Later on my father told me they had indeed called and said we looked good and seemed to be okay. I have always remembered that kindness and hoped someday to be in a position to do that for some young kid who is away from home and in a dangerous situation.

Larsen elected to go back to the ship early for some reason, and Sager and I decided to have a couple of the local talent come and spend some quality time with us in our rooms. After that I decided I would stick to "round eyes." There's something nice about being able to hold a conversation with your partner, even if you really don't have a hell of a lot to say.

A dummy MK-46 torpedo is fired from the tube at Gould Island, Rhode Island. (Photo by Steve Waterman)

HMC Algeo of UDT-13 crosses a small stream in a defoliated area of the Ca Mau Peninsula, South Vietnam. (Photo by Steve Waterman)

The *Bay King* rests in the slings after being salvaged from the bottom of the Chesapeake Bay off Solomons, Maryland. (Photo by Steve Waterman)

Members of UDT-13 Bravo Detachment off the USS *Cook* perform a hydrographic recon. (Photo by Steve Waterman)

Lt. Bruce Dyer, UDT-21, crossing a small stream in the Ca Mau area of South Vietnam. (Photo by Steve Waterman)

PH1 Steve Waterman rigged for beach security and photography off the USS *Cook*. Note the fins shoved up under the back life jacket straps. They came in quite handy a couple of times. (Photo by SN Pete Carolan, UDT-13)

Award ceremony for UDT-13, January 1970. Left to right: John Lowry, John Campbell, Robbie Robertson, Steve Nash, Mike Sandlin, Pat Broderick, Randy Piper, Bill Morterud, and Steve Waterman. (Photo by SMC Lou Boyles, NSWG)

Steve Waterman crossing a stream in South Vietnam. (Photo by Larry Whitehead, UDT-21)

PHC (DV) Richard Johnson, my friend and the man in charge of the Underwater Photo Team and Atlantic Fleet Combat Camera Group. (Photo by PH1 Bob Woods, AFCCG)

Petty Officers Turok and Hill dress a diver in the Mark V Mod 1 HeO$_2$ diving rig in preparation for a training dive in the pressure pot at Naval School Diving and Salvage at the Navy Yard in Washington, D.C. (Photo by Steve Waterman)

A member of the Navy's HAL-3 fires an M-60 machine gun at Viet Cong on the ground. (Photo by Steve Waterman)

Lt. Bruce Dyer and PO Dean Nelson during a search-and-destroy mission in the Ca Mau Peninsula, South Vietnam. (Photo by Steve Waterman)

Lt. Carl Flack Logan and Steve Waterman preparing to climb into Flack's F-4 Phantom for some photo sessions during the fortieth reunion of the Red Rippers, VF-11. (Photo by PH2 Charles Famuliner)

GMCM Everett Barrett and Hospital Corpsman Doc Pacuirk rig a charge during some explosive tests on Piñeros Island, Puerto Rico, 1973. (Photo by Steve Waterman)

Inside the Regulus hangar on the deck of the USS *Tunny*. This was where the SDV was kept and the Frogmen from UDT lived. (Photo by Steve Waterman)

EN2 John Porter of SEAL Team Two jumps from a CH-46 helicopter over Little Creek Amphibious Base during a UDT/SEAL demonstration. (Photo by Steve Waterman)

A Navy diver installs a salvage balloon on a sunken fuel barge off Puerto Rico. (Photo by Steve Waterman)

GMCM Everett Barrett and Lt. Joe DiMartino have a technical discussion over cocktails at the SEAL compound at Roosevelt Roads, Puerto Rico. (Photo by Steve Waterman)

Larry Theorine is lowered to the water to search the China Wreck for valuable items to salvage. (Photo by Steve Waterman)

Most of the members of the AFCCG Underwater Photo Team sitting on the stern of a sunken Navy landing craft off Small Hope Bay, Andros Island, Bahamas. (Photo by Steve Waterman)

Steve Waterman and Von, a South Vietnamese Frogman, in the crew compartment of the USS *Terrell County*. (Photo by Moki Martin, SEAL Team One)

Lt. Brian Barbata, Lt. Comdr. Chuck LeMoyne, and Comdr. Shaoul Ziv (Israeli navy) prepare to dive the GE experimental Mark 1500 closed-circuit scuba, Puerto Rico, 1973. (Photo by Steve Waterman)

The schooner *Lister* heading up the bay toward Lewes, Delaware, on the treasure hunt for the China Wreck. Shortly after this photo was taken, I was working on my record for being seasick. (Photo by Steve Waterman)

BM3 Bob Lewis, UDT-21, fires his M-60 machine gun at a bunker installation on the bank of the Song Ong Doc, South Vietnam. (Photo by Steve Waterman)

The *Lister* started taking seas over the bow a few hours after this photo was taken. Here the 110-foot schooner is heading under power up the Atlantic coast. (Photo by Steve Waterman)

A Huey helicopter from HAL-3 approaches the deck of the USS *Terrell County*. (Photo by Steve Waterman)

The author getting ready to leave the USS *Cook* for a beach recon mission, about as hard-core as he ever looked. (Photo by STG2 Steve Nash)

STG2 Steve Nash and the author, sitting near the rail of the USS *Cook*. (Photo by SN Pete Carolan, UDT-13)

The author receives the only personal award he got in Vietnam, the Navy Achievement Medal with Combat Distinguishing Device for Outstanding Combat Photography. (Photo by SMC Lou Boyles, NSWG)

Members of UDT work their way inland from the banks of a river in South Vietnam. (Photo by Steve Waterman)

RD3 Walter "Mole" Roberts clears the door sill during a static line jump at the Castillejos DZ, Philippines. (Photo by Steve Waterman)

ADJ2 Stanley Neal operates an SDV on a practice run at Subic Bay, Philippines. (Photo by Steve Waterman)

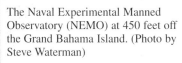

The Naval Experimental Manned Observatory (NEMO) at 450 feet off the Grand Bahama Island. (Photo by Steve Waterman)

The NEMO in Freeport City, Grand Bahama Island, Bahamas. Dr. Jerry Stachiw, the developer of the Plexiglas dome for manned submersibles, is seen standing in the hatch alongside a support diver from the Perry ship, the *Undersea Hunter*. (Photo by Steve Waterman)

The author's class at First Class Diving School. The big guy in the front is Lt. Comdr. Tony Esau, the commanding officer. He would become the skipper of the USS *Ortolan*, ASR-22, later on. (U.S. Navy Photo)

Members of a UDT-13 beach recon party board the landing craft for a ride back to the USS *Cook*. (Photo by Steve Waterman)

The remains of Swift Boat PCF-43. This boat was destroyed during an ambush on the Duong Keo River. HMC Robert Worthington, of UDT-13, LTJG Don Droz, the boat's skipper, and QM3 Tom Holloway, the coxwain, were killed. Numerous members of UDT-13 were wounded. SM3 John Lowry was awarded the Silver Star for heroism as a result of action he took in saving the life of teammate Art Ruiz. He recovered an M-60 machine gun and used it to destroy the VC who were throwing grenades at the crew. (Photo by HM2 Jim Myers, UDT-21)

The author with some explosives and ever-present camera bag on Piñeros Island, Puerto Rico. (Photo by Lt. Comdr. Pat Badger)

Stanley Neal and Pete Upton give some pointers to a group of Army Special Forces troops who had come to Subic to learn scuba. (Photo by Steve Waterman)

Comdr. Jerry Pulley, CO of Atlantic Fleet Combat Camera Group. He is the person who helped me get into underwater photography. (U.S. Navy Photo)

RFPFs by day. Viet Cong by night? (Photo by Steve Waterman)

Lieutenant, junior grade Robertson climbs the ladder to the Regulus hangar where UDT worked and slept aboard the USS *Tunny*. (Photo by Steve Waterman)

Petty Officer Burton stands watch on the SHAD (Shallow Habitat Air Dive) chamber in Groton, Connecticut, 1974. (Photo by Steve Waterman)

Left to right: Gary Seibert and Ray Fine (human guinea pigs) have a conversation with Comdr. Claude Harvey, MC, USN in the chamber during the SHAD at the Naval Submarine Medical Research Lab in Groton, Connecticut, 1974. (Photo by Steve Waterman)

HMC Robert Worthington injects SM3 Mike Sandlin with one of the shots we were required to have prior to deploying. Doc Worthington was killed and Mike Sandlin was wounded in the same firefight in which Swift Boat PCF-43 was destroyed by the Viet Cong. (Photo by Steve Waterman)

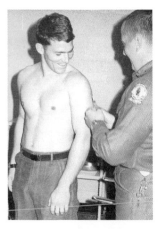

Lt. Paul Plumb, UDT-13, with radio, Charlie "Tobacco" Lewis, and Mickey Holland after we were ambushed on the beach. This was the day that Steve Nash saved our bacon by spotting the ambush before the Viet Cong had time to properly set up. (Photo by Steve Waterman)

Crossing a damp area in the Ca Mau Peninsula. The man with the boonie hat is the U.S. Army Special Forces advisor to the Ruff Puffs. (Photo by Steve Waterman)

Outside the U.S. Naval School, Underwater Swimmers, Key West, Florida. (Photo by PHC Dick Johnson)

Some of the guys in UDT-13 clowning around. Left to right: Marvin Dukes, Bob Barton, Bill Pozzi, Steve Waterman, Al Starr, Phil Czerwiec, and Pete Carolan. (Photo by Lt. George Green)

Members of the diving gang on the schooner *Lister* undress Larry Theorine after a dive to the China Wreck. (Photo by Beldon Little)

The author taking a break during a trek inland off the Song Ong Doc to do some "destruction" of VC assets. (Photo by HMC Algeo)

A member of UDT-21 runs out a trunk line that is hooked to explosives set on underwater obstacles, Puerto Rico, 1973. (Photo by Steve Waterman)

The author on the escape trunk ladder of the submerged USS *Tunny* as he prepares to lock out to support SDV operations on deck. (Photo by LTJG Robbie Robertson, UDT-21)

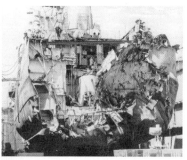

The stern section of the USS *Evans* in dry dock in Subic Bay, Philippines, after she was cut in two one dark night in June 1969 by an Australian aircraft carrier. Seventy-four American sailors were killed. It turned out to have been the fault of the *Evans*. (Photo by Steve Waterman)

The author with his two younger sisters, Cheryl and Heather. Cheryl later retired from the Naval Reserves as a commander. Heather left the Navy as a lieutenant. (Photo by NAS Norfolk Photo Lab)

The *Cook* returned to Subic and I learned I would be advanced to photographer's mate, first class (I had taken the test in the fall before I left Combat Camera Group. This, in the Navy, is pay grade E-6, one grade below chief petty officer). I would be advanced on 16 April 1969. I had been eighteen when I joined the Navy and had over four years in when I headed for Vietnam so I was a little bit older than most of the guys in the team except for the chiefs and officers.

I spent a few days in Subic, got laid a few times, caught a "gentleman's cold," got it cured, and prepared to go back to Vietnam to see action with the other detachments. I hated sitting around when there might be some action going on; it's hard to shoot combat photos if you aren't in combat. I caught a bus to Clark Air Force Base and would be flying out on a C-141. When we got aboard, I realized there were no seats; the passengers had to sit on aluminum pallets with a strap across their laps. I thought that really sucked. I looked to my left and there was a warrant officer, on my right was an Army major. I guess rank has no privileges when it comes to being cannon fodder.

We landed in Da Nang at night and somebody from Frogsville—the name of our compound—came out to the field to pick us up. We went to our Quonset huts and found our racks. The berthing area was well air-conditioned and I damn near froze to death the first night. After that I found a blanket. The Da Nang detachment didn't do much. They mostly went up rivers and blew things up and sometimes got shot at a little bit. Mostly the guys there water-skied, laid around, and went over to Camp Tien Sha to try to meet the nurses. I, of course, did not partake of any of this, with the exception of going over to to the EOD compound at Tien Sha with Steve Nash to drink a little beer. Tien Sha was chickenshit and you were supposed to have your boots bloused and all that REMF crap. There were even white picket fences around some of the officers' buildings. The frog types, of course, did not subscribe to peacetime standards.

One night one of the Army sentries stopped our OIC (officer in charge), LTJG Robbie Robertson, at the gate between Tien Sha and our area and asked where his pass was. Robbie was drunk and just leaned over and grabbed his left lapel and shook his silver LTJG (O-2) bars at him. "There's my fucking pass," he said, and drove on. A Vietnamese woman we called Mouse worked at the compound doing laundry and cooking. Her cooking sucked and I guess she did, too, according to one of the guys. I mean, I knew about the cooking sucking, but not the other. One day Larry Whitehead, on loan from UDT-21, got pissed off at Mouse for her poor cooking. From what I hear he was about to shoot her until one of the more rational types talked him out of it. I guess I was just naive or something, but I missed out on a lot of probably not-so-hot fun. Some of the men used to go out and smoke dope in one of the bunkers. I could hear them out there laughing and listening to "In a Gadda Da Vida" by Iron Butterfly all night long. They were West Coast types and that was in their blood.

I got pretty bored at Da Nang and needed to do something interesting if not dangerous. One day I made some crack to Tom Winter of UDT-21 about needing to go down to Ca Mau and kill somebody. He looked at me with a strange look. "You're nuts, Waterman." I felt kind of stupid for making that remark.

VC bunkers were located up a river (the Song Bo De, I think) and somebody higher up decided they needed to be destroyed. We had some outdated demolitions in the bunker, so we loaded them onto a Swift boat and steamed up the river and blew up the bunkers. We took a few stray rounds that day, but nobody even shot back. We thought the shots were from some firefight off in the distance, as we could barely hear the weapons as they discharged. The best part about going out with the Swift boats was that they always had great chow. We raided their freezers when we went with them because they had frozen steaks, ice cream, and other goodies we didn't have access to. The crew didn't mind as we usually had something to trade, and chow was not hard for them to get. We would go up rivers and look for bunkers that had been spotted from the air, or that had fired upon boats in the rivers. I went on three operations without incident. One day we had to blow up a little section that separated two different parts of a river. As it was, the Swift boats could not cross to the other part of the river and chase the VC. The little bar between the two sections became nothing but a column of water, mud, and sand shooting straight up into the air.[4]

4. In 1993 I met the skipper of this boat in a restaurant in Rockland, Maine. I was eating with my son and the guy noticed the SEAL TEAM shirt I had on. He asked me if I used to be in SEAL Team or was just wearing the shirt. When I told him I was an admin puke in UDT-13 in 1969, he said I looked like one of the guys who blew up the sandbar for him in the river near Da Nang. Small world, ain't it?

The frogmen in Da Nang had built themselves a great compound, Frogsville. When I was there they were putting a chain-link fence around it. I think that was so nobody could get in and steal the cold beer. A Marine in a vehicle had run over a flare locker by the Freedom Hill Exchange and that set the field on fire. It was blamed on the Viet Cong. The fire had burned down the exchange and destroyed most of the beer, but a bunch of enterprising frogmen had gone up with a truck and gathered the cans that hadn't burst. They washed them off and chilled them. Then the beer was sold to sailors on the boats down at the deep-water piers. A couple of the boys also stole a brand-new outboard still in the crate. It was sitting on the dock just inviting somebody to take it. They beat it up a little with some chain, painted it flat black, then mounted it on our Boston Whaler. It towed many a UDT water skier around the harbor, including this author. I had a photo of Stanley Neal being towed behind the boat. We used it in the cruise book and were going to entitle it "Trolling for Alligators," but LTJG Pete Upton, my partner in the creation of the cruise book, thought it might offend him. I don't think it would have, as Neal had a hell of a sense of humor. He used to love to give the PT and swim test to guys who wanted to try out for the teams. He liked to squash the stereotype of the black guy who couldn't swim. Neal looked like a real seal when he got in the water and probably could have outswam one.

One of the scariest things I did while in Da Nang was go out diving with MR3 Gary Cronin. He was a rugged little guy who was always getting into trouble for either catching VD or beating up fleet-type officers.

We didn't have anything to do one day, so Robbie, the OIC, asked us if we wanted to go look for a fifteen-thousand-pound anchor the Seabees had lost. We figured it would be a chance to do a little diving and cool off, and maybe the Seabees had something to trade. At the very least they'd owe us one. Gary and I checked out a handheld sonar and took the truck to the area where we met the Seabees and put our gear on their boat. We burned a set of double tanks each, and the whole dive all I could think about was some gung ho boat crewman dropping a grenade on our bubbles, thinking we were VC frogmen. That didn't happen and we did find the anchor. That was good for obtaining more building materials for the compound. We could always trade something when we needed gear, paint, fencing, weapons, most anything.

Another scary thing that happened with Gary Cronin was on a search-and-destroy operation when Gary had an M-79 grenade launcher. We were crossing an area of bunkers made from blocks of stone. Gary said, "Hey, watch this," and fired an HE (high explosive) round at the entrance to one only a few yards away. The round hit the bunker's stone entrance and bounced back without exploding. Before I could act, Gary picked the dented M-79 round up off the ground and threw it into the river.

"Jesus Christ, Gary, that could have gone off when you picked it up. Don't ever do that shit again!"

He just grinned.

Detachment Charlie was aboard the USS *Tunny*, which had pulled into the harbor one Friday for liberty for the crew. I planned on going aboard to document some of the swimmer delivery vehicle (SDV) operations there. I already knew all the guys in the detachment, so it would not be a big change of pace for me.

On Monday morning I went aboard the USS *Tunny*, LPSS-282, an old diesel-powered fleet submarine of World War II vintage. I'd read a lot about submarines and seen them in World War II movies, but until I served with UDT-13 in Vietnam I'd never been aboard one. My first experience on board the *Tunny* was to be led to the "UDT bunk room." The guys in the team were quartered in the hangar. The *Tunny* had been converted to firing the Regulus missile and then back to an SS boat. In January 1969 she'd been converted from an SS boat to an LPSS. Her sole purpose was to support UDT operations and insert commandos on special operations.

To get to the bunk room we had to go down a hatch in the *Tunny*'s deck, through the control room, and up through a hatch in the crew's mess. The hangar was a big steel cylindrical tank with a huge, hydraulically operated door on the aft end. Two large hydraulic rams opened the door and, in the old days of the Regulus missile, the crew rolled a missile out onto the aft deck along tracks and set it up, cleared the decks, and fire control cranked it off. Once the weapon had been launched, the deck crew rolled the launcher back into the hangar, the door closed, the sub dove, and everybody would live happily ever after— except maybe the guys downrange. The Regulus missile was never used in combat and designed after the World War II German V-1 buzz bomb so fondly remembered by the civilian population of London. The Regulus missile was relegated to the dust heap of outmoded military equipment, and the *Tunny*, being not the latest or greatest example of our underseas technology, was assigned to support UDTs so they'd be able to use it as a shelter for SDV operations. LTJG Robbie Robertson, of UDT-21, was OIC of that UDT detachment, and the only UDT officer with us.

UDTs used the swimmer delivery vehicles for clandestine beach recons. The SDV motored in, submerged, toward the beach, with two swimmers and a driver. The driver would sit it on the bottom in thirty feet of water and the two frogs in the backseat would swim toward the beach on a compass heading. They'd be attached to the SDV by a heavy fishing line wound on a huge reel. The SDV driver would just let it reel out as they swam toward the beach, then reel them in as they started back. That was about the only part of the operation nearly free from Murphy.

One of the swimmers carried a little Plexiglas tube containing a clock mechanism. One end was closed off with a fairly heavy latex material. As the depth changed, the rubber end would respond to the pressure change by being pushed in or out. A stylus connected to the rubber marked a roll of paper. The paper moved at a known rate, so it acted as a clock. The stylus made a black line on the paper that was representative of the gradient of the bottom. All the cartographers had to know was how deep the thing was when the swimmer turned it on, and they could extrapolate the depths from there. In spite of it being a primitive piece of gear, it worked very well.

The *Tunny* pointed her bow to sea and we headed out of Da Nang harbor. That night we steamed toward our area of operation. The sub, being conventional, was just a submersible surface ship, so it was more at home on the surface. We made our way offshore and, after dark, started creeping shoreward toward our objective.

At about three in the morning, the sub dived. It was just like in the movies. I was sleeping in my bunk up in the hangar and the klaxon horn blew, *Ahoogah! Ahoogah!* followed by the command, *"Dive! Dive!"* I could hear the rumble of the diesel engines' rpms drop quickly—then silence. The sub's main induction valve closed and my ears popped a little. In a few short moments the water was sloshing up under the hangar and then beside and over it. The gurgling passed by the steel outside of the hangar past my head and then all became quiet as the sub completely submerged. It was eerie to hear that sound and feel the slight downward angle of the boat as she slipped quietly beneath the South China Sea. Now I knew what Captain Nemo felt like on board the *Nautilus*, safe and out of sight of the bad guys.

We needed to conduct SDV operations during daylight hours, but had to be in place to launch the minisub before the sun came up. The skipper of the *Tunny* ran his boat toward shore until we were at a depth of around ninety feet. As the sub touched down on the seabed, I felt the slight jarring as we bounced along the bottom and finally came to rest. The submarine crew secured the electric propulsion motors and went to other tasks. By then the UDTs had crawled out of their racks and had the scuba gear ready for the day's work.

On that day, ace SDV driver QM2 (Quartermaster, Second Class) Bill "Jake" Jakubowski would be at the controls. SN Bill Shearer and SN Steve Abney were the swimmers who'd ride in the backseat.

In the SDV, on top of the battery containers, was an array of aluminum ninety-cubic-foot scuba bottles. These were the "boat air." On the way in to the beach and back out, the crew of the SDV breathed from those bottles. In spite of the telltale bubble trail left by the rigs, open-circuit scuba was being used on these operations. Although classified at the time, our SDV operations were not conducted north of the DMZ (demilitarized zone) and the topside Vietnamese were thought to be "friendly." Each man wore a set of double 90s on his back and the usual belt, Ka-bar knife, flare, and UDT life vest. They kept their duck feet stashed in the sub when not using them. On those operations the men wore, at the very least, a wet suit top. Although the water was warm, they would be in it for a long period of time.

All the support divers and SDV crew moved to the forward torpedo room. I would be locking out and working with the SDV deck crew. RD3 (Radarman, Third Class) Walter "Mole" Roberts and I climbed up into the escape trunk and stood back to back in that very confined space. Neither one of us was a little guy, and I want to tell you, the escape trunk is no place for one who can even spell claustrophobia. We almost had to take turns inhaling. It was tight. Mole and I had to do a little dance so the submariners in the torpedo room below could get the lower hatch shut. Then we were in total darkness. Then the valve was opened to flood the trunk. The water started to rush in around our feet and quickly rose to our chests. Just before it reached my mouth, I yelled out, "Trunk's flooded, secure the flood," and we shoved our scuba regulators into our mouths, hoping we'd remembered to turn on the air before we donned our rigs. The operator acknowledged by securing the flood valve leading to the trunk. Then he opened the air valve to pressurize the trunk to ambient sea pressure. I put my foot against the door of the trunk and leaned on it lightly so that when the pressure outside and inside the trunk were equal, the door would easily swing open on its hinges. The door opened and I sounded off, "Door's open, secure the blow," and then ducked down and swam out and onto the deck of the submarine. I turned back to make sure Mole was right behind me. We stopped at the edge of the opening in the sub's deck long enough to pull on our fins and then continued aft toward the conning tower looming up in the clear water.

I'd been diving since I was thirteen years old, but had never locked out of a submarine before. All the "real" UDT guys had done lockouts in training. It is an eerie feeling to swim along the deck of a submerged submarine and realize that the only place you are safe is inside that gray, steel hulk beneath you. Above you is the unknown and maybe death, but under you in that gray slab of U.S. government-issue steel is hot chow, a rack, a place to take showers, your teammates, and the crew that is there to support your mission.

Mole and I swam aft along the deck toward where the SDV was secured on deck behind the hangar. He was on my left and I was near the edge of the sub's deck. As we passed the conning tower, I looked to my right. A yellow sea snake was swimming in formation with us about five feet away. I'd read about sea snakes and how they could kill you if they bit you and all that, but I'd never seen a live one. All of a sudden the damn thing pulled a ninety-degree turn and swam straight at me. It came right at my face and bounced off my face mask. I was too scared to panic, so I just kept swimming. He turned and swam away. I guess he thought his reflection was either mating material or the enemy. I don't care. He went away.

Mole and I moved to the SDV and started loosening the chains holding it to the deck. The scuba tanks and the batteries in the SDV had been charged the night before. In a very few minutes two more guys locked out and swam up on deck beside us. We were only about fifty feet below the surface, so we had plenty of air in our tanks to do whatever we needed. When the crew was sure the SDV was ready to go, they made a series of taps on the hull and Jake, Bill Shearer, and Steve Abney locked out. They wasted no time in getting to the craft and climbing in. Jake gave it a quick preflight check and nodded with a thumbs-up. We released the chains and he flew the small submarine off the deck and into the hazy green gloom of early morning.

None of us had been outside the sub long enough to worry about decompression, so I locked back in with MM1 (Machinist's Mate, First Class) Harry Lapping, another guy on the deck crew. Mole locked in with the second member of the deck crew.

Chow on board a submarine is the best in the entire U.S. military. They have four meals a day, plus "soup down" in the afternoon when you can go by the galley and grab a bowl of soup and a sandwich. To us guys in UDT-13, that was hog heaven. We ate about all we could hold. They had steaks, ham, french fries, even ice cream.

LTJG Robbie Robertson and MM1 Harry Lapping (borrowed from UDT-21), and a couple more of us stationed ourselves up in the conning tower. The UQC (underwater communications unit) transceiver was there. The SDV trailed a thin, disposable wire that was connected to the UQC on the *Tunny*. The *Tunny* had two-way communication with Jake in the SDV—for a while—and then it went dead. Robbie kept messing with it and trying to raise Jake, but no luck, the wire must have broken. We all started grabbing quick glances at our watches as the time passed slowly. Pretty soon we realized the boys would be out of boat air and have to go on scuba. This meant that pretty soon the SDV would have to surface.

By now the sub was rolling gently back and forth, side to side in a groundswell. It got pretty quiet in the darkness of the dimly lit conning tower, and the serious expression on everyone's face added to the solemnness of the situation. There was no question that things were getting tense. The skipper ran up the periscope and we all took turns watching the surface toward the beach for signs of our little sub and three-man crew. Daylight was rapidly fading and the sky was overcast. The seas were getting rougher and nobody was talking who didn't have something to say.

Finally, Robbie shouted, "There they are, I see a flare!"

He had just taken over the periscope when he spotted the SDV on the surface. Jake had an MK-13 day/night distress flare burning hotly in his hand. The skipper surfaced *Tunny* to decks awash and we rushed out on deck, pulled the small sub on board, and chained it down. The SDV crew had run out of air and they were nearly exhausted and getting cold. We helped them get below to warmth and hot chow. They were happy to be home.

We got some good hydrographic data even though the mission was compromised, and the after-action report showed some points needing improvement on future missions.[5]

Thanks to these Vietnam missions, SDV operations nowadays have a whole new set of procedures, equipment, and operations. The attitudes of the men on UDT/SEAL teams are the same now as then, and their spirit is universal within the U.S. naval special warfare community. They just don't make sailors any better.

After a week on the *Tunny*, I went ashore and back to Frogsville in Da Nang. But it got boring hanging around the Quonset hut there, so I caught a flight down to Saigon and from there a flight to Phu Quoc Island. There was a Swift boat base there, where I got on a boat and rode down to the USS *Terrell County*, LST-1157, an old LST (landing ship, tank) at a two-point moor off the mouth of the Ong Doc River. That was where Detachment Golf was based. The following action happened just prior to my arrival at Detachment Golf. The *Terrell County* had shortly before replaced the *Westchester County* as the base of operations for UDT-13, Detachment Golf, and a SEAL Team One detachment.

On the evening of 12 April 1969, around 1700, Detachment Golf of Team-13 suffered several casualties on the Duong Keo River. They were on board PCF-43 (patrol craft, fast), which was the trail boat in a group of four (the others being PCF-5, PCF-31, and PCF-38). Before the day was out, PCF-43 was totally destroyed. It carried the full complement of UDT-13's men. The VC were set up in thick vegetation on the west bank of the river and waited until the other three boats had passed their

5. RD3 Walter "Mole" Roberts of Burley, Idaho, was the last person ever to lock in aboard the USS *Tunny*. He was number 3,860. In June 1969 the LPSS *Tunny* was decommissioned. On 19 June 1970 she was used as a target and sunk by a torpedo fired from the USS *Valodor* (SS-490).

position, headed upriver. It was assumed that once they opened fire on the boats, the ones upriver would turn to run and have to pass through the kill zone to escape.

The first two rockets struck PCF-43. "Doc" Worthington was killed when he was hit by a B-40 rocket during the first minutes of the ambush. The shrapnel from that rocket also wounded SN William "Randy" Piper, and his helmet was blown off. The steel pot flew straight up in the air and fell back on the deck. He didn't know he'd been hit until blood started to run down his forehead. GMG3 (Gunner's Mate Guns, Third Class) Ricky Hinson took some shrapnel from the same blast. Seaman Mike Sandlin from Roosevelt, Utah, one of the youngest members of UDT-13, took an AK-47 round through the thigh. The corpsman gave Sandlin a shot of morphine and an M-16, and two frogmen carried him forward where he could fire back without moving around too much.

The only one of Team-13 who had to be discharged for his wounds was SM3 Art Ruiz from Tulare, California. He took some shrapnel in the abdomen. Art later returned to active duty and served again with naval special warfare. LTJG Pete Upton was also wounded by shrapnel during the firefight.[6] Lieutenant Lomas ran to the pilothouse to give first aid to the wounded there. The skipper of the PCF-43, LTJG Don Droz, and the coxswain, QM3 Tom Holloway, were instantly killed by a second rocket that entered the wheelhouse. With nobody at the controls, PCF-43 ran onto the bank at full throttle and careened onto its starboard side almost on top of the VC bunkers. From that position its .50-caliber machine guns were useless as they could not be depressed enough to fire at the enemy, but the thick foliage prevented the VC from using more rockets and its proximity to their position precluded using the mortar on board the '43.

Signalman, Third Class John Lowry, of Spokane, Washington, and Art Ruiz were trying to set up the crew's M-60, but Ruiz was seriously wounded in the abdomen by grenade fragments during the attempt. Lowry dragged him back to the boat and went after the M-60 he had dropped in the shallow water by the bow of the grounded Swift boat. The VC kept throwing grenades at him, but Lowry was determined to get the M-60 and take out

6. Pete Upton is now a lawyer, and he wrote up this story for the UDT-13 *Cruise Book*.

those VC. He got into a snowball fight (with concussion grenades) with two VC in a spider hole who were shooting at the men on the disabled Swift boat. Finally, Lowry lobbed a concussion grenade into their hole and blew them physically out of it. After some time, another one of the Swifts came and took off the survivors. PCF-43 caught fire, exploded, and burned so there was nothing left but a hull with two Detroit diesels sticking out of it. The name "PCF-43" was still visible on the stern, but that was about all. The men of Detachment Golf stayed the night on the river so as not to risk a night transit back to the *Westchester County*.

For that action, Lowry earned the Silver Star. To look at the kid, you'd have thought he should be out delivering newspapers or bagging groceries instead of throwing hand grenades at the bad guys, but he came through and most likely saved the lives of many of his fellow frogmen. Later in his tour he picked up the Purple Heart on another operation. The only men not wounded on this operation were SM1 John Campbell, QM3 Patrick Broderick, and SM3 John Lowry.

When I went aboard the USS *Terrell County*, no bunks were available in the UDT compartment. Actually there were; I just had to share mine with somebody from SEAL Team One. The SEALs slept during the day. As we got back from operations, the SEALs would be getting up to go out at night. By the time they got back in the morning, the UDTs would be getting ready to go. In the Navy, that is called hot bunking. The SEAL officer in charge, Lt. Tim Wettack, was a decent guy. None of us wore any rank insignia and sometimes it was a joke to see who the other guys thought was in charge. I remember some of the guys in that detachment, a Richard Solano, Jim Gore, Lance Farmer, "Moki" Martin, and a skinny guy by the name of Dwight Daigle. Later on, some of those guys were killed when a helicopter's transmission seized and the entire crew went in.

While we were there we heard of some guys in a SEAL team platoon getting blown up in an accident involving the removal of the demolition charge from a Chicom 82mm mortar. It was a foolish accident and never should have happened.

Two Navy Seawolf helicopters from HAL-3 (Helicopter Attack [Light]) were on board the *Terrell County*. These gave us close air support and medevac if we needed it, and the crew let me fly with them whenever I wanted to. On days when the OIC didn't think there would be any action, I would go with them and shoot pictures and try to shoot seagulls from above with the M-60 door gun. Some fun. Sometimes when we were up high we would throw out white phosphorous grenades to watch them explode in midair. Expensive fireworks, but impressive.

Our officer in charge there was Lt. Bruce Dyer, a graduate of the Naval Academy. He was as fair a person as I had ever seen and gave everybody the chance to work to their full potential. The second in command was a nice enough guy, but somewhat of a wimp when it came to standing up to brass.

Lt. Tim Wettack and the Army lieutenant adviser to the RFPFs (Regional Forces and Popular Forces, commonly called Ruff Puffs) had flown upriver in the LOACH (Light Observation Helicopter). They landed when they saw footprints going into a bunker. After several attempts to get whoever was inside to come out, one of them threw a concussion grenade into the bunker. It turned out to be a woman in her early thirties. She was not badly injured, but when the LOACH flew her back to the ship for medical help the skipper told everybody to get the cameras off the flight deck. I felt, due to the fact I was an official Navy photographer and had the credentials to prove it, that I was exempt from this order. I shot about six or eight shots of them unloading her from the helo. The captain called me up to the bridge and asked me what the fuck I thought I was doing out there with a camera after he had ordered everyone to stop taking pictures. I told him I was an official photographer and that it was my job to document everything that happened.

He said, "Well, official Navy photographer, give me that fucking official Navy film out of your fucking official Navy camera!"

Then he threw it overboard out the window of the wheelhouse and told me to get off his bridge. Fortunately, I had control of my temper. Plus we were in a war zone and I was not sure just what my rights were. I shut up and left. If the situation ever occurred again, I'd have a dummy roll to give the captain. Hindsight truly is 20/20.

After a couple of days there, I went on my first operation with Detachment Golf. The Ong Doc River (Song Ong Doc) runs through the Ca Mau peninsula on the southern tip of Vietnam. It drains into the Gulf of Thailand adjacent to the South China

Sea. One day in May 1969 we were to travel up the river with a small flotilla of six Swift boats, take aboard some RFPFs, then proceed farther upriver to locate and destroy bunkers and other structures that could give the Viet Cong cover during their attempts to ambush and destroy American and South Vietnamese riverine craft.

At approximately 0400 the members of Underwater Demolition Team Thirteen, Detachment Golf and six Swift boat crews ate chow, checked gear, and went on deck to prepare. The SOP was: reveille; eat chow; load magazines; assist the boat crews in loading demolitions and munitions aboard the Swift boats (PCF). We would carry several cases of C-4 plastic explosive; 5.56mm ammunition for the M-16s; 81mm mortar rounds; high explosive rounds for the M-79 grenade launchers; concussion, fragmentation, CS (a harassing agent), and a few smoke grenades. Usually, about then the squad from SEAL Team One, which was also operating from the *Terrell County*, would return from night operations, often with a prisoner or two for interrogation.

On some other operations, we brought the Ruff Puffs to the ship and fed them, showed them movies at night, and so on. None of the team members had a warm, safe, fuzzy feeling about living offshore on a ship carrying both Vietnamese troops and tons of high explosives. One evening I took a detour through the tank deck[7] on my way to the galley. I walked along admiring the numerous stacks of ammo and explosives. As I approached the door that led off the tank deck toward the galley, I heard a sound. A sailor who was supposed to be on watch was sleeping on top of a pallet of ammo, snoring away. A real confidence builder! And we had Vietnamese troops on board! Any one of them could have been Nguyen Van Hardcore. All he would need was a length of time fuse, a cap, and a match. In a heartbeat he would have been a hero and we would have been history.

My mind raced back to the year before. The USS *Westchester County* had been moored in a similar fashion off the coast of Vietnam and was also being used as a base for the Riverine Forces. Viet Cong sappers had sneaked up and planted limpet mines on the hull. The ensuing explosions killed twenty-five

7. The area used for carrying tanks and other vehicles prior to making an amphibious landing. The ship's company stored all the ammunition there because it was a large, open, and well-ventilated space.

Americans, making this the "U.S. Navy's greatest loss of life in a single incident as the result of enemy action during the entire Vietnam War." Heroic action on the part of the crew and others on board the *Westchester County* kept the ammunition stored on its tank deck from going off. I think my concern over that guy sleeping on watch was pretty well justified.

The sun was creeping up toward the horizon and we were anxious to get the operation under way. The boats were loaded and the crews briefed. Diesel engines were fired up and the formation of Swift boats struck out for the mouth of the Song Ong Doc, a few miles inshore from our anchorage. The plan was to take the VN troops who were on the ship with us and to pick up a few more from a village up the river a few klicks (kilometers). The two Seawolf helicopters on the *Terrell County* would come in later. Their crews would be monitoring our radio frequencies and wouldn't take off until after we had left the pickup point with the Vietnamese troops; no sense orbiting around, burning fuel. With Murphy's Law the order of the day, they would most likely run low on fuel about the time the action started.

The Song Ong Doc was a typical Vietnamese river—brown, shallow, and meandering slowly toward the ocean. The vegetation was heavy on both banks. We stopped at our rendezvous point near a small village and picked up the Ruff Puffs who would be operating with us.

Our boat's skipper pushed the bow onto the mud of the riverbank and some of us jumped off. The officer in charge of the Ruff Puffs was standing a few yards away. He motioned for us to get off the boat and follow him. An Army captain on board our boat—the adviser and interpreter for the Vietnamese troops—turned and invited us into the village. Our OIC, Lt. Bruce Dyer,[8] didn't relish the idea. We agreed; the less time we spent screwing around, the less time the Viet Cong would have to set up surprises for us. The RFPFs, a slack-looking bunch, climbed on board several of the boats and we headed upriver. They were equipped with World War II–vintage M-1 (small .30-caliber semi-

8. Bruce Dyer, a graduate of the Naval Academy, stayed with the naval special warfare community and recently retired as a captain. Bruce was a good leader. If he had mentioned he was planning to go to hell to put out the fire, his men would have fought over the buckets.

automatic) and M-2 (automatic .30-caliber) carbines. Some of them wore sandals and had brightly colored scarves around their necks, a method of unit designation. I got the distinct impression they were not crack troops.

We took them aboard and left the village. The sun had broken over the horizon and was beginning to cast its oppressive heat. The sunlight reflected off the brown river water and made it difficult to make out the details on the east bank of the river. The heat was an omnipresent thing, and I never got used to it, I just quit bitching about it. The UDT men wore flak vests and steel pots while on the boat but, when disembarked, shed the extra weight. That way we wouldn't sink any farther into the mud than necessary.

The stern of the Swift boat was crowded with the members of Detachment Golf and the crew members of the Swift. A .50-caliber machine gun was mounted on the stern deck and a twin-fifty was mounted in the gun tub topside behind the wheelhouse. I was sitting under the stern fifty with my back against its mount. We were all trying to make believe nobody could see us, that the Viet Cong didn't know we were coming. It is the most naked feeling in the world to be sitting on the deck of a fifty-foot aluminum-hulled boat with two GM diesels screaming underneath, hoping nobody knows you are around. There's no place to hide. You try to get real small. We called it the "fishbowl effect." You can't sneak up on anybody. With the noise of the engines there's no way you can even tell you're being shot at. Maybe we'd see rounds hitting the water or catch a glimpse of muzzle flashes. That's what I thought, anyway.

Without warning a huge geyser of water erupted fifty feet astern, equidistant between us and the boat to our rear. Nearly every weapon on the boats opened up. I didn't have a clue what the hell was going on, but figured I better get involved. From where I was sitting, a few feet back from the rail, I didn't have a clear field of fire, so couldn't bring my weapon to bear on the riverbank. Suddenly I felt a searing pain in my back. I thought I had been hit but it was just the hot .50-caliber shell casings falling between my flak vest and my shirt. I rolled over and got the vest off rather hurriedly. No harm was done, but I understood why the place where I had been sitting was so readily available. The skipper of the boat pushed the throttles wide open and the sound of the twin diesels increased from a roar to a scream. The boat forged ahead and muddy brown water churned from under the stern in a froth as we sped upriver to get clear of the kill zone. We traveled nearly a hundred yards around a slight bend, then the skipper throttled back and pushed the bow ashore on the riverbank.

Six boats were in our formation, and ours was second from the front. When the ambush started the three lead boats sped upriver, and the three in the rear did one-eighties, turning downriver. The boats with Ruff Puffs and UDTs aboard hit the bank in order to insert and encircle the bad guys.

The boat mushed to a halt in the soft mud of the riverbank. Equipment Operator, First Class Oliver Dean "O. D." Nelson, on loan from UDT-21, moved to the bow and told the Ruff Puffs' adviser to get his troops off the boat. They just milled around indecisively as if they had no direction and were afraid to get off. O. D. then told the adviser he would open fire on them if they didn't disembark. That message was understood.

I made a graceful non-Hollywood exit from the bow by jumping down and driving both legs into the soft mud clear up to my knees. Then I fell forward onto my rifle. Anywhere else that would have elicited laughter, but most of the others landed the same way. We pulled each other out of the mud, then moved inland as quickly as possible, having no idea what size force we might be fighting if the enemy had not run off.

The Seawolves were airborne and heading our way. We could hear the Hueys a few minutes before they were in sight. They had spotted some Viet Cong running away from the riverbank. The staccato sound of their M-60 flex guns could be heard coming from the sky as they took the Viet Cong under fire. We watched the smoky trails shooting earthward as the Seawolves fired rockets at a position hidden from us by the foliage. Over the radio one of the commanders on the ground ordered the Seawolves to hold their fire unless they were well away from our ground forces, as the flex guns' brass casings were landing around the troops on the ground. Getting hit by brass dropping from a thousand feet can ruin your whole day.

Paths crisscrossed the swampy area. The one I chose to follow intersected a small stream where tree branches hung low to the ground. I passed under one and it brushed the top of my head and shoulders. Suddenly the back of my neck felt like it had been hit with a bucket of hot coals. I grabbed for my neck and went down on my knees. When I pulled my hand down it came back full of big red ants. The damn things were three quarters on an inch long and it felt like at least a third of that was teeth. I cleared them off, buttoned my collar and sleeves, and packed handfuls of gray mud around my neck and wrists. Then I smeared it over all the exposed skin of my face and hands. In the sun, the mud poultice soon dried to a consistency like concrete. I didn't much care what it looked like, as long as I didn't hurt. That was my last problem with ants.

Boatswain's Mate, Third Class Bob "Machine Gun" Lewis[9] from UDT-21, Hospital Corpsman, Third Class Larry Williams,[10] and I moved out ahead and to the right of the Ruff Puffs. They didn't have our aggressive attitude, or they knew something we didn't. We were moving across a small open area when I heard a loud explosion. I learned afterward that a Viet Cong in the bushes to our front had fired a B-40 rocket that passed harmlessly between Lewis and Doc and me and hit the trees yards behind us. Nobody was hurt. Lewis opened fire with his M-60. "Rambo" was back in the States then making X-rated movies, but if he could have seen Lewis with that '60 on his shoulder and the bandoleers of ammunition crisscrossing his body Pancho Villa style, he would have been inspired. Doc Williams and I were moving forward on either side of Lewis. We spotted movement in the bushes, but hesitated for a moment before opening fire because Bruce Dyer was somewhere on our left flank with the Ruff Puff adviser, and Larry Whitehead, Dean, and some others were on the right. We also knew we had three boatloads of good guys coming in from somewhere in front of us, and we didn't want to take a chance on shooting our own men. All that decision-making took place in the course of a few seconds; it didn't take Doc and me long to realize that the movements in the bushes

9. Master Chief Boatswain's Mate Bob Lewis retired from active duty with the SEALs in 1993. His retirement came shortly after the fiftieth anniversary of Naval Special Warfare at Little Creek, Virginia. He had taken part in other operations in Vietnam and also Grenada and elsewhere. One of his favorite stories is about fast roping into Grenada with a machine gun and a chain saw.

10. Hospital Corpsman, Third Class Larry Williams had served with the Marines, where he was awarded a Purple Heart. Doc used to say if he ever received another one, it would be given to his mother, not him. We laughed about this. UDT-13 returned to Vietnam for one more tour in 1970. Larry tripped a booby trap and he and another kid, Luco Palma, were killed. Lt. Ernie Jahncke III was wounded and Tim Nichols lost an eye.

were not friendlies. The Ruff Puffs were firing randomly past us. Lewis got off about thirty rounds when he stopped firing and went down on one knee. Doc Williams and I were firing our M-16s to cover him, and I moved over, kneeling beside Lew to see what was wrong. Then I realized that he was trying to clear his weapon. The extractor had broken off the end of a shell casing and the brass was stuck in the chamber. He couldn't clear it and had no spare barrel.

At that time the Ruff Puffs moved past our position, firing their weapons sporadically. Lewis gave up on the M-60. By then the firefight was over. The Ruff Puffs ran by us and into the bushes. As I moved closer I could see the body of a dead Viet Cong lying nearly hidden in the bushes. One of the little Ruff Puffs ran up to where he was lying and emptied a full magazine into the guy's chest. They dragged his body and two others out of the bushes. The dead Viet Cong looked like they were in their late teens or early twenties. There was an AK-47 plus a few magazines beside one of them. Beside another was a B-40 launcher and two rockets. The third Viet Cong had been running toward a small canal when he was killed. We found more weapons in the canal. Apparently some of the Viet Cong had ditched their weapons and made a run for safety. Some were killed on the other side of the canal. One of the Ruff Puffs came up and pointed to the Buck knife on my belt. He was asking to borrow it. Not knowing what he was going to do, I let him use it. He returned shortly with a big betel-nut-stained grin and showed me the set of testicles he had cut off one of the dead Viet Cong. I was not impressed.

As we worked our way down to the riverbank, in a small depression we found two more B-40 rounds and a bamboo frame full of G.I. batteries, about twelve D-cell batteries, in series, fitted into a long tube of bamboo strips held together by rubber bands. That was the power source used to fire the command-detonated mine that had exploded astern of our Swift boat. A pair of wires led into the water and revealed where the mine had been placed. Apparently the man who fired it had his timing off. Luck was with us on that one.

Following SOP we got a body count. It is difficult to comprehend how those numbers meant anything. There were actually thirteen dead Viet Cong, but by the time the numbers were added that each separate unit wanted to claim, the total in the message traffic far exceeded the actual number of dead. That was typical, and I believe it was done to make our efforts look more productive than they actually were. Somehow the politicians equated military victory with how many of the enemy were killed versus how many of us were lost. It was kind of like we were nothing but points on the scoreboard of some permanent basketball game.

The captured weapons were gathered up before we slogged back through the mud to the Swift boats. We stopped at the village to drop off the Ruff Puffs. That time we went ashore and drank some Coke. Since the Ruff Puffs kept the captured weapons, we joked that we would probably be shot at again with them the next time we went out.

The villagers were very impressed with the little anatomical packages their macho heroes brought back. I felt only revulsion for anyone who could cut up the dead from his own country. Men are killed in combat. Having achieved all he could ever do for his cause, once a soldier is dead, he should be afforded the privacy of death. Those false heroes should have saved their energy for running the country after the war was over. Then bravery, character, and fortitude can truly shine, even if it is all a facade.

As an afterthought, some of us totaled the cost in ammunition for that day's operation. As nearly as we could estimate, it came to twenty thousand dollars per dead Viet Cong. If there had been some way to offer the Viet Cong a reward just to forget the war, we all might have been better off. But soldiers don't fight for financial gain. Only the politicians reap the rewards from the efforts of the warriors.

We were back aboard the *Terrell County* in time for steak, french fries, and ice cream. What a way to fight a war! From death, mud, mosquitoes, huge ants, and defoliated swamps to movies, a shower, hot food, and bunks. Talk about culture shock.

On another foray into the jungle with Detachment Golf, we came upon a small hootch where some Viet Cong had been staying. We found empty ammunition and crates that had contained U.S.-issue C-4 explosive. I made note of the lot number and date on the crate. When I got back to the ship, I checked the numbers against the inventory we hadn't used up yet. They were the same. The VC had been salvaging the stuff we threw off the ship and carrying it back to their hootches. Pretty industrious, I thought. It was so hot that day that HMC Doc Algeo passed out from the heat. He came around shortly after and we didn't have to hump (carry) him out. That would have been a bitch. Seemed like the bigger guys always had more trouble with the heat.

We were supposed to make any VC bunkers we encountered unusable. On one foray up the river we planted bags of CS powder (an irritant) in bunkers and stuck a sock of C-4 under them with a length of time fuse. Then we ran back to the Swift boat that had inserted us. But the goddamn boat was aground and when the C-4 went off and blew the CS all around the bunker, we were downwind of it. Needless to say, we were crying a little before we got the boat off the bank. After that we always grounded the boat upwind, if possible, when we blew CS.

On one trip down the Song Ong Doc we had to walk point for a Navy captain (O-6), who was there with some other men to survey the area in preparation for putting in a kind of floating Naval base. It was set up later that year and SEALs were stationed on board.

When I got ready to leave Detachment Golf and head back to Subic Bay, it was time for a number of others to rotate out. I was not actually due to rotate, but I was making a tour of the detachments to shoot pictures. We rode a Swift boat back to Phu Quoc Island. The boat had been in many firefights and had a number of holes that had not been patched because they were above the waterline. At least they were until we got into rougher seas. We had a twenty-three-hour boat ride ahead of us. The whole SEAL detachment was seasick and I was wishing I was dead. The only two who were not sick were Dean "O. D." Nelson of UDT-21 and the commodore, the captain in charge of the squadron of Swift boats. I was lying on the port engine cover on the stern deck. On the other was a man from the CIA we had picked up from some obscure island. I was puking straight up, as was he. We would throw up and then the next wave would wash it away. At one point I looked over at him and said, "I sure hope dying doesn't hurt this bad." He agreed. When we got to the base on Phu Quoc Island, we ate some half decent chow. I couldn't believe the guys there had Vietnamese women making their beds and cleaning the hootches. Talk about lax security.

From there I caught a C-123[11] and went back to Da Nang. Then I took a flight back to Clark Air Force Base in the Philippines, a very easy place to get in and out of. Usually a bus ran about every day from Clark AFB to Subic, so it was not difficult to catch a ride.

I had been able to make some illegal parachute jumps while in Subic Bay. The skipper, Lt. Comdr. Jim Wilson, didn't stand on formality when it came to operating. I'd had about 135 parachute jumps by the time I went to UDT-13, but they were all sport jumps. We used to jump out of any aircraft we could get. I jumped out of amphibious planes, transports, and helicopters. A couple of us even managed to make a demonstration jump trailing smoke at the San Miguel Naval Station on July 4th. I landed up to my knees in a large puddle, but I didn't care about that; the chow was pretty good. We just made the jump, ate a hamburger, and got on the helicopter to go back to Subic.

We had the usual PT (physical training) every day during our time in Subic. It got incredibly hot just a short time after dawn and during the runs, guys, usually hung over, would sweat incredibly. Some of us would take off ahead of the pack and hide behind a bus stop, and when the more dedicated members of the team ran back down the hill we sneaked out and joined them from the rear. It didn't take them long to figure that out. Some days we would play "jungle rules" water polo in the swimming pool near the Quonset huts where we were headquartered. The goal was to try to drown the skipper, or get the ball into the makeshift net at the end of the pool. I never had much luck doing either one, but I could keep up with the best of them in the water. That was a serious workout and served as a more realistic evolution than just doing PT in the oppressive heat.

We had our share of beer parties in Olongapo. I really missed American women, "round eyes." It wasn't the physical relationships with them I missed—at least that's what I thought—but being able to hold a good conversation with somebody who spoke the same language and had basically the same background. The girlfriend, Mary, who I was going with in high school, was in college somewhere. And Chris, who I had been

11. The C-123 had two turboprops and two jet engines and looked like a smaller version of the C-130.

going out with off and on in San Diego, wrote me that she had gotten married, so I burned her picture in a big glass ashtray in the barracks in Subic Bay.

During the trips to and from Vietnam, we had time to do PT, go into town for "sporting events," and get our gear squared away. After my experience in the Ca Mau Peninsula and since I didn't need a handgun, I had entertained thoughts of selling my Browning Hi Power 9mm. In conversation, I had offered to sell it to some of the guys in the team. The only one who had made me an offer on it was "Moki" Martin, when I was aboard the *Terrell County*. He had offered me an AK-47, a thousand rounds of ammo, and a couple of M-1 carbines. I would have taken him up on it, except I had no way to smuggle the fully automatic weapon back to Subic and then on to the States, so I declined the offer.

One of my teammates told me that he might be able to get me a good price for the weapon from some Filipinos that he knew. He and I went into town and dropped in at the U & I, where Crazy Amy worked. I talked to her for a few minutes and told her that I would sell the pistol, both magazines, and the shoulder holster for $250; I had about $75 invested at that time. She told me she would talk with her contact and see if that was a reasonable price.

While I was waiting, I decided that perhaps it was not a really bright idea to sell a weapon to a civilian in a country like the Philippines, so by the time I got the word from Crazy Amy that the price was too high, I had already decided not to make the deal.

There is a very good chance that my intuition saved my bacon. Later on, when returning to the States, I found out that there had been persons prosecuted for what I had contemplated doing. My good judgment finally paid off.

While I was in Subic Bay, Parachute Rigger, First Class Al Flud, a rather large Indian from Okmulgee, Oklahoma, and I went up to Camp Magsaysay in the Philippines to train some of the Underwater Operations Unit of the Philippine Navy in static-line parachute jumping. That was an experience. We rode to Camp Magsaysay in the back of a truck with the UOU men. It must have been a hundred or so miles. I remember the view from the back of that truck: being able to look straight down the side of a mountain. I noticed that the UOU guys had live ammo in their weapons. When I asked them about that, one of them explained that they got ambushed by the Huks all the time and had to be ready to defend themselves. I guess I should have brought something besides a pocketful of pesos and a camera. During the long ride to Camp Magsaysay we sat in the back of the truck listening to dirty jokes I had heard in high school. There's something funny about old dirty jokes told by a guy who barely speaks English—even if the jokes aren't that funny.

We arrived at the barracks where we would stay for a couple of nights. There was no running water, the toilets were overflowing, and the showers, of course, were inoperable. There were no mattresses on the beds; I stretched a blanket over the springs and slept on that. The insects nearly ate us alive. We ate lots of rice and whatever kind of meat it was they put in it. Real good bunch of guys, though, and we had fun doing this. Most of them would end up being pretty safe when they jumped, providing they remembered to wear a parachute. The UOU guys were quite good. And they looked out for us when we were in town. One of our guys, Dave Hosteter, was breaking up a fight between a Filipino and his girlfriend when somebody stabbed him with a butterfly knife. When he went down, the guy stole his Rolex watch. While Dave was recovering in the hospital from his near-fatal wound, one of the UOU men came to visit him. He grinned and tossed the Rolex on his bed. Hosteter asked where he had found it. The Filipino grinned and told him somebody shot the guy and left him in a ditch; all he did was recover the watch.

Some Special Forces troops from Okinawa came over to Subic so UDT could teach them how to do cast and recovery and scuba diving. While they were in Subic, we took them into town to knock back a few cold ones. When we were at the U & I club or Ding's, I can't remember which, a fleet sailor threw something at an SF sergeant. The sergeant calmly walked over and asked the sailor if he had really thrown something at him or had he imagined it? The sailor said, "Yeah. What the fuck are you gonna do about it?" Needless to say, the sailor didn't wait long to find out. The place instantly erupted into a typical TV-type free-for-all. Chairs and bottles were being thrown, some people were being knocked out, and others just ran from the club. At one point the Filipino singer on the bandstand threw down the microphone, pulled a piece of tubing from the mike stand, and started swinging at the crowd.

Now, mind you, I am not prone to violence, so I just stood up, stepped back, walked over to the bar, and ordered another San Miguel. A young hostess walked over to me and asked me to sit down. About then a Filipino came running at me with a chair to hit me, so I grabbed the chair out of his hands and made believe I was going to hit him with it. Then I sat down in it and started drinking my beer. About that time the "hardhats," full-time shore patrol (Navy policemen), came into the bar. They had guns and some of them carried M-3 "grease guns."[12] They looked around the bar and walked directly over to me.

"Let me see some I.D., sailor," a lieutenant commander said.

"I'm not in the military."

"Word is you started this fight."

"That's a crock of shit. But if you insist, I'll go with you."

"We insist," one of them said.

I walked down the stairs with two first class petty officers. As we walked down the street toward their paddy wagon, each one held one of my arms. I was talking real friendly and all of a sudden I jumped forward like I was trying to get away. They tried to hold me back and I just pushed my arms back against their grips. They weren't expecting the reversal and they lost their grip on me. I jumped back and hauled ass up the street. I could run pretty fast in those days and had no fear that they would catch me. However, there were other SPs on the street that night who were far thinner and in better shape than the two clods who had captured me. One of them, a real track star, came after me from the sidewalk across the street. I knew he would catch me, so I slowed down to save a little energy and feigned being tired. I waited until he ran up behind me. As soon as I felt his hands on me, I elbowed him in the face and he went down. I started running again but ran into the hood of a stopped Jeepney. By the time I got my shit together the other two had caught up with me. This time they held me a little tighter. I told them I hadn't meant to hurt the guy who caught me and that I hoped he was all right. They relaxed their grip a little and I pulled the same reversal thing again. This time I ran only about twenty feet and stopped and turned around.

"See, I could have gotten away."

That pissed them off. Now I knew I was in deep trouble. They got me to the paddy wagon and put me in with a kid who was in

12. A World War II–era .45-caliber automatic weapon, the M-3 looks like a caulking gun on steroids.

for drinking as a minor. The driver took every back road in Olongapo and bounced us around for about an hour. We finally ended up at the shore patrol headquarters inside the gate. When they opened the back door and I got out, two rows of SPs holding clubs out were waiting for me to try any crap.

"Nice night, ain't it fellas?" was my only remark as I quietly walked the gauntlet and into the shore patrol building, where I quickly produced my I.D. card.

The next day YN1 DeLorme came up to me with a sheet of paper. He handed it to me and asked me if I had done all that stuff. I read it and handed it back to him. He asked if I wanted it in my record.

I said, "No, I don't think so."

"Well, you better get rid of it then."

I did.

Around June some new guys checked in to UDT-13. They were Gilles, Gillen, Baresciano, Czerwiec, Dudley, and Kozlowski. All of them were fresh out of Coronado's BUD/S (Basic Underwater Demolition/SEAL) Class 50 and had not been to jump school. On about the second or third operation off the USS *Cook*, with Detachment Bravo, second group, they got in a firefight on the beach and Kozlowski jumped up to run from a bad place with no cover to try to get to the water (there is not much cover on a white sand beach, anyway) and was shot in the arm. As a result he was medevacked and had about an inch taken out of his arm, so that one was shorter than the other. He soon received a medical discharge with disability.[13]

Some time later I was in the barracks. Parachute Rigger Al Flud had the duty as the officer of the day. He went to the club and got drunk. When he returned to the barracks we were all asleep. He came into the barracks and started making noise about somebody taking the extension cord to his fan or something to that effect. I woke up and told him to go to sleep and worry about it in the morning. He mentioned something about

13. He went on to become a surf bum and successful commercial diver. Fate brought us together in 1993, when we worked the same diving job in Vermont. By then the story of his wounding had gotten better and he claimed to have been shot twice instead of just once. Well, they didn't choose frogmen for their mathematical ability.

"your generation," then started talking about how he had fought in the Korean War. I had the jump on him there. I had heard his stories before and thought they were bullshit, so I had asked DeLorme, the yeoman, to look up Al's record. He told me that Al had joined the Army after the Korean War was over and had then crossed over to the Navy after his hitch was up. Al kept on ranting. He was pissed off because I was twenty-three and had made E-6 only six months after him, when he was thirty-three.

Finally I said, "Al, you're full of shit. I've been shot at more than you've been fucked."

It was nearly pitch dark in the barracks. Al walked over to where I was lying in the top bunk. I had my eyes closed and had started to go back to sleep. All of a sudden he punched me in the face and broke my nose. I jumped out of the rack, blood streaming.

"Good job, asshole, you broke my nose."

Al was standing there ready to hit me again. I told him to go to bed before he screwed himself further. I think he might have sobered up a little. I opened my locker, got some clothes on, and went to sick bay. The corpsman there told me my nose wasn't broken! Christ, it was sideways. I could feel the bone crunch when I tried to straighten it. The next morning I went to the medical clinic at Cubi Point Naval Air Station. The corpsman there had a different diagnosis. The next thing I knew I was sitting in a dentist's chair with a drumstick or similar item in my nostril. The dentist had sprayed some novocaine solution up there to numb it, but might as well have not bothered for all the good it did. I think he lifted me out of the chair by my nose during the procedure. I heard the bone snap back in place and then the pain lowered to a dull roar. My nose has never been the same since.

About six weeks before we were due to go back to the States, Pete Upton and I gathered up all the material we would need to create the cruise book. Peter Carolan, known as "Pete the Pirate," gave us some of his cartoons.

LTJG Pete Upton was one hell of a writer. He could put things into words better than anybody I have ever known. I had shot a lot of pictures for it and we hoped to produce a good book. We lined up the well-known Dai Nippon Printing Company to do the work. We had asked all the guys in the team to write stories, draw pictures, and get out their souvenirs for us to put in the book, so Pete and I went to Tokyo with a briefcase full of memorabilia of our tour.

I had a room at the Akahane Hotel in Tokyo for a few nights. One evening I was sitting in the bar on the first floor when I struck up a conversation with two Japanese men. Well, it wasn't much of a conversation because we didn't speak each other's language. One of the hostesses did the translating. The men were with the Teijin Tire Cord Company, manufacturers of Bridgestone Tires, and they were inviting me to come with them to a Japanese country & western bar. How could I turn down an invitation like that? We left and walked to the train station. After a short train ride, we walked some more to a place that had Hank Williams music blasting out the door. The patrons were singing in English, but they couldn't speak a word of it, just memorized the words. We went inside and my hosts wouldn't let me take out my wallet, the party was on them. Tokens were purchased from the girl at the door and we paid for everything with them. That way no money changed hands except at the front counter, where the cash register was.

We had a few drinks and ate some sashimi, my first and last. Then we started back to the hotel. By then the subway was about deserted. We stopped at a little stand to get some fried tofu or something and I heard a violin being played. I looked around and saw an old man playing a violin, begging for money. This was too good to be true, since I play the fiddle. So I walked up to him and tried to convince him to let me play his violin. He was very reluctant to part with it, but the two guys with me told him I was okay. So there I was, a six-foot-three American, drunk, in a Tokyo subway after midnight, playing country music on a Japanese fiddle. After that I told people I was an internationally acclaimed violinist.

Back at the hotel, the Japanese asked me if I would like to go out again the next night. I told them I would and we agreed on a time. The next night they showed up with a girl, the sister of one of them. I kind of got the picture that she wanted to marry an American. I didn't feel comfortable in that situation, but went with them to the Tiger Beer Garden for some Japanese entertainment. Once again my wallet could not be removed from my pocket. Great people, but I never saw them again and did not get their addresses.

Pete Upton arranged for us to stay at the BOQ at Camp Oji, the site of an Army hospital where men with orthopedic wounds were operated on and stayed during recovery. There were men all over the place in wheelchairs, with limbs missing and horrible chunks removed from their bodies. Pete, myself, and several men who were going to Tokyo to study karate at the Shodokan ended up staying at the BOQ at Camp Oji. It cost us fifty cents a day for the room and we had maid service and a refrigerator. I thought that was great. The food in the chow hall was very good because the officers and enlisted ate together.

Every day we'd take a cab or train down to Dai Nippon to work on the book, and we made friends with the Japanese men who helped us, Naoyoshi Saato and Hiroyoshi Mizogui. Mr. Saato took us to one of the top floors and introduced us to the president of Dai Nippon, which even then was the second-largest printing company in the world. I was impressed by the work ethic I saw all around Dai Nippon and found out they printed the Far East versions of *Time* magazine and other publications for American publishers.

One night on the way back from Tokyo, where I had been watching the guys at the Shodokan work out in their karate class, we stopped by a bar outside the gate at Camp Oji. Before long we had made the acquaintance of the kickboxing champion of Japan. And we started drinking absinthe. An American had told us not to drink the stuff as it contained a narcotic we weren't supposed to drink. Anyway, by the time I left the bar that night I was wide awake and drunk and the kickboxing champion was passed out in the corner on his hands and knees with his face on the floor in a puddle of his own vomit. So much for the Japanese being able to drink.

During some of my time off I went into downtown Tokyo and purchased Nikon camera equipment. I had owned a Nikon when I first joined the Navy, but had sold it when I had access to free equipment as a photographer's mate. But I wanted my own again. The price was right, so I spent most of the money I had been saving since I reenlisted in December 1968 on camera gear. I still have that camera.

Pete and I, and our cases of cruise books, needed a hop back to Clark Air Force Base. When we tried to get a flight out of Tachikawa Air Force Base, the Air Force sergeant at the desk told us the "no-cost" orders we had were worse than no orders at all, so he threw them away and told us to say we had lost them. He got us on the next plane out. When we got back to Subic, the guys of UDT-11 had already started moving their gear into our spaces.

When I looked for the negatives that I had stored in a filing cabinet in the office, I could not find them and nobody seemed to know what happened to them. All the black-and-white photographs I'd shot during my tour were gone. I had only a few dozen eight-by-ten prints as a result of all that work. I was upset and to this day wonder who took them. I expect to see them in print sometime. Then I will know who the culprit is.

My sport-parachute rig had been stolen as well, the Paracommander in a Crossbow piggyback rig. The reserve chute was a tri-conical of a special design. I didn't have the serial numbers, but I knew I could get them from the dealer I had bought the rig from (Hugh Bergeron, in West Point, Virginia). The parachute theft pissed me off as much as the theft of my negatives. But right now I would give about ten of those parachutes to get my negatives back.

We drank our way back to the States, via naval aviation. When we got off the plane in San Francisco at the Air Force base, some of us didn't want to screw around waiting for a military flight, so we hired a cab and headed for the PSA (Pacific Southwest Airlines) terminal at the San Francisco airport. We'd put on civilian clothes by then and bought tickets for San Diego. Most of us had rings in our ears and didn't look too military, so we didn't catch any garbage from the antiwar types. When I arrived at the airport, I called Tom Hummer. He came out to pick me up in his Jaguar and took me to his place in South Mission Beach. I took a shower, changed clothes, and walked down to the Beachcomber, my favorite hangout in those days. I walked in and sat down at the bar and one of the guys I knew looked over at me and said, "Hi Steve, ain't seen you around for a while. Where you been?"

"Vietnam," I answered.

"Well, Jesus Christ! Welcome home! Let me buy you a beer."

CHAPTER FIFTEEN

Back in the States, San Diego

When we arrived back in the States, some of the new guys who had come to Vietnam with us and some of the men who were just reporting to the teams out of training had to get jump qualified. There were men from UDT-13, UDT-12, and SEAL Team One. Lieutenant Commander Wilson, our skipper, told me I could go to Fort Benning and attend basic airborne training with them. That was referred to by the guys in the teams as "Navy Appreciation School."

We were given commercial airline tickets and flew to Georgia in our civilian clothes. An ex-enlisted LTJG named Jim Dentice, of UDT-11, was in charge of our detachment.

We checked in and got basically the same lecture the skipper gave us before we left: we were guests of the Army and they would not put up with any crap from the Navy, Marines, Air Force, or even the Coast Guard if there were any of them here. The chow was awful and the instructors, although quite professional, were pretty much on the numb side. The officers didn't have to do anything except show up for class. They stood no duty that I knew of. Before long all the Army E-6s had quit or dropped out for some medical reason and I became the company first sergeant. I didn't have a clue what a first sergeant was. All they told me was that I was in charge of my company—half the class. There were 640 men (no women in those days) in the class. The first day I was in charge, the instructor, SFC Nuñez, told us there would be a police call. We had to pick up all the cigarette butts between the parade grounds and the PX. Well, being the fair-minded individual that I am, I decided that anybody who didn't smoke shouldn't have to pick up cigarette butts, so I had all the men fall out who wanted to have a cigarette. When they did so, I told the rest of the guys to go back and shine their boots and work on getting their uniforms squared away. I quickly learned that was *not* the Army way of doing things, and I was advised that everybody goes to police call.

During the runs, sometimes guys from the teams would fall out and run circles around the Army formation as they ran along the road. On hot days that kind of hot-dogging could be a real bitch, but we tried not to show it.

I had a private room with Al Starr, a second class storekeeper from Team-13. He was fresh out of training and a former fleet sailor. One night I was awakened by Starr, who told me that some lieutenant was giving somebody some shit in our barracks. I jumped out of my rack and put on a pair of pants. Then I walked out into the squad bay to confront an Army second lieutenant by the name of Fox, who was chewing out one of the men in my barracks. Most of the soldiers in that barracks were Army reservist parachute riggers who were required to go through jump school to fully appreciate the importance of what they were doing. Most of them had college degrees and they were about as squared away as any Army types I have met. The man who was bearing the brunt of the lieutenant's harassment happened to have a master's degree and owned a chain of barbershops with his father. He flew his own personal plane to attend jump school and was a sharp troop. To make a long story short, on inspecting the barracks after taps, the lieutenant had found the man in the latrine polishing his boots and was chewing him out for not being in his bunk after lights-out.

I lost it. I told Lieutenant Fox that the Army had decided to put me in charge of the barracks, the men in it were my responsibility, and I expected to be notified prior to anybody coming in and even talking to them. In the future any infractions of that rule would be met by me or my men physically throwing the son of a bitch out of the building. Fox just looked at me with disbelief and left. The men, awakened by the sound of loud voices, slowly made their way back to their bunks, shaking their heads in that "Oh, shit" manner.

Damn, I thought to myself, I'll get it in the morning. I figured they would probably throw me out of jump school. The skipper of Thirteen, Jim Wilson, had told us that anybody who got shit-canned from jump school, for any reason other than physical injury, would be back in the fleet as soon as he could cut the orders. The next morning at formation, Lieutenant Fox came up to me, took me aside, and quietly apologized for coming into the barracks without checking with me first. He said he had been out of line and shook my hand. I said no problem and that I shouldn't have jumped on his shit so hard. I humbly accepted his apology, we saluted, and parted amiably.

One of the guys on light duty who worked in the office, a Spec Four, had hurt himself playing touch football. He ran messages and drove the instructors around. He seemed like a pretty decent guy. We became buddies after a while. One night he asked me if I had any civilian clothes. I told him I did. He wanted to know if I wanted to go to some joint where they had a band. It was against regulations for students to go off base or even be seen in civilian clothes, so, for about ten seconds, I hesitated.

"How we gonna get there?" I asked.

"I've got a car," he said.

"Well, as long as we don't get into any trouble, I can handle it," was my response.

I went back to the barracks and slipped into Levi's and a shirt and a pair of shoes. When we walked to the parking lot, I saw that the kid drove a brand-new Corvette.

"Where in hell did you get this?" I asked.

"Bought it."

"Jesus, are you a rich guy or something?"

"Well, my dad gave me the American Music Corporation for my twenty-first birthday and told me not to piss it away."

"What the hell are you doing in the Army?" I asked.

"I thought I should serve like everybody else," he said. "I got fed up with those chickenshit assholes running away to Canada and the like. Besides that, I always wanted to be a paratrooper."

We ended up in some redneck, shit-kicking place down in Alabama. I was dancing with some reasonably good-looking woman and he was with another one. I noticed some guy watching us and asked her who he was. She said it was just her husband, he was kind of jealous. The Spec Four and I left shortly after that and drove back to the base. He scared the shit out of me the way he drove because we were doing a hundred at times. After that I figured I would stick to jumping out of airplanes. It was safer.

The only other time I went on liberty from jump school was with all the other guys from the teams. Lieutenant Dentice and the rest of us ended up in some other bar in Alabama. We were in there drinking beer and trying not to draw fire from the indigenous population. Before long the cops came in and dragged some woman out in handcuffs. I asked the waitress what that was all about and she said it had something to do with the woman's having shot her husband. We left after a while and got cabs back to the base.

We all graduated from jump school en masse. We had to sit in a very hot auditorium—I guess the air-conditioning was broken—and one of the instructors handed us a cigar box full of jump wings. We passed it up and down the rows and each took one. Well, some of us took two. Then they drove us Navy guys out to the airport and we flew back to San Diego.

We no sooner got back when the word was passed that we were going to Hawaii for training in the submarine escape tank and surf training. In other words, we were going to screw the Navy out of a vacation. I really didn't want to go, as I figured it would be a classic clusterfuck, but that was the way it was. After about three false starts we were on a four-engine prop job for Hawaii. We landed at Barber's Point Naval Air Station and soon were ensconced in the barracks at Pearl Harbor Naval Base. It was hot. We had to go out to Sunset Beach and "train" in the surf. That meant body surfing and learning to handle the big waves. I didn't have a lot of use for that because I wanted to chase women. But most of the women there were already being chased and, for the most part, didn't like sailors.

The best part of the trip was working in the submarine escape tank. It's one hundred feet deep and there are locks at the bottom and at various depths along the sides. Submarine sailors are trained to make free and buoyant ascents from it. They put the sailors in the locks, pressurize them, and then, one at a time, the men are released to go to the surface. Instructors stationed at various depths inside the tank ensure that students do not hold their breath and embolize as a result.

Some of us, of course, had to prove how hard-assed we were by making a free dive to the bottom of the tank. We would tie our sneakers together and throw them in. When they hit bottom we would grab the cable that went down and pull ourselves to the bottom. The goal was to grab your sneakers and have them on by the time you reached the surface. I made it to the bottom and succeeded in getting my sneakers, but the knot stuck where I had them tied together and I damn near blew out my sinuses. I didn't get them on. My mask was half full of blood when I got out of the water. So much for that trick. Only about twenty of us made it to the bottom. That's because most of the guys thought it was a dumb idea and didn't bother to attempt it.

When I got back from Hawaii, I started hanging out more and more in the photo lab. Officially it was known as the Naval Special Warfare Photographic Laboratory. Those of us who hung out there, SMC Lou Boyles, a SEAL, and PH2 Charlie Renaud, an admin type, used it almost strictly for cumshaw. Now to the uninitiated civilian, cumshaw is just another word for grand theft, but in the Navy cumshaw is frequently the only way to get stuff you need to do your job. But not always. It's an informal system of barter, exchange, and deception. The word "cumshaw" is what sailors called beach time in Hong Kong. They thought it was a Chinese word, and few knew it was a slurred contraction that native hawkers once yelled to entice sailors into their dice, girl, and opium action—"Come ashore." Since I was not "ship's company" in the lab, Lou asked me if I'd shoot the photo for the annual SPECWAR photo lab Christmas card. Lou said we needed a couple of weapons so I should go over to the SEAL team armory and check out some. Well, I went there and the chief in charge gave me an AK-47, an M-3 grease gun, and a Swedish-K with a silencer attached. I got back and showed them to Lou. I asked him what about the Swedish-K; I thought silencers were against the Geneva Convention or some shit like that. His eyebrows jumped a little and I took the 'K' back to the armory. We had this little Oriental-looking guy who would play the captured Viet Cong for the Christmas card. I shot the picture and we printed a bunch of them. They were mailed throughout the Navy to all the photo labs, to our friends, and to other members of the SPECWAR community.

Underwater Demolition Team-13 was selected to be on the recovery team for Apollo 12, and PH3 Bill Pozzi, one of the guys I had trained to become a photographer, was going along. He asked me if he could borrow a Nikonos, as he would be jumping into the water and actually helping the astronauts out of the capsule and then assisting them into the sling for the lift to the helicopter. I told him I would let him have a Nikonos and all the film he wanted, but I wanted first choice of his best shot. I would get to keep the original and would give him the rest. He kept his word. When he came back he told me they had confiscated all his film except the first roll he shot, and he gave that to me. I processed it and to this day I have the slide, one shot that has all the astronauts, the capsule, the recovery helicopter, and the ship they would be flown to. Great photo, never been published.

In Southern California, the teams made all their land parachute jumps at Roll's Farm Drop Zone, south of San Diego near the Mexican border. I made a couple of night jumps there and during one of the Boy Scout demonstrations made two water jumps into San Diego Bay. That's about the most fun you can have parachuting. I guess the Boy Scouts loved it. As soon as we hit the water and were recovered by the boats, we had to wash the saltwater out of our chutes and hang them up to dry. Then we all hit the beach for some cold beer.

When I had first arrived back in the States, I purchased a Honda 350 from Lieutenant Jahncke, who needed the money for a car. The bike had only a couple thousand miles on it and I think I paid five hundred dollars for it. On that bike I made a trip through Big Sur and almost all the way to San Francisco. I shot a lot of film and made some good photographs. But while I was traveling through Santa Barbara, somebody took a shot at me. I wouldn't have recognized what it was had I not had some experience at getting shot at. I was zipping down the road when I heard the shot snap by and then the crack of the weapon. It happened only once, but it was enough. I don't have a clue as to why or who it was. I just kept going.

When I returned to my apartment, two new kids from Team-13 were walking down the stairs from my door. I asked them what they wanted.

"Master Chief Walsh, the command master chief, sent us to tell you that you have shore patrol duty in San Diego." I went back to Coronado and checked in early off leave. I talked to BMCM (Master Chief Boatswain's Mate) George Walsh about it. He told me that they needed a first class petty officer to stand shore patrol. It was a rotating thing and we had to take our turn. No problem, I said, happy to do it. It would be for thirty days and I wouldn't have to pay the toll to cross the Coronado Bay Bridge. I knew Master Chief Walsh was a real operator. He had been one of the frogmen in the old days and was a friend of Roy Boehm—who founded the SEALs—and Hoot Andrews, an original SEAL. Some of those "old" guys had gone into Cuba with closed-circuit rigs from a submarine—not one of your average swims. I figured if George

Walsh wanted me to do this, then I would gladly do it, no questions asked.

I went in the office, picked up my orders, and jumped on my bike—I had traded the Honda to QM2 Bill Jakubowski of Thirteen for a Triumph 650 Bonneville—and headed to the shore patrol station in downtown San Diego. I checked in with a chief by the name of Sims.

"Jesus, they sent us a first class," he stated.

"They told me that's what you guys requested," I answered.

"Hell, all we ever ask for is a petty officer over twenty-one. I guess they felt they didn't need you around that bad."

I began to see the handwriting on the wall and knew that my time with peacetime special warfare was going to be short-lived.

Chief Sims was on light duty as he was recovering from a wound. Sims introduced me to the shore patrol officer, who turned out to be Marine captain Dave Hamilton, a guy I had spent many a night drinking beer with at the Beachcomber. I had never known what he did for a living. He recognized me and stood up, shook my hand, and told me to have a seat. He advised me that it was really a great job with not much to it. I should consider it almost a vacation. I would be assigned to booking. I would lock up military personnel who were brought in, ensure they were not in need of medical attention, and make sure they didn't have weapons. That sort of thing. Not too hard.

About a week after I checked in at San Diego shore patrol headquarters, I was walking in through the front door—I usually came around the back—and a young-looking Marine first lieutenant was sitting on the settee in the reception area. I took a quick squint at the ribbons he was wearing. He had about three rows, but the thing that stood out was the little light blue one on top with the five little white stars—the Medal of Honor. I had never seen one on anybody before. I walked into Dave Hamilton's office and told him about it. He came out and walked over to the lieutenant.

"Hello, I'm Captain Hamilton, the shore patrol officer," he stated.

The lieutenant stood up and shook his hand and introduced himself.

"What can I do for you, Lieutenant?" asked Dave.

"I just got out of Balboa Naval Hospital—I got wounded—

and I'm on light duty for thirty days, so they sent me here to work with you on shore patrol until I go back to my unit."

"That's the Medal of Honor, isn't it?" queried Dave, knowing exactly what it was.

"Yes, sir."

"Where is your home?"

"I live up the coast a little this side of L.A."

"Tell you what, Lieutenant, no Medal of Honor winner is going to be working shore patrol while I'm in charge here. You go home and give me a call once a week and let me know how you're enjoying your vacation. I'll see you in thirty days."

I was really impressed that Dave would do something like that, considering he was a gung ho Marine. He definitely earned my respect.

My job there wasn't too rough. Sometimes staying awake was the hardest part. The biggest crime most of the kids committed was drinking underage. The vice squad of the San Diego Police Department would bring in several of them every night. Usually there was no problem. We tried to explain to the sailors that it was a courtesy to turn them over and that the police did not have to give them to us. But one night, the cops brought in a real asshole in handcuffs. He had been in a fight and was quite belligerent. The cop who had arrested him was a decent guy about forty years old. When he took the cuffs off the sailor took a swing at him. One of the guys grabbed him. I looked at the cop and shrugged. The SP chief just said, "You can have him; he just fucked up. Now you can get him for assault and being drunk underage."

Another time they brought in a guy who had been in a fight and had cut his lip. When the corpsman went to ask him if he would like to have the cut looked at, the guy spit a mouthful of blood all over the corpsman's white uniform. I did not think much of that. I went into the cellblock and opened the cell door. I asked the guy if he'd spat on the corpsman.

"Yeah, what the fuck's it to ya?" he snarled.

"Well, I'll tell you what, pal, nobody spits on a corpsman on my watch. The guy's just trying to help you. You can either come out here, or I'm coming in there after you, asshole."

The guy just gave me that "fuck you" look. I walked in and dropped him with one punch. I made sure he was still breathing, then left the cell. Then next day when I showed up for watch, Captain Hamilton wanted to see me.

"Some guy we had locked up last night claims you hit him."

I'm sure Dave was expecting me to tell a story about how the guy must have slipped and fell and hit his face against the bars.

"Goddamn right I hit him, sir. The cocksucker spit on the corpsman when he went to look at a cut on his mouth. I knocked the prick on his ass."

"Well, his division officer is coming here with him to lodge a complaint against us for that. Are you sure that's how you want to leave it?"

"Yes, sir. That's what happened and I'd do it again."

A couple of hours later a namby-pamby lieutenant in khakis and thick glasses drove up in a gray Navy-issue pickup truck, parked out front, and he and the sailor I had punched walked in. Captain Hamilton sent for me. I walked to the door of his office, knocked, and was invited in.

"Petty Officer Waterman, this lieutenant is from the USS *Whatever*. He is Seaman Dipshit's division officer. Seaman Dipshit claims he was punched in the face by somebody who fits your description. Do you know anything about this incident?"

I stated, "Yes, sir. I knocked the son of a bitch on his ass last night."

The lieutenant's eyes lit up a little. He was thinking, Ah, I'm gonna get these fucking shore patrol assholes now.

"Petty Officer Waterman, please tell the lieutenant why you hit Seaman Dipshit," Hamilton said.

"Well, sir, I just got back from Vietnam. I served with Underwater Demolition Team-Thirteen. One of the things we did when I was with the teams is treat medical personnel with respect. After all, sir, they were sometimes the only thing between us and one of those sleeveless gowns made of waterproof fabric we know as body bags. Anyway, sir, this guy spit on the duty corpsman when the corpsman went to him to offer medical aid. Something just snapped, sir. I had to hit the bastard."

By that time the seaman had tried to crawl down into the top of his jumper.

The lieutenant glared at him. "Did you spit on the corpsman?" he yelled.

"Well, er, ah, yes, sir," he answered sheepishly.

"Get your sorry ass out to the truck. You're goddamn lucky it wasn't me here last night when you pulled that shit. Captain Hamilton, Petty Officer Waterman, I'm sorry to have wasted your time. You guys keep up the good work. I don't think you'll see Seaman Dipshit in here anymore."

That was the end of that.

Another time a young kid about eighteen was brought in drunk by the vice squad. He was about six-foot-three and probably weighed two-fifty. From looking at him I could tell he was most likely 100 percent American Indian. The vice cops were treating him like shit. When we took the kid's stuff from him, wallet, cigarettes, and all that, he went apeshit. One of the vice cops jumped on his back and choked him out. While he was unconscious they put handcuffs on him. When he came to I explained to him that we were going to put all his stuff in an envelope and seal it. He would sign across the back of the seal. When he got out, he would get all his property back. He couldn't seem to grasp that concept. He had a picture of his little kid in there and he was upset that we were not going to let him have that. I guess he thought he would not get it back. I couldn't understand why that would be a problem as we planned to give it to him as soon as the vice cop assholes left. In the meantime we put him in a cell and took off the handcuffs. He settled down on the bunk and went to sleep. The vice cops filled out the release forms and left. On the way out one of them stood on a plastic milk crate and sprayed Mace on the kid through the bars of the window. I didn't think too much of that and it gave me something of an attitude about San Diego vice squad cops.

A day or so after I returned to UDT-13, there came another challenge. One morning after PT, BMCM George Walsh informed Seaman Dudley and me that we had a mission. The Black Panthers or a bunch of radical bikers or some other organization might try to steal explosives from our military magazines. The teams needed a couple of us to "volunteer" to go up to Miramar Naval Air Station, where we kept our explosives, and make sure they were well-guarded.

"No problem, Chief. What do we draw for weapons?"

I thought they would probably give us M-16s.

"Go see the chief in the armory and draw a .38 and a box of ammo."

"You gotta be shitting me, Master Chief. I'm supposed to guard a fucking magazine full of TNT and C-4 against a radical group of crazed biker assholes, and you're sending me up there armed with a little pissant .38?"

"We can't send you down the road in a civilian vehicle carrying a fully automatic weapon. Besides, Dudley hasn't been in combat so I am having just one weapon issued."

I guess that made sense. So Seaman Dudley and I jumped on my Harley (I had traded "up" from my Triumph), with our sleeping bags tied on the back and the .38 stuck in my belt, and went up to Miramar to guard the magazine. I hid the Harley in a building in the same area as the magazine, and he and I crawled under another building that overlooked the magazine. We were going to just lay in there and gather intelligence if they broke through; there was no fucking way I was going to launch an offensive with just two of us and one beat-up Smith & Wesson .38. Fortunately nothing happened. That assignment lasted only two days. Then base security rigged up some type of alarm for the magazine.

I wasn't back at the teams for more than a week when Master Chief Walsh told me I would be the new barracks master-at-arms. I was to maintain law and order in the UDT barracks on the base. This was one straw that was putting a hell of a strain on the camel's back. I asked him if I had "fuck me" stenciled on my forehead or what was going on. He told me that I wasn't a UDT operator and therefore was kind of expendable as far as they were concerned. These jobs really weren't considered shit details as they were almost work-free and had no adverse effects on my record. I could still jump and dive with the teams and was still drawing my diving pay. Still, I didn't like it. I think he was under orders to coerce me into requesting UDT training. I went out and ran the obstacle course one day. I didn't see how the hell those guys did it so fast. I talked to one or two and asked them if they had had that much trouble running it. They laughed and said that some of them could just barely do it when they started training. After that I didn't feel like such a pussy.

During the latter part of February 1970, a woman moved into the apartment two doors down from me in South Mission Beach. Her name was Rosalyn Clausen. I helped her carry some of her heavy stuff up the stairs to her apartment. She lived there by herself and worked in San Diego. She invited me in for a cup of coffee (the only time I drank the stuff was when it gave me an excuse to talk to a woman) and told me she had to introduce me to her daughter. A few days later I met her daughter, Judy. We started hanging out together and jumping one another's bones with increasing frequency. It got serious when she started taking birth control pills. I asked her to marry me, under the impression that I had jumped out of airplanes, locked out of submarines, been shot at, and now it was time to do something *really* dangerous. She, of course, accepted. A few nights later I got shitfaced and called Mary, my old girlfriend back home. I asked her to come out to San Diego. She said she couldn't right then. I took that to mean she had other plans. Judy and I went to Fairhaven, California, to one of those instant marriage operations and got married on March 21, 1970. A civilian friend of mine loaned me his Corvette for the occasion. On the way back I got a ticket for speeding and the vehicle turned out to be unregistered. I should have taken that as a hint of things to come.

I requested a transfer back to Combat Camera Group and it had gone through. I would be going back to the East Coast in April 1970.

In March, UDT-11 returned from its six-month WESPAC tour. One of the men in the team, PH2 Terry Muehlenback, told me he knew who stole my parachute. I didn't even think about inquiring into my negatives. He told me that a parachute rigger by the name of PR2 Craig had done it. I went to SMC Lou Boyles, who ran the photo lab at Special Warfare Group, and asked him for advice on how to handle it. He told me to go see Lieutenant Commander Bell, the CO of UDT-11, and tell him the situation. I then went to PHCM Gene Gagliardi, who ran the parachute loft,[1] and told him about it. He said he would impound Craig's gear when it came back in the Conex box with the other stuff. Meanwhile, Lt. Comdr. Ron Bell talked to Craig and tried to get him to admit that he stole my stuff. Craig said he didn't do it.

When the gear came back from overseas, Master Chief Gagliardi impounded it and I got the serial number off the canopy of the Paracommander. Then I called Pioneer Parachute Company in New Jersey and asked them to run the number. The person I talked to said that the number was bogus, as they had

---

1. Things are really different in the teams. There was a master chief photographer's mate, PHCM Gene Gagliardi, running the parachute loft and a chief signalman, SMC Lou Boyles, in charge of the photo lab. Both of them were eminently qualified to do the jobs they held.

never issued a Paracommander with that number. When confronted by this information, Craig broke down and admitted that he had stolen my gear. I asked him where the piggyback rig and the reserve chute were. He said he had the reserve at home and that the piggyback rig had been burned. I tried to get Bell to put it to the guy hard, but he gave me a song and dance about how courts-martial take a long time and we might not even get a conviction. He asked, what would be my second choice? I told him that it would be better if I just got all my gear back and all Craig's gear, and that Craig should be transferred and never serve with Naval Special Warfare again. Bell said he could do that. I got my canopy, my reserve chute, and some other stuff that Craig had. I sold all but his reserve chute and my stuff. I had a feeling that Bell might be lacking in some areas of leadership, but he was still a lieutenant commander. I didn't think he showed the aggressiveness that many other SEAL officers would have under the same conditions. Thievery was not looked upon lightly among team members.

I was ready to head back to the East Coast. I tried to sell my Harley. I even left it outside my apartment, hoping somebody would steal it, but no such luck. So I arranged to have somebody ship it to me in a crate. That turned out to be a stupid move.

In a couple of weeks I had moved out of my apartment, and I stayed with Judy at hers for a few days until I flew to the East Coast. She would come east after I found a place for us to live.

I checked out of the team and said good-bye to all my friends there. I knew I'd miss operating with those guys. The skipper, Lt. Comdr. Jim Wilson, had told me he would send me TAD (temporary additional duty) across the street to training, but being an underwater photographer was looking like a much better deal than being a peacetime frogman. Most of us realized that the war in Vietnam was soon to be over, with us in second place. I told Lieutenant Commander Wilson that I appreciated his confidence, but I had a pretty good deal as an underwater photographer. There were only about fifteen of us in the whole Navy. What he didn't know was that my eyesight was a well-kept secret; I couldn't pass the physical without my contact lenses. Knowing the amount of time spent in the sand, mud, and water during BUD/S training, I was pretty sure there would be no chance I could see well enough to function on some of the training evolutions, especially at night. In retrospect I should have stayed and made another tour with Team-13, but that is history now.

I said good-bye to Judy's mother, Rosalyn,[2] then Judy gave me a ride to the airport and we kissed good-bye. The flight was nonstop to New York. From there I had to take Allegheny or some other treetop airline to Norfolk.

---

2. I saw Judy's mother one more time, when she came to Norfolk to visit. She contracted cancer and killed herself a few years later.

CHAPTER SIXTEEN

Combat Camera Group Again

When I arrived at Norfolk airport, Dick Johnson came out and picked me up. Christ, was I glad to get back to the East Coast. Things seemed more realistic there.

After I checked in at Combat Camera Group and settled in at Dick's place, I found an apartment on Waco Street in Norfolk. Two brothers named Wright, "the Wright brothers," were developers and had recently completed several apartment buildings. I talked to one of them and he said he had a place. He asked me if I had one of those "mixed marriages." I told him that I didn't. I guess nowadays he could get into trouble for even asking that question. The apartment I rented was on the first floor and close to a large supermarket, the Giant Open Air Market, and only about two miles to work.

Judy flew to Norfolk and we purchased a used car, a Coronet 440. As a wedding present, her grandmother had given us the money to buy it. We didn't own it very long before we traded it in on a bright yellow VW Super Beetle. The thing cost just under two thousand dollars brand new.

My Harley Sportster hadn't arrived from San Diego. There was a truckers strike on and no one had a clue when it would end. When the bike finally arrived, it had rust on it and had obviously been sitting out in some back lot in storage. I couldn't get even the headlight to work without killing the engine. I took it to a Harley shop in Norfolk and they screwed around and bypassed the light switch so I could at least run the headlight. Eventually I got some guy to buy it, but I have to say that Harley was the worst piece of machinery I have ever owned. I know they make them better now, but I still can't get the nasty taste out of my mouth from that experience.

During May 1970, Dick Johnson, Bill Curtsinger, Charlie Curtis, and I went to Freeport on Grand Bahama Island. We would be working with the inventor of the Plexiglas dome, Dr. Jerry Stachiw, a Russian engineer. Jerry had developed a method of taking thick sheets of Rohm & Haas Plexiglas cut into pentagons and, using a heating and vacuum process, bending them into a spherical shape that was capable of withstanding enormous pressure. The Navy had built a sphere out of these plastic pentagons at Southwest Research Institute. A couple of their physicists came up and would be diving this thing to five hundred feet. The Perry Oceanographics submersible and the support vessel *Shelf Diver* were on-site for support. I talked my way into a dive in the *Shelf Diver*.

The pilot and I sat on the bottom in about five hundred feet of water and waited for the NEMO (Naval Experimental Manned Observatory) to come down beside us while I shot movie footage and still photos of it. I was shooting High Speed Ektachrome out of the forward port in the *Shelf Diver*. The light was pretty dim and I had to rate the film at 400 and push-process it when I got back. It was my first experience in a small, dry, one-atmosphere submersible, but would not be my last.

My assigned job was underwater cinematography. Bill Curtsinger would be shooting stills underwater and each of the other men on the crew would shoot whatever was required topside. Charlie Curtis was the motion picture guy, and Dick Johnson ran around shooting cut shots with the handheld 16mm camera.

Whenever I could, topside, I would shoot stills. One of my color photos was used on the cover of *Navy* magazine. And some of my footage was used in the Navy production *Eyes Under the Sea*, a movie we made about the Navy's underwater photographers. The script had started out very corny, but by the time we gave it a reality check, one could actually believe it. The writer had beautiful women coming out of the surf with cameras and that sort of thing. We read it with a jaundiced eye and made so much fun of it that Volker "Hasi" Seifert, an optical engineer we were working with from the Naval Photographic Center, told us to just go ahead and shoot wild footage with no script and then have our editors see what they could do with it. We did, and the editors pulled off a hat trick and made a good documentary of it. The scriptwriter was sent to Adak, Alaska, I think.

A lot of the footage for it was shot topside back in Norfolk. I had a motorcycle with a sidecar and PH2 Rick Mason shot motion picture film from it as we drove alongside guys running PT.

Some other footage was filmed in the diving locker. All together, it was not a bad production and we got some good reviews on it within the military filmmaking community.

There wasn't much to do in the Bahamas. Except for the Chinese at the International Marketplace, the food was not gourmet quality, and the British beer was always warm and I couldn't get used to that. Other than the diving I had no use for the place. A civilian named Flip Schulke came down to work with us. He was making a film about the NEMO testing. Things like that used to really piss us off. We had the best equipment in the world, yet they would assign some civilian with a trust fund or government grant to do a story on us. Or somebody who was into "film" would decide they wanted to tell the "true" story of some operation we were on. They, or their crew, would then show up with an old Bolex wind-up camera, bum film off us, and, without possessing the necessary technical expertise, write about and document what was "really" going on.

My motorcycle at the time was a BMW R-60 with a Steib sidecar, a thing of beauty. I used to ride it to Suffolk when I went parachute jumping. It was silver and the sidecar had red upholstery. Early on I broke the sidecar's windshield by trying to bend it too quickly to snap it into place. So I went to a plastics shop in Norfolk that specialized in making custom objects out of Plexiglas. The fellow who owned the shop was named Emanuelson. I vaguely remembered his name from somewhere, then I recognized his son, Bo, one of the kids who had hung out at Al's Surf Shop when I lived in Virginia Beach.

Mr. Emanuelson made me a new windshield from smoked Plexiglas and it fit perfectly. On one of the first long rides on the bike after that, Rick Mason and I decided to go out to the backwater area of Virginia Beach and just ride the roads a little. Rick was small and easily fit into the sidecar. Well, we got going along and ended up in Pungo, Virginia. Jay Bender, a friend from Virginia Beach who used to own the Steamer, a small restaurant that served steamed corn and hot dogs, lived out there in a big house. We found his driveway, a long one that looked like something out of a swamp-setting for a Stephen King movie. The house looked like it was about to fall down. The outside was all faded and weatherworn. It was hard to tell if somebody actually lived there.

We rode up the driveway and to the front door. As I got closer

I could see that the windows and all the doors were fairly new, they just didn't look it. Jay came to the door and invited us in. I introduced him and Rick and we sat and talked for a while. Jay asked us if we would like some homemade bourbon.

I looked at Rick. He had a shit-eating grin on his face. I looked back at Jay and he already knew the answer. Jay broke out a Mason jar full of clear liquid. First he gave us a small shot of that. It was pure moonshine of good quality. Then he put some sugar in a frying pan and burned it on the stove. He poured the moonshine in the pan after the sugar had cooled off and then poured us some more over ice. Jesus, that stuff was smooth. Pretty soon we had quite a buzz on. Next thing Jay asked us if we wanted to go for a boat ride. Sure, we could go for that.

He led us outside to a small, decrepit, unpainted boathouse. Inside was an airboat with a 180 horsepower Lycoming airplane engine. Jay pushed it out of the shed and we hopped aboard as he cranked her up. We spent about an hour zooming through the swamps outside of Virginia Beach. By the time we returned to Jay's house the effects of the moonshine were starting to wear off, so Jay gave us a little more and some to take with us. Rick and I made it back to Norfolk, but I don't know why I am still alive.

The antiwar movement was going full blast, and almost every weekend there was some kind of rally in Washington, D.C. PH2 Jim Call, one of my photo mate friends from combat camera, and I decided we would see if we could get some good photos of the situation there. I wore a pair of combat boots and Levi's, and Jim dressed about the same. We each carried a couple of Nikon Fs and shot color slides. We found just about every denomination of radical church, and anything else we could imagine. A lot of the kids were smoking dope, and the religious right was there with Reverend Carl McIntyre, the supposed guru of patriotism. We just wandered around trying to get good photographs. I didn't have an opinion and thought some of it was pretty humorous. One guy tried to recruit me into a white supremacist organization called ROWP, Rights of White People. I don't think they went very far with their recruitment. I think the head of it was a Marine sergeant in North Carolina. Jim and I went up to D.C. twice that I recall, and decided it was not a productive way to spend our time. We slept in the car and ate at whatever hot dog stand was available.

Later in the summer, Jim and I went to Little Creek and photographed Class 49's UDT/R (Underwater Demolition Team/Replacement training) Hell Week. We made up an audiovisual presentation that used two projectors and the song "Raindrops Keep Falling on My Head" as background music. At the graduation party for that class, Jim showed the production to the new frogmen as I was out of town on a job. They loved it.

I still did some parachute jumping out at Suffolk. The first time my new wife, Judy, had come out to watch me I had a bad partial malfunction. I jumped with a guy named Fred Farrington, who we called Fred Farkel after a character on *Laugh-In*, the TV show. We went out at twelve thousand feet and were going to hook up and do some relative work. I blew the exit and he got away from me, so I decided to just pull high and screw around. I dumped my main at about thirty-five hundred feet, which is a thousand feet higher than the normal parachute opening in sport jumping. As soon as I got the shock, I looked up and saw a ball of colored rags where I should have had a Paracommander parachute. The thing was really tangled up. I pulled the steering toggles down and alternated them. Then I pulled on the back risers and tried to shake the thing loose. I looked over to where Fred was and noticed I had fallen past him, even though I had opened way above him.

Oh, shit, I thought, the reserve I have is the one I got from that dickhead who stole my parachute in the Philippines.

I wondered if there was even a parachute in the damned pack, as I had not had it repacked since I got it from him. I figured I would die either way, so I cut away from my main and opened the reserve. It was a twenty-six-foot conical parachute. However, he had cut a modification in it to make it steerable and in doing so had cut to within about thirty inches of the apex of the chute. This made it come down like a rock. I had on my blue tennis shoes, Levi's, a Navy-issue leather flight jacket, and, of course, my Bell helmet. I knew I was going to hit like a ton of shit and could see people running out to where I was going to land. All their faces were turned skyward. My legs started to shake as I approached the sun-dried, plowed ground between the runways of Suffolk Airport. I was making a maximum effort to execute the perfect parachute landing fall (PLF). I hit in a front left PLF and rolled over so quickly that I actually bounced back up off the ground. As I got to my feet I heard somebody exclaim, "Jesus, he got up!" I knew then that I had hit pretty hard. My left shoulder hurt back by my shoulder blade, but I was not hurt otherwise.

Fred landed not far from me a couple of minutes later. He came over and congratulated me on living through a real bastard of a landing. He had seen how fast I was coming down and figured I would at least break a leg.

The fellow who sold me the BMW motorcycle had told me that he wouldn't sell it to me unless I promised him that I would sell it back to him if I wanted to get rid of it. I did so after a while and he ended up selling the thing anyway and getting another bike. I bought Judy an MG Midget. The damned thing was so small I could hardly ride in it. She had always wanted an MG and one of the chiefs—one of the smaller chiefs—was selling his. He was being transferred and needed to get rid of it. I gave him seven hundred dollars or so for it and Judy had her sports car. We used the VW whenever both of us went somewhere; I could get in the MG, but couldn't move around enough to scratch my ass.

A new guy, PH1 Eugene McCraw, transferred into the Underwater Photo Team. A short, stocky guy, he had finagled his way into being a saturation diver while stationed at Experimental Diving Unit in DC. Mac smoked at least a pack and a half a day and was usually last on the runs at PT, but he could fix anything mechanical and was one hell of a nice guy. He was one of the best cumshaw artists around. His wife, Jeannie, was from somewhere in Texas, too, I think and she could cook as well as anybody I have ever met. They made one hell of a fine pair, both of them real characters.

We were needed in Puerto Rico for another underwater photo job. I can't remember what the job was, but I remember that we somehow sneaked Mac's 90cc motorcycle into one of the packing crates. I remember that Mac was so drunk he passed out on the plane before we took off and woke up just enough to drink some more. We had vodka and cranberry juice in one of those thermos-type coolers. We all partook of the spirits on occasion.

When we got to Puerto Rico we were put up in some barracks way the hell away from the rest of civilization. There was a bowling alley nearby and I used to go over there and make phone calls home and drink beer. I remember that the cook there made a hell of a good grilled ham-and-cheese sandwich.

One night, after going to Fajardo to consume vast quantities of malt beverage, I was walking down the road to the back gate. The back gate is very desolate and the road that runs to it goes through a large cane field. Behind me in the darkness I saw a single point of light coming my way. Then I realized it was a motorcycle. Pretty soon I saw that it was Mac. There aren't any buddy pegs on a Honda 90. Even so, Mac stopped and I got on behind him. At the time I weighed about 235 and Mac probably was pushing 190. Somehow both of us got on the bike. I think Mac was sitting on the gas tank and I had the back two inches of the seat. My heels were on the nuts that held the back wheel on. We were cruising about fifteen to twenty miles per hour down the paved road and managed to get through the gate and past the Marine sentry when I noted a car following us. We had to stop at a sign where the road branched off. I waved the car by. The guy didn't move. I waved again. He still didn't move. I jumped off the bike and walked back to the car. There was a lone person in the vehicle.

"What the hell are you doing, goddamn it! Why don't you come around us and get the hell out of here. If I fall off this bike I don't want some dickhead running over me."

"Watch your language, sailor," he said. "I'm Lieutenant So-and-So and I'm president of the base motorcycle club. I don't want to see anybody get hurt."

"Well I don't give a flying fuck who you are, you're the only one that's going to get hurt if you don't get the hell out of here right now."

He left. I never heard another word about it. Mac and I made it back to the barracks in one piece.

I decided that if I was going to stay in the Navy, I should probably go to 2d Class Diver's School, as I eventually wanted to become a diver first class. One of the prerequisites for first class school is to be a second class diver when you apply. The course was at YFNB-17 at Little Creek Amphibious Base. The school was ten weeks and covered every aspect of air diving and salvage theory, and a small amount of demolitions training. I put in a chit and it was approved. I ended up in a class with about fifteen other guys. A couple of them, Rex Davis and Fred Keener, were from SEAL Team Two. Rex was a pretty big guy but out of shape. Fred was a quiet blond man and a hell of a good guy. He had been a heavy-duty operator in Vietnam and stories about him are told to this day. Our class instructor was a Mexican-American by the name of Hernandez, a bosun's mate first class. We had others there, Bill Manning and a guy by the name of Royce who looked like Howdy Doody. The chief at the school was named Ross, a short little prick nobody liked. One day when we were going out for PT, I said, "Hey guys, Chief Ross is gonna lead the run today." He looked at me with fire in his eyes. The guy couldn't have run if his ass was on fire. After that, since I had poked fun at him in front of the class, he was out to get me. One day we were swimming underwater in the pool over at Norfolk with scuba gear. We had taken our masks off to practice swimming without them but the pool had recently been chlorinated and our eyes started to really burn. I felt there was no need to screw up our eyes for the sake of a stupid drill. I stood up in the pool and told him that if he wanted to screw with us, why didn't he just get us out of the pool and make us do flutterkicks or something. He said, "You really like it here, don't you, Waterman?" I said, "Yeah, Chief, I really love this place."

Next day they called me into the office and told me I had to quit school or they would shitcan me. I told them they would have to shitcan me as I wouldn't quit under any circumstances. You guessed it, I was gone the next day. Hernandez had been on leave for a family emergency when that happened. When he came back he asked somebody where Waterman was. "He got shitcanned for having a bad attitude," one of my former classmates said. "Shit, he was the only one in this whole goddamn class who had the right attitude," Hernandez retorted. Meanwhile I returned to Combat Camera Group and explained what had happened. I told them that I would like to go back later and take the course again. Nobody gave me any shit and they said I could when things were right.

In late summer 1970, I went home to Maine and ended up seeing Mary a lot. Her father warned her not to become correspondent in a divorce and she, of course, took his advice seriously. I had brought my two Nikons and lots of Uncle Sam's film, so I spent a week on Graffam Island shooting pictures of an old lobster fisherman I had known as a kid. He and I had some long conversations about life, women, war, and things of that nature. After some time out there, I returned to the mainland and headed back to Norfolk. A few weeks later I got a phone call from my old friend Bill McClellan. It seems that Beldon Little, of salvage fame, had another idea about how we could make some serious money. Somebody had located an old shipwreck off the coast of Delaware that was loaded with ironstone china. Beldon did some checking around and thought we could make a few thousand dollars apiece if we cleaned out the wreck and sold the dishes on the antiques market. The crew would consist of Beldon, Bill, me, Jerry Smith, Larry Theorine, and Ray Curraco. Ray would be the cook, the rest of us would be divers, and Beldon was the brains behind the operation. He had lined up an old Nova Scotia–built schooner, the *Lister*, that we would use as a platform to operate from. The owners, Lem Brigman and Riley Davis, had bought the 110-foot vessel and were living on it over at the old ferry dock near Little Creek. We removed its sails, put them in storage, and loaded aboard all the supplies, compressors, diving gear, and so forth that we would need for this adventure.

In addition to being a crewman and a diver, I was going to be the photographer. I put in for a week's leave and it was approved. Then I "borrowed" a couple of Navy underwater cameras and "requisitioned" film for "training," assembled my diving gear, and loaded everything aboard the *Lister*.

The *Lister* was an old schooner built in Lunenburg, Nova Scotia, for swordfish fishing on the Grand Banks. She was wood and had a Rolls-Royce diesel engine. The reason she was named the *Lister* was that the Lister diesel company offered to give the owners a Lister generator for free if they'd name her after the company. That was easy. She had been lying there at the wharf in calm conditions for several months. Water had not touched her above the waterline for quite a spell. The seams above the waterline had dried out and started to open up a bit. Beldon had allowed for this, so he had rented a large air compressor and a couple of submersible air-driven pumps. We knew she would leak badly once we got under way.

We left the ferry dock the next morning and headed up the bay. After passing over the Chesapeake Bay Bridge Tunnel, we hung a left and steamed along the eastern shore of Virginia and Maryland. I had started to get a little queasy as we passed the first point of land off Virginia. Before long I was throwing up. The swells kept increasing until we were taking green water over the bow. We stood two-man watches every two hours. Beldon had gone ahead of us in his truck as he didn't want the people in Delaware to know what we were up to. He had loaded a case of dynamite or two on board in case we had to blow the wreck to get at the cargo. The China Wreck, as we called it, was a favorite spot for charter fishermen to take their parties. It was out of sight of land but still pretty shallow, about fifty feet. As we progressed up the coast, it got dark and the wind picked up. Before long all of us except Riley and Lem were puking. Bill was so sick he was lying under a piece of canvas back on the lazarette. Soon we were getting soaked by the water coming over the deck with every other wave or so as the bow plunged into the swells. The wind was howling at about forty knots and I was wondering if it might be my last voyage. Lem's cabin was just forward of the steering station. Lem came up and looked around to see if he could spot any landmarks or red lights on radio towers. His electronics consisted of an old HF radio and a Loran A receiver.

He calculated our position and started back down the steps. Just then a large wave broke over the bow and green water washed down both sides of the trunk cabin along the deck. He felt the thud as the bow dug into the swell and jumped back up to where I was steering. We both grabbed for Bill just as he started to float back over the stern rail. Lem rolled him down the steps to the trunk cabin, and that's where he stayed until we got to the wreck. That was close. Had Bill slipped overboard, I doubt very much that we could have recovered him under those conditions. Even Larry and Jerry, both ex-Navy frogmen, were throwing up, and we were all cold and miserable but had no choice except to stand our watches every two hours. It was fifty-seven degrees and I was as cold as I have ever been before or since.

By the next morning we had recovered, and the seas and wind had abated to reveal a very nice day. We got the word from Beldon over the radio not to show up at the site of the wreck, but to just lay over the horizon until he had pinpointed its location. After a while he gave us the "secret code" and we steamed for it. Beldon had marked the spot with a buoy thrown from the fishing boat he had conned into taking him to the site. He paid the skipper of the boat fifty bucks and loaded his gear onto the *Lister* from the party boat. The charter fisherman left and went back into Lewes, Delaware. The get-rich-quick part of the trip commenced. When I signed on, my cut was to be 12.5 percent of the take, plus whatever I would make for doing the photography. Ray, the cook, had chosen to get paid a salary of $125 for the trip.

Larry and I set up the gear, and he was going to dive in Mark

V hardhat while I would dive scuba. Larry had no hardhat training, but he was a good diver and could use any kind of gear quite handily. We got rigged up and loaded Larry into the big steel box we would use to bring up the "treasure." Lem lowered him into the water using the *Lister*'s main boom, and he rolled out of the bucket. As soon as I heard him say he was on the bottom, I jumped over the side and followed his air hose down to him. We prowled around the wreck and started to load dishes into the bucket by the armload. We finished getting what we thought was a full load, and Larry told Beldon over the diver's radio to take up the bucket. It disappeared from view and in a few minutes came back down near where we were. Larry and I dragged it across the bottom to another location and filled it again. We had been hoping that we would find some silverware or something valuable, but did not. We loaded the bucket a few more times and then Larry climbed in with the dishes and they hauled him up. After he got out of the bucket, they dropped it down and I climbed in and they recovered me from the water. We had picked up around 275 plates and various dishes from the wreck. We called it a day as we felt we had cleaned out whatever was there. The dishes had been packed in hay inside wooden barrels, which, of course, had rotted away over the years. Many were broken, but a large number were intact.

We hauled anchor and steamed for Lewes. My Vietnam record of twenty-three hours of being seasick had been broken, and I got one plate out of the recovery. I had to be back at work in a day, so I rode back to Norfolk with Beldon in his pickup truck. We later found out that the type of dishes on that ship were the cheapest that could be made as they were heading for a prison. In those days, of course, paper plates had not been invented. Our dishes were the ironstone equivalent of paper plates.[1]

I got to Norfolk and made it to work on time, checked in off leave, and things were back to normal again.

Judy and I decided to go to Maine for a few days so she could meet my family. We drove up in the VW and made the rounds. My mother treated her quite badly and it upset her a lot. So we didn't stay in Maine long and soon drove back to Norfolk.

---

1. Years later the wreck *Whydah* was recovered from an area not far from where we had been working the China Wreck. Of course, we all speculated on how rich we could have become had we stumbled onto that treasure instead.

I got a call from Lane Briggs of Rebel Marine. Lane was a good old boy from Virginia who owned Rebel Marina on Willoughby Spit. He also had a small diving company called Rebel Marine Service. He just did whatever work was required. Lane never had any full-time divers, he just hired people when he needed them. This time he had a job in North Carolina shoring up a small dam on a river. The bottom of the river had washed out underneath the dam and we had to go down and put fiber-form bags under the downstream side and pump them full of a cement mix. That took three or four days. I had lots of leave on the books so I had no trouble taking some time off.[2]

Judy and I did not have any big problems and seemed to get along well for a while. I think probably our biggest difficulty was not communicating with each other. One week Judy took off and drove to Akron to visit her grandmother. She called me and asked me to come up and be with her. I did and things seemed to go well for a while, but I think we both knew her trip was the beginning of the end.

The Salvage of the *Bay King*

In the summer of 1971, I was asked to go on another salvage diving job with Beldon Little. A tug, the *Bay King*, had sunk up the bay off Solomons, Maryland. The *Bay King* had been towing a barge loaded with sand when it had simply rolled over and sunk right out from under the crew. The skipper, a North Carolina native by the nickname of Jitterbug, barely got off the boat alive. He couldn't swim a stroke. Later he told me what had happened.

They'd been steaming for Solomons towing a sand barge. Jitterbug made a slight turn to port and the *Bay King* just kept on rolling over to starboard as they made the turn. "I knew she was full of water. The cook and the engineer were standing in the wheelhouse and their eyes started getting real big. They headed for the open wheelhouse window and began to squeeze out through it. I knew I'd never have time enough to wait for them, so I dove for

2. A few years later Lane got a grant from the federal government to test the feasibility of a sail-powered tugboat that would use wind power to supplement the diesel engines. He named this boat the *Norfolk Rebel* and has been on many adventures with it. It has come to Maine a couple of times in the past few years.

the open wheelhouse door. By now the water was coming in through the door. I pulled myself out the door and, just as I started pulling myself up the rigging for the surface, I felt the stern of the boat hit bottom. When I got to the surface, the cook was hanging onto the bow of the tug. Air was bubbling up all around him and I knew the bow was going down any second. There was some wood and stuff floating in the water that washed off the *Bay King*. I had a sheet of plywood and just shoved it toward the cook, who grabbed onto it just as she went down. The engineer was hanging onto another piece of blocking that had washed up from the tug."

Some local fishermen had seen the mishap and rescued the three men from the water. Later on the Coast Guard came out, cut the hawser hooked to the tug, towed the barge to Solomons, and put a lighted wreck buoy on the place where the oil slick was forming. The *Bay King* was diesel-powered, and a continuous upwelling of fuel oil leaked to the surface, marking the spot with a wide sheen on the water.

Before we could do the job, we had to outfit a barge over at Lockwood Brothers in Hampton, Virginia. Beldon and I went over and figured out what would be needed. His plan was to find the tug, rig slings under it using divers, pull it to the surface using two cranes—one on the stern and the other on the bow—pump it out, and tow it back to Norfolk.

It took a couple of days to rig the barge with the two cranes and the diving gear. We then went aboard the tug for the ride to the *Bay King*. I slept most of the way and the other divers, Skip Barber and Larry Theorine, did, too. We came into the wheelhouse to inquire about our position once in a while. We anchored the barge near the site the next morning and I suited up in a wet suit and scuba gear. Beldon rigged a circling line on a cinder block, threw the block overboard, and passed me the end of the line. I jumped into the water off the side of the tug and started searching for the wreck. In spite of its having a buoy nearby, it took me almost a full tank of air to find it. Pretty soon I ran into it in the limited visibility of Chesapeake Bay, tied the circling line to it, and surfaced. The tug came over and I handed the line to Beldon. He tied on a Clorox bottle as a float and I climbed aboard. We had a small discussion as to which direction the *Bay King* was lying on the bottom. I told him what part of the boat I had tied the line to and Beldon had the tugboat go over and hook up to the crane barge.

They pulled it back over the *Bay King* and, using a bow and stern anchor, placed the barge just about over the top of the *Bay King*. The water there was fifty-five feet deep at high tide.

I got out of my diving gear and we rigged the dive station. Larry got into his long underwear and his canvas diving suit. We bolted him into the breastplate and Beldon gave him instructions as to what he wanted him to do. Larry was a good man in the water and had no trouble figuring out exactly what we were up to. We lowered him into the water with one of the cranes and he went to work. After he had done a survey on the *Bay King* and checked around to see how much of what Beldon wanted could actually be accomplished, he passed word up that he was ready to have me come down and help him. I climbed back into my wet suit, strapped another bottle of air on my back, and jumped overboard. I followed Larry's air hose to the bottom and tapped on his helmet to let him know I was there. Using a rope, the deck crew lowered a steel cable sling to us. Larry took one end and walked around the side of the stern. I grabbed the other end and fed it through between the shaft and the bottom of the tug. Then I swam back and gave him a thumbs-up. The topside crew lowered the hook the rest of the way and we pulled it to us using the same rope that the sling had been tied to. I helped him get his end of the sling onto the hook and went over to retrieve mine.

By then it was getting late and Beldon decided to call it a day because Larry and I were pushing our bottom times. We left the barge and tug there and went ashore in shifts in the outboard. The crew of the tug stayed aboard. Beldon, Skip, Larry, Jitterbug, and a couple of other guys from Lockwood Brothers came ashore and we stayed on the third floor of some firetrap hotel. Unfortunately, Beldon smoked all the time and would fall asleep in bed while smoking. That scared me more than any part of the job. I went in to wake him in the morning and he was lying there on his back with the burned stub of a cigarette between his fingers. The cigarette had two inches of ash on it that had burned clear back to his fingers before going out. Scary. If that wooden building had gone up, I might not be around today.

After a large breakfast at a nearby diner—Beldon had just coffee and a doughnut—we headed back to the barge. The weather was flat calm and the water was glassy smooth. The first thing we did was make sure that the crane was still hooked to the tug.

Before surfacing, I had mouthed the hook with a piece of manila rope to make sure the hook did not slip off the slings.

We got the compressor fueled up and started the Moretrench pumps to make sure they would run when we needed them later in the day. Then I suited up in the hardhat rig and got ready to dive. The crane took a strain on the sling under the stern and lifted it off the bottom. Then they lowered me into the water with the other crane and I started down to the wreck. A second sling was lowered to me and it was my job to pull it as far forward as I could under the bow, working forward from the stern of the *Bay King*. The *Bay King* was seventy feet long and had been built in the 1800s out of iron plate. Not welded but riveted, it was an extremely heavy boat. I worked my way along the hull and put the loop of one end of the sling over one of the bitts near the bow. I then went back as far as I could and shoved the other end back under the keel of the sunken tug. Next, I had to walk around the bow and find the end and pull it out and forward as far as possible. That took a while to accomplish, and the compressor kept quitting. I would feel my air decrease in volume and ask them topside what was going on. When Beldon replied, I would notice the lack of compressor noise in the background.

"Now, Steve," Beldon would say over the dive radio in his North Carolina drawl, "we got a little problem with the compressor—nothing to worry about, we'll have her running in a minute, just take a little breather and we'll have her cranked up in just a second."

In a couple of minutes, the airflow volume increased slightly. I had the air control valve on the suit all the way open and there was never any danger of me blowing up to the surface. I was getting just barely enough air to survive. I was sweating and had a headache from carbon dioxide buildup, but managed to get the sling under the bow. It was then a simple matter to rig a third sling back under the keel near where the original sling had been rigged under the hull. We wanted the full weight of the boat to be on the keel, so the crew lowered the tug back onto another sling I had put under the keel and tied off to the bitts. Then I took the hook off the uppermost one and rehooked it to the one that went under the boat. Now we were ready to lift her up. I made one final check, then told Beldon I was ready to leave the bottom. Before I did, I ensured that the shackles in the rigging were secure so there was no chance we would drop the tug once we started to lift it.

"Steve, where are those decompression tables?" Beldon inquired over the diver's radio.

"I think they are in the toolbox with the spare fittings."

I heard nothing for a few minutes and then he came back. "They ain't in there. You got any idea what the decompression schedule is for three hours at sixty feet?"

"No, but I better take a long stop at ten feet," I offered.

They ended up hanging me off at ten feet for about a half hour, and then I surfaced. I didn't seem to suffer any bends and felt none the worse for wear. After I surfaced I kept imagining that I was getting pains in my legs or arms or was about to pass out from some kind of central nervous system hit, but it never happened.

It was then about 1030 on Friday morning and we were ready to lift the *Bay King* and pump her out. With the help of the tenders, I got out of my diving rig and headed for the galley to get some chow. I was hungry as hell from that long working dive, heaving around on cables and trying to get enough air to breathe. I went back out with my cameras and started shooting pictures as the two cranes took a strain and began lifting the *Bay King* from its temporary watery grave. The antennas started showing above the water and pretty soon the top of the wheelhouse broke the surface. We had the pumps all rigged with hose and were ready to drop the suction ends into the tug as soon as she came up. I put my wet suit back on and prepared to go aboard to help get the suction heads placed where they needed to be.

As soon as the main deck was awash, Larry and I went aboard and opened up the engine room hatch. We shoved the hose down through and Beldon lit off the eight-inch Moretrench pump. Water started flying out of the discharge hose and we could see the water level dropping in the engine room. Before long the boat was lively in the slings and we knew she would stay afloat.

It was time to explore. Larry went up into the galley area. Next thing I knew he was out on deck, puking over the side. I asked him what was wrong. He said he didn't know, but when he opened the refrigerator door something made him throw up. I went in and opened the same door. My stomach knotted up and I heaved as he had done. Later in my diving career I understood what had happened. A package of steaks and some hamburger meat had rotted in there in an anaerobic[3] environment. Hydrogen sulfide formed and when we smelled it, the natural thing for our bodies to do was reject it. Four years later I was taught in 1st Class Diver's School that it can be fatal to breathe hydrogen sulfide. What you don't know *can* hurt you. We finished stripping the water out of all the compartments other than the engine room, then the crew and the insurance adjuster, who had come aboard that morning, went down and tried to find the reason for sinking. We located it. What had happened was pretty simple and pretty stupid. One through-hull fitting did not have the shutoff valve directly connected to it. Instead there was a piece of rubber hose between it and the hull. The hose had rotted off and a small stream of water, about the size of a garden hose, had filled up the engine room to just below the breather. When Jitterbug made that last left turn in the calm sea, the free surface of the water in the engine room caused the *Bay King* to roll to starboard. The engine room hatch had been open and propped up so the engine would get plenty of air. Seawater cascaded into the large opening and the *Bay King* went to the bottom in a hurry.

The tug was rigged to be towed alongside the barge. Beldon and I went ashore and drove back to Norfolk in his truck. Another adventure in the life of an amateur salvor. I was paid three hundred dollars for my part in the operation. Beldon made ten thousand bucks, which was pretty cheap for what we had done. I went down to Bay Towing some time later and went aboard the *Bay King*. She was all outfitted just like new—they even had fresh meat in the reefer.

Late in the fall of 1971 word came down that a crew was to go to the Naval Underwater Sound Lab, Naval Station Newport, Rhode Island, and do missed-distance studies for the Naval Ordnance Lab on the Mark 48 torpedo. It was a photo-instrumentation job and boring as hell, but Newport was a pretty good place compared to Norfolk, and we'd be living in a motel and drawing per diem, then about sixteen dollars a day. Big money. I was there about a week when I got a call from Judy. She told me she was leaving and going back to California. I felt bad about her leaving, but we were not hitting it off well. We had no children and it was probably better that she went on to finish her life elsewhere.

3. Oxygen starved.

A few weeks before she decided to leave, I was driving to the Outer Banks to photograph a hurricane when I hit a deep puddle, hydroplaned, rolled the VW, and landed it back on its wheels. The wreck caved the roof in and broke out all the windows. Neither the guy with me, PH2 Don Middleton, or I got hurt. I put some rags over my face to protect it from the driving rain and drove back to Norfolk through the storm. The damage estimate was $1,400, and we had paid only $1,900 for the car. I wanted the insurance company to declare it a total loss but they wouldn't do it. The car never was right after that, and the repair shop wouldn't fix it right.

So I asked Judy what she was taking when she left. She told me the stereo and the VW. I tried to get her to take the MG as I couldn't fit into it, but no, her mother talked her into taking the VW. I had wanted to stick it to the guys who repaired it and make them eat the goddamned thing if they couldn't fix it right.

Judy took the Volkswagen back to the West Coast and I got stuck with the frigging MG. I didn't know what to do with it, so I put an ad in the *Trading Post*, a local sell-it paper. Soon I got a call from Jerry George, the guy who I had bought the bike from back a ways. He told me he was looking for an MG Midget, so I traded Jerry the MG for the bike. Now I had one vehicle with only two wheels. So I got some other junk together and traded a rifle and some money for a Datsun pickup truck.

I didn't need the big apartment anymore so I moved to a third-floor place in Ocean View. PH2 Larry Cregger was getting out, so I took over his place. The rent was cheaper, the utilities were free, and it was not far from the back gate to NAS Norfolk. I spent about a year there in that snake ranch. I was single again and trying to make up for lost time.

I had a queen-size waterbed there on the third floor, which was probably not too smart as it weighed a ton and the building was very old and not too sturdy. My landlord, a Navy chief, used to "borrow" my place to screw his girlfriend. I would come back and find money under the pillow, usually nearly a month's rent, so it was a good deal.

While stationed at Combat Camera Group, we always had time for Friday afternoon beer parties. The money for these would come either from passing the hat among the people there, or from the "recreation fund." Well, it so happened that I became, I think by default, the manager of the recreation fund. My job, as such, was to raise money for this noble cause. The usual method was running a raffle, with the prize generally being something like a shotgun or a "six-pack" of half gallons of liquor. I wanted to make a lasting impression, so I decided to try something a little different—I would raffle off a hooker. The holder of the winning ticket would get to go to my apartment, when I had duty, and the woman would show up at the assigned time and take care of business. At this time, there were no women assigned to Combat Camera Group, as it was considered sea duty, and that was the way things were.

I called my buddy Medford Taylor, a reporter/photographer down at *The Virginian-Pilot/Ledger-Star*, the largest newspaper in the Tidewater area, and asked if, in his travels, he had found a woman of this particular occupation who might like to be the prize in this raffle. Med told me he didn't know anyone, but he sure as hell knew somebody who would know. He hooked me up with Bill Abourjille, a reporter who worked the crime scene with the local cops. Bill gave me the name of a woman who, he thought, would like to be the prize in the raffle.

I drove down to her place and told her what I had in mind. Donna was a tall woman and built well. I could tell that she had some education by the way our conversation went. She told me she owned a motel and the apartment that she lived in and was planning to retire with her boyfriend before she was thirty. We talked for a while and I told her that I'd call her with the address to my place when the time came.

Everything went like clockwork. Most of the guys bought tickets, married or not. Due to the nature of the mission at hand, I decided to rig the lottery so a married guy would not win. I figured I would be in enough trouble if the word got out about this, without contributing to some marital strife on the part of a shipmate.

I drew the lottery on the date as specified—on a day when I had the duty, and would be staying at Combat Camera for the night. I didn't have to rig it after all, as the first name I drew was of a single guy who claimed he had not been laid in months. It was a simple matter to give him the keys to my place, call Donna, and just wait for a report back. I gave him half the money from the lottery, as agreed upon with Donna, and he was on his way. I think the total take was around $150, so Donna ended up with a bit more than her usual fee, and my buddy got taken care of. It was not long before I was replaced as the manager of the recreation fund.

In the early part of 1972, I had to go to St. Croix in the Virgin Islands to do some underwater motion picture work of a fast-attack submarine. They were having a problem with the wire that fed the guiding signal to the Mark 48 torpedo. It would vibrate and send a harmonic signal down its length and mess up the guidance. The Navy engineers had designed this stuff that looked like plastic seaweed to cover the wire so it would not set up these vibrations, and they needed motion picture photography of it while the sub was steaming along at about ten knots.

We loaded our gear and headed down on a civilian flight. While on the plane I met JoAnne, a girl who worked for the Peace Corps on St. Kitts. She was on her way back from visiting her parents in Tempe, Arizona. She told me I should visit some time and that I could stay with her in a large farmhouse they rented near Basseterre on St. Kitts. Some months later, I went down to visit for ten days. We did a lot of exploring of the Brimstone Hill fort and climbed Mount Misery, which was an active volcano not long before. There were still sulfur pits and hot sulfur boiling up out of the ground down in the crater. That was my first experience in the crater of a volcano. We took the ferry over to the neighboring island of Nevis, the birthplace of Alexander Hamilton, and spent a few days there.

On the way home I flew from St. Kitts to San Juan. In San Juan, I climbed aboard the plane in my dress blues to get the standby rate and changed into civilian clothes as soon as the seat belt sign went out. There were kids on board smoking pot and carrying on, as they had just come from some big rock concert in Puerto Rico. The flight attendants told them they had better get rid of it before New York as the narcotics people would be waiting. I had never seen anybody smoking dope on a commercial airliner before.

During the trip to St. Kitts I had shot about fifty rolls of Kodachrome. When my slides came back from the lab my friend Rita and I went through them and picked out the best ones. These I sent to my agency, Photo Researchers, a stock photo agency in New York. Later that year I went there and visited Clifford Dolfinger, the man who handled my photos, and Jane Kinne, one of the owners of the agency. I always figured a face-to-face meeting could not hurt. While in New York, I met Linda Blazer, a food writer for a magazine. She wrote a story on a recipe that I had for fish chowder and also did an article about me being an underwater photographer.

Meanwhile, back in Norfolk, I was calling Mary Ware on the phone and talking with her on a fairly regular basis. I knew her background and her parents, and figured that if I was gonna have kids they might as well be from genetic material that was a known factor. I called her one night and asked her to come down and live with me. She agreed and flew down a couple of weeks later after quitting her job, putting her old horse to sleep, and selling her VW.

We got married a few days later. The day before we got married I went to the bike shop and bought a brand new BMW motorcycle for about $1,700. The next day was payday, so I got my check, got off early, and we drove to Elizabeth City, North Carolina, and got married. Turned out there was another couple there and the woman's name was Miriam Ware. She was from Canada and the two of them were sailing south and had stopped at Elizabeth City to get married. Pretty strange coincidence, another Ware and with almost the same first name as my girlfriend. We said the words, paid the money, and then went and had some fried fish and drank a couple of beers before heading back to Virginia Beach.

Rita, the optometrist's assistant I had been dating since shortly after Judy left, was very upset that I had married Mary without at least warning her but she and Mary later became good friends and remain so to this day.

Back at Combat Camera Group, I received a set of orders to Naval Special Warfare Group, Atlantic. That command was at Little Creek and was the parent command of SEALs, UDT, Beach Jumpers, Boat Support Unit, and a couple others.

Before Mary came down I had moved my stuff to an apartment off Shore Drive, on the other side of Little Creek Amphibious Base. I thought I would probably die in a car wreck if I had to drive facing the sun both directions. The roads are lined up so that the sun, in the summer, sets and rises almost directly in front of you depending on which way you are heading.

The place where Mary and I first lived was near Fort Story, off Shore Drive, which ran along the coast to Norfolk from Virginia Beach. The house was about a hundred yards or so from the beach and we could hear the surf pounding at night almost as loudly as the cars roaring by on Shore Drive.

About a month before my orders went into effect I was hanging out in the office at combat camera. I told them I wanted to check my record and make sure everything was in there. As I was going through it I noticed the sheet of paper that said I had been involuntarily disenrolled from 2d Class Diving School. I jokingly said, "I guess I don't need this shit in here," pulled the paper out and, without crumpling it up, threw it into the nearby trash can. The administration officer, a Lieutenant Williams, wrote me up for that. He called it "intentionally destroying official military records." I got a captain's mast[4] out of it and a suspended bust from first class to second class petty officer. Now that was meant as a joke; I had no intention of destroying that piece of paper. If I had, I could have easily done it with nobody watching, and no one would have known. However, I had made a nasty remark about a friend of the administration officer's some time back. The friend had made warrant officer, and he was a good enough guy but a consummate ass-kisser of extreme skill. He had been to all the right schools and punched his ticket quite effectively. I made the loud comment one day, "If that guy can make warrant, any asshole can." I was wrong about that. I never made warrant or limited duty officer.

Some weeks later, prior to taking my orders to Little Creek, I was late to work due to the power having gone off and my electric alarm clock not firing. I was about thirty minutes late, something not at all uncommon for most people. I had not been late before in my entire time there except in cases of auto trouble on the way. Even then, that had happened maybe only twice. This time though, they had a hard-on for me and were gonna stick it to me. I came in and went to the administration office.

"Am I on report for being late?" I asked.

"Well, er, I, er, guess so," was the answer I got.

Immediately, if not sooner, I was across the hall and in the operations officer's office. I did not ask to see him and he did not ask me to close the door. I just walked in, closed the door, and sat down in a chair opposite his desk. Lieutenant Commander Dixon, an ex-enlisted puke, was the operations officer. I leaned over his desk and looked him in the eye. "I understand that I am on report for being late this morning."

4. Nonjudicial punishment issued by the commanding officer.

"Well, er, I, er, guess that's the story," he offered.

"Tell you what, sir, I ain't standing by to get busted a pay grade for this chickenshit rap. If you want a stripe, don't stop there. Keep ripping until you have the crow, the uniform, the seabag, I.D. card, and even the fucking dog tags. And furthermore, this ship ain't gonna go down without taking some of the rats with it. Perhaps you would like the NIS (Naval Investigative Service) looking into all of the travel claims from this command."

He started to mellow out, even turned a little pale.

"I know some things about people here that would really embarrass the hell out of this command all the way up to AIRLANT (Naval Air Forces, Atlantic Fleet). I would hate to do it, as I have a lot of friends here. If Commander Pulley were still CO, this shit would never have happened."

He sat back and looked at his fingernails.

"Tell you what, Waterman. I think perhaps I can see a way out of this for both of us. The skipper wants your ass, and so does the administration officer for that remark you made about his warrant officer asshole buddy. I'll recommend that they drop this stuff if you'll go see a shrink. I'll tell them you were still upset over your wife taking off."

I was too easy and went along with it. A couple of weeks later I was checking out and heading for my new command, Naval Special Warfare Group. I thought they would forget all about the shrink part.

Wrong again.

CHAPTER SEVENTEEN

NavSpecWarGruLant

I checked in at NSWG and met the guy who was running the photo lab. That would be my job. Ryder was a radarman third class who had a knack for photography, so they had assigned him there. He was transferred out a short time after I arrived. There was also a real doofus type who was a PHAN (Photographer's Mate, Airman). He shuffled when he walked, wore glasses thicker than mine, and couldn't pour piss out of a boot with the instructions written on the heel. But he was a good kid and you had to like him, though—there wasn't an evil bone in his body.

The photo lab was located out behind SEAL Team Two in a windowless gray trailer. It had wooden steps leading up to it and didn't even have a sign to identify it. Fortunately, the air-conditioning worked most of the time. Hot weather was never a problem.

It had a phone, so I could make calls anywhere, on the base and off. We had a setup for color slide processing and any kind of black-and-white. The budget was not too restrictive and I usually didn't have any problem getting materials.

My actual boss was PTC (Chief Photographic Intelligenceman) Scotty McLean, a SEAL who had changed his rating from cook to photographic intelligenceman. McLean thought he was some kind of Ansel Adams when it came to photography. He had a cute little beard and was always sucking on his pipe as though deep in thought. I believe he was deep in thought all right, but most likely he was thinking, "How can I fuck Waterman this time?"

His boss was a more mature version of my PHAN, with many of the same physical characteristics. Lieutenant Williams was supposed to be an intelligence officer but he never exhibited any intelligence that I could detect. Between Williams and Scotty McLean, I made the determination that I would not go to the administration building if I did not absolutely have to. A couple of days after I checked in, PH1 Joe Leo, my old buddy from Oceana days, showed up at the door of the lab. Turns out he was the duty PAO (Public Affairs Office) photographer for the admiral. It was a great job and he loved it. All he had to do was shoot "grips and grins"—award ceremonies—and reenlistments.

One day I got a call from the commodore of NSWG, Capt. Bill Thede. He wanted to see me in his office. Seems he had gotten a call from Combat Camera Group. They wanted to know if Waterman had contacted a psychiatrist yet about his "problem." I told him that I intended to go down to the clinic as soon as I got my things in order. He looked at me over the top of his reading glasses and advised that I do it pretty soon. I said I would.

Next thing I know, Leo is in the lab asking me if I am nuts or something. I laughed and told him the story. He told me that the chief, McLean, had asked him to keep an eye on me to see if I exhibited any irrational behavior.

"What the hell ever happened to doctor-patient confidentiality?" I asked him. He just shrugged.

I called the neurological department at Boone Clinic ("Boone's Farm," we called it) and made an appointment with a shrink. A couple of days later I went to see the doctor. Ryder went with me for something to do. I walked in and told the Gray Lady volunteer that I had an appointment. Two doctors shared one receptionist so she didn't know whether I had an appointment with the shrink or the neurologist. After a few minutes she asked if I was there to see "Doctor Green" or "Doctor White." I told her I was there to see Doctor White, the shrink. There was an obvious change in her demeanor. She started talking down to me like I was a little kid or a deranged maniac about to go apeshit with a chain saw.

"Well, just have a seat over there. There are some nice magazines to read until it is time for you to see the doctor."

I expected her to give me a fucking coloring book and a handful of crayons.

"Jesus Christ, lady, I don't need a straitjacket—yet. I just have to have an evaluation."

She kept looking up at me in fear the whole time I was in that chair. I guess some real winners had gone through there.

Finally it was my turn. I walked into the office, sat in the chair facing his desk, leaned forward, and started asking the young-looking shrink some questions.

"How old are you?"

"Twenty-eight."

"Ever been shot at?"

"No."

"How much time have you spent in the real world—I mean not actually in school?"

"Not much, but probably enough."

I leaned farther over the desk and asked him how the hell anybody who was only twenty-eight years old and had eight years of college, had never left the warm comfort of academia, and worked in a room without any windows could possibly relate to anything in the real world.

Apparently he felt I was hostile or a menace, as he put me down as being dangerous to myself and others and pulled my jump and diving status. This pissed me off, not only because of the money lost but because of the stigma and the fact that people would start to look at me like I had tits on my forehead. I was pretty pissed off when I left. He had given me a chit to take back to the CO. It said that I was to be removed from jump and diving status. I had been able to draw only jump pay at this command as it was not a diving billet. Jump pay was $55 a month then and diving pay for scuba divers was $65. The guys in the teams got double hazardous-duty pay, jump and demo, of $110. The officers got $220, which was not fair to the enlisted SEALs as they did more jumping than most of the officers, and most of them intended to make the teams a career. Most of the officers were there for the thrills and chills of being a frogman, and then went on to the fleet. In those days, being an officer in the teams was akin to being a leper. There were no career paths in special warfare for officers.

Now I was a marked man. Mentally unstable, dangerous to myself and others, who knows what else. Joe Leo joked about it and told me I wasn't anywhere near as crazy as himself and almost everybody he knew. I agreed that I was not nuts, but once you had the name, that was all there was to it.

Mary, my wife, did not think very highly of my being railroaded into going to a shrink and felt it would screw up my naval career.

"Now that's a crock of shit, it won't have any effect," I responded. She was right, I found out later.

Scotty McLean had Leo watching me, and I began to catch curious looks from some of the other people on the staff. The asshole I worked for, Lieutenant Williams, was one of those types you just want to grab and pound into a mess of goo. Later I found out that I was one of a large number who felt exactly that way, including a few senior officers.

Occasionally my photographic duties would take me to the SPECWAR sick bay. Working there was a young doctor by the name of Kent MeWha. He was a physical kind of guy and worked out with the teams when he could. He drank, chased women, and did all the other stuff that would ingratiate him with SEALs and UDTs. One day I was telling him about my medical record and the stuff in it that had me painted as a "liability" to myself and others. He looked my record up, said something derogatory about shrinks, and proceeded to write a recommendation that ended up placing me back on full status. Kent added that, of all the people he had come in contact with in NavSpecWar, I was probably one of the sanest and most reliable. That took care of that bullshit and I started to draw jump pay again. I thought he was doing this just as a friend until one day I walked by sick bay and overheard a SEAL chief in there crying, I mean "boo hoo" crying, about "not being able to hack it anymore." I never found out who he was, and didn't care to.

A few weeks after Mary and I had married, I found out I was going to be sent to Puerto Rico with UDT-21 and then work with RDT&E.[1] I would be riding down on a ship, the USS *Barnstable County*, with a detachment of guys from UDT-21 and staying at the UDT barracks in Roosevelt Roads. Whew! I thought, I'll be getting out of here and away from this bunch of staff jerks.

Then Lieutenant Williams told me that I was to report back to him weekly and keep a daily logbook of all my activities. This guy wanted me to shit and fall back in it. Just to get him off my back, I told him I would. I asked him if he had one of those green logbooks I could take. He took that as a sign that I was "coming around."

I packed my gear, drew some film, and loaded my things aboard the LSD we would ride to Puerto Rico.

The officer in charge of the UDT detachment was Lt. Brian Barbata. He was a regular guy and liked to do all the frogman stuff although I could tell he was not the career type. On the ride down we played cards, ate, slept, did PT—all that boring stuff that passengers do on Navy ships when their mission is ashore.

1. Research, Development, Testing and Evaluation, part of Naval Special Warfare.

The chow was good and we watched movies at night and did not stand watches. All of us hated standing watches.

We stopped in Guantánamo Bay, Cuba, to drop off some Marines and vehicles, stayed there for about two pitchers of beer, and got under way again.

When we arrived in Puerto Rico we were met at the dock by one of the support guys who was stationed there permanently to maintain the area. We loaded our gear on the trucks and they took us to the barracks.

A swimming pool out back of the place was away from the rest of the base. The two buildings had been there for UDT training, but that was all on the West Coast by then so they were used as places for UDTs to stay when they were in Puerto Rico.

Each day we had PT in the morning or played jungle-rules volleyball, or ran. The rest of the day we would do something that "needed to be done." That could be anything from making a swim to lining up beer for a party.

Atlantic Fleet Combat Camera Group had a detachment on the other side of Roosevelt Roads Naval Station and I went there to meet the crew. They didn't have a photo lab, so the chief at combat camera told me to go to the base photo lab and talk with PHCS (Senior Chief Photographer's Mate) Don Husman, he would take care of me. Husman was a great guy and let me use the lab for processing black-and-white and color.

We had a problem with rats in the other UDT barracks—not the building we lived in, but the one we used for storage. EMC (Chief Electrician's Mate) Scotty Slaughter, a crazy bastard like myself, liked to play with explosives. So he rigged a rattrap with a couple pieces of wire, an electric blasting cap, a battery, and a piece of cheese. We set it up so the cheese was on a piece of wire hanging down through another loop of wire. The blasting cap was placed on the floor near the cheese. When the rat moved the cheese, the wire would swing and make contact with the loop, closing the circuit. At that close range, the rat would be demolished. We would set it up and go in the other building and drink beer and wait for the explosion. It worked about twice before the other rats figured it out and stayed away from it. Rat guts were everywhere.

I had brought my ten-speed bicycle with me so I had a way to get around the base. I eventually sold the bike after I moved to the SEAL area, as I could use the SEAL vehicles whenever I needed to and they were much easier to pedal.

One day about noon the chief got us all together and asked if any of us would volunteer to go out to Loquillo Beach and look for a young boy who had drowned. Nearly all of us offered to go, and the chief picked those who were a little older and had done body searches before. I was one. We ran a pattern parallel to the beach but we never found him. I was sad that we had not found him, but happy that if he had been found that I was not the one to stumble across his body. The senior person in the Civil Defense unit there wrote all of us a personal thank-you letter.

In a couple of weeks I moved from the UDT barracks to the SEAL area by the Chiefs' Club on the beach. The SEALs lived in what had been the old Chiefs' Club. It had a bar and a lot of little rooms, and an area like a bunkroom, with two-tiered bunks.

Lt. Terry Grumley, whose class I had photographed during Hell Week, was OIC of the SEAL area. His presence was just that, he was only there putting in his time. There was no fooling anybody into thinking he was a career officer. He didn't get in our way and just did his job, low profile. Things ran a lot smoother that way.

My friend Dick Stauffacher, a petty officer in UDT-21 at Little Creek, had asked Mary if we wanted to take over his house when he got out of the Navy. It was on Lauderdale Avenue off the end of Pleasure House Road, which is the first road going toward the beach east of Little Creek. Lauderdale Avenue dead-ends against the chain-link fence of the amphibious base. She and Dick moved all our stuff out of the place on Hatton Street and into the little two-bedroom place almost on the beach. The rent was ninety dollars a month and included all the sand we could track into the house.

Meanwhile, Mary decided to fly down and visit me. I thought that would be a good idea as she had not been to Puerto Rico before. When she arrived at the airport in San Juan, I wangled a truck and driver out of somebody at the SEAL area and they drove me to pick her up. I was glad to see her and she looked good. We drove back to RR and took her gear over to the house of PH1 Hudson, a black guy who worked in combat camera and a hell of a nice guy who had offered to put us up if Mary came down. We stayed there a few days and then I was able to get a private room over at RDT&E in sick bay. The corpsman, HM1 "Doc" Pacuirk, told me I could use that space. There was a shower and a bunk there, so he gave me the key and things worked out quite well.

Mary rode the chase boat on a few operations with SDVs and during testing of some new closed-circuit scuba gear, and another time when we were testing a new handheld sonar. At first they weren't going to let her go, then BMCM Corney Leyden, the master chief in charge of RDT&E, said if Lt. Tommy Hawkins's wife (who was there visiting him) could go, then he guessed maybe Mary could go, too. That took care of it. She hit it off with the frogs and we had a good time. I still have my wife, but I hear Tommy replaced his later on.

Master Chief Gunner's Mate Everett Barrett, Lt. Joe DiMartino, Lt. Comdr. Pat Badger, and Lt. Jim Harper were some of the older frogs in RDT&E. Except for Harper, who was somewhat younger and a former enlisted man, they had been in World War II. Barrett and DiMartino were the salt of the earth. It was a pleasure to operate with them. One of the missions we had was to test some new explosive hose. This stuff was not like Mark 8 hose, which is nothing more than fire hose filled with granulated TNT. The new hose used a plastic explosive that looked like olive-drab modeling clay, except that it was more rugged and came in hose form. On each end of the hose was a valve that could be used to let water in. That way a swimmer could flood the hose and tow it along underwater. It didn't work very well for the swimmer, but it sure as hell was powerful enough as an explosive. We shot the hell out of it and thought it was a good product—if you didn't have to tow it underwater very far. On the surface it was okay, you could drag quite a few lengths of it behind you.

We took a Mark IV boat over to Piñeros Island, a small island UDT had been using for demolition operations for years, and set off some large charges. There was a restriction on the size of the charge we could use, but we never paid a lot of attention to it. One day we shot about a thousand pounds in one shot. We had Mark 8 hose, C-4, the new hose, and a couple of ammonium nitrate cratering charges all linked together with primacord. When it went off, the shock wave went skyward, reflected off the low cloud cover, and came back down right about where the UDT barracks were, a few miles away. One of the guys was in the shower there, and the shock wave focused directly onto the building he was in and knocked the light fixture off the ceiling. It came crashing down around him and glass went everywhere. It scared the shit out of him but nobody was injured.

A representative from General Electric was at RDT&E to run tests on the new GE Mark 1500 closed-circuit scuba. A number of companies were vying for the contract to produce that equipment and he was there to oversee it. The GE guy was a former Navy diver so he fit right in with the frogs. Lt. Comdr. Chuck LeMoyne flew in with a couple of guys with funny accents. Turns out they were Israelis, here to learn about our SDVs and to try out the closed-circuit rigs. They were on tourist visas so they were not really supposed to be there at all. One of them, Shaoul Ziv, was the CO of the Israeli Navy Commandos. He was a commander and a nice guy. He had seen a lot of combat and lost a few men, both from accidents or combat casualties. The Israelis had a good time while there and the men liked them. Later on, I met a whole platoon of them in Little Creek when they were training with SEAL Team Two.

The Mark 1500 was a mixed-gas, closed-circuit rig with two small flasks of gas and a baralyme canister in a fiberglass shroud the diver wore on his back. On the left wrist, an instrument console was worn that gave the status of the gas mix and the supply, battery life, and other information. By today's standards it was primitive. But it worked. I don't know who got the contract, but I know the thing worked pretty well and nobody drowned swimming it.

RDT&E made a run to Vieques Island using this rig in one of the SDVs and I got to ride over in the backseat. During the long ride I read a paperback crotch novel and tore out the pages and let them float away as I went. The chase boat on the surface could tell what chapter I was in by the debris left behind.

Many nights at the SEAL bar I almost drank myself into a coma. We had a rule: The bartender got to drink for free but had to relinquish the job when he got too drunk to make change. Some of the SEALs and divers would sit and drink until we closed and then get up and go run PT the next morning. That, I could not do. Many mornings I paid the price for having sat there too long, having too much fun. Sometimes the nurses from the base came down and danced to the jukebox. I don't know where the jukebox came from and never asked.

Joe DiMartino could hold his own with the boys. He could slam down rum and Coke or beer until the sun came up and his personality never seemed to change except, perhaps, that he had a little problem with certain words. But that usually came quite late in the night. Joe was an icon in the teams and everybody loved him except, for some reason, the promotion board. Joe was an ex-enlisted guy and never made it past lieutenant. I guess he must have pissed somebody off down the line. Joe told me that his Hell Week was on Omaha Beach during the Normandy invasion.

I had been working with RDT&E for about a week and a half when Barrett or DiMartino called up Lieutenant Williams back at SPECWAR and told him that I would not be sending him any situation reports or keeping a logbook. They told him that the work I was doing was classified and that I had enough to do without keeping any stupid records. That took care of that.

One of the men working out of the SEAL area was EMC "Filthy Phil" Phillips, a fat chief electrician's mate from Indian Head, Maryland, home of EOD (Explosive Ordnance Disposal). Phil was a sharp cookie. When his civilian flight landed at San Juan airport, he called and asked for a driver to be sent up to pick him up. The kid on the phone asked him his name and rank. Phil said he was a chief.

The kid replied, "I'm sorry, Chief, we are only allowed to provide transportation for commanders and above."

Phillips called back in a few minutes and with his voice disguised he told the dispatcher that he was a "Commander Clump." (A clump is the weight on the end of a downline to keep it taut when divers descend. It is usually a lump of lead or steel with an eyebolt cast in it to tie a line to. All divers recognized the term. Not so the admin pukes.) They sent up a truck. Phil bought the driver a meal on the way back and he never said anything about it. So from that day on, Filthy Phil was also known as Commander Clump.

Phil had a lot of money. His father had died some time back and left him about fifty grand. Phil knew he'd piss it away otherwise, so he gave it to a broker and told him to make him rich. The guy did. He put the money in soybean futures when that was a hot investment, sold at the right time, and Phil ended up with a shitload of money. When one of the guys asked Phil if he was going to get out of the Navy now that he was rich, Phil replied,

"What, and let them screw me out of my retirement?" The only visible toy he purchased was a new pickup truck.

I spent a good deal of time at the base photo lab near the airfield. PHCS Don Husman, the senior chief in charge of the Roosevelt Roads photo lab, took great care of me there and made sure that I had everything I needed. When I had to order more photographic supplies, he had his supply guy fill out the paperwork for me and made sure it was right. Then I would take it back to the SEAL complex, requisition a vehicle ("Hey, Chief, I need the truck") and head up to Bayamón, where Kodak was located. It was a good ride and we'd stop along the way to take pictures or eat at a restaurant.

Time flew while I was in Puerto Rico. Even the work was fun down there. Mary was still with me and we were trying to figure out how to get her home without spending money to do it. Finally, Corney Leyden said we'd just put her on the frigging airplane. We didn't have much gear and there were only about seven of us going home. So we just went over to air operations, loaded our gear on a big C-141, climbed aboard, and took off. We managed to slip a little cocktail material on board to help the time go faster. Mary ended up sitting in the flight engineer's seat up in the cockpit, shooting the shit with the pilot, who had to fly the plane manually because the autopilot had died. We landed at Norfolk Naval Air Station and threw all the gear on a stake truck from Little Creek. One of the guys had left his car there and gave us a ride back to the house. Things continued on as usual at NavSpecWar.

There were usually a few foreign military personnel at Little Creek training with the SEALs. At a beer party one afternoon I happened to meet a couple of men from the Pakistani Navy. One, Ali Khan, was an officer, and the other, Sham Din, was a chief petty officer.[2] Sham Din had been on board a ship that the Indians shot out from under him and he'd been hit in the foot while running to get his fins to swim for it. I felt sorry for him and had him out to the house for supper and to meet Mary. A few days

---

2. In 1991, I was hired by a civilian diving company to go to Pakistan and help install trash racks in the intake structure of Tarbela Dam, on the Indus River. Some Pakistani divers were there to "assist" us. I asked them if they knew a Navy diver named Sham Din. Their eyes nearly came out of their heads. "Sham Din was our instructor," they replied. Small world.

later I had him out there again. Then he started showing up at the house *after* I had left for work; he told Mary he was in love with her and wanted her to go back to Pakistan with him. Despite having proved her lack of taste in men by marrying me, Mary didn't think much of that idea; I thought it was pretty humorous.

One day I wandered into Lieutenant Williams's office. Williams had a new guy working for him, a senior chief yeoman. I guess he was an intelligence specialist as he handled all the top secret material. As I walked into the office I saw a top secret item lying on the desk. Although I didn't have a top secret clearance then, I walked over to it and started to read. Then I started laughing.

"Waterman, you aren't supposed to be in here when we have top secret stuff out," Williams said.

"Well, you're gonna look like an asshole if you send this report in."

"Oh yeah, why's that?" Williams asked, cocking his pointed little head to one side.

"Well, you've got the wrong pictures with the wrong bios."

"How do you know that?"

"'Cause I drank with these guys for a week; I ought to know their names by now."

His face turned red and he went over and switched the photographs of the two Israelis to where they should be. He had mixed up Ziv's picture and the engineer's. I turned and walked out of the office. I couldn't get the grin off my face.

My parachute jumping continued and I made some friends down at the parachute loft. Pierre Ponson, Stan Janecka, Norm Olson, Danny Zmuda, Ty Zellers, Hershel Davis, and some of the others still jumped a lot. They were going to have a short version of HALO (high altitude/low opening) school taught at Little Creek. The real HALO school in Fort Bragg was too much money for their budget, so they talked SpecWar into funding the school there. We would take a short ground course and then go out to Suffolk and jump out of C-1As or helicopters. Lt. Norm Carley, Lt. Al Horner, Lt. Tom Steffens,[3] and some enlisted guys were all going to take the course. I conned my way in with my camera, as usual; all of them liked to have pictures of themselves doing manly things. We made four or five jumps with oxygen

3. Tom Steffens is now an admiral.

equipment and a parachute bag full of sawdust strapped to our asses. We jumped T-10 parachutes and, for those of us who had had experience with it, the olive-drab Paracommander. I don't remember if I had a PC or a T-10, but I remember that I managed to find my way to the ground and didn't pull my rip cord too late. The worst part was that our goggles and oxygen masks completely blocked the view of the altimeter strapped to the top of the chest-mounted reserve. If I cocked my head to one side and pulled my chin way over, I could just make it out. I decided I would trust the team leader and just pull on him—unless I got so low I could read labels on beer cans lying on the ground. Nobody got hurt, except the taxpayers.

I had by that time spent a little more than two years at NSWG and my shore-duty stint was about up, so I decided I would like to go back to Combat Camera Group, which was considered sea duty. The Navy had decommissioned Naval Special Warfare Group while I was in Puerto Rico and all of us were transferred to NAVINSWARLANT, "Naval Inshore Warfare, Atlantic." I never figured out why they did that, but they have since recommissioned Naval Special Warfare Group.

I put in a chit and asked to transfer to Atlantic Fleet Combat Camera Group via the 2d Class Diving School. I got my orders and checked in at YFNB-17, the school. YNC Ross, my old nemesis, had since retired or been transferred. One of the first stories I heard was about him getting the shit kicked out of him in a bar by a guy he had mouthed off to while in the Navy. I liked it and wished I could have been there to see, or even take part in, it.

Several Puerto Rican State Police officers were in my class. Most of them were not high-speed, but some were good people and tried to do what they were supposed to and didn't act like they were just along for the ride. In this school we didn't have permanent swim buddies, so we rotated. I never had any problem outswimming and outdiving anybody in the class, but that was not the challenge. The challenge was keeping my mouth shut when I saw somebody screwing off.

One of the duties I had was standing junior officer of the deck (JOOD) watches, four-hour exercises in staying awake, drinking coffee, and fielding phone calls to guys who were "supposed to be on watch," according to the wives who called to talk with them. One night I had the eight-to-twelve watch and a seaman from Maine came up to the quarterdeck. We were just talking

when another kid came up and started harassing him verbally.
Before long the second kid hauled off and slugged the kid from
Maine. I grabbed the asshole and nailed him a couple of times,
pretty hard, but that didn't take him down. Instead, he ran down
the brow and onto the pier with me in hot pursuit.

"Nobody starts a fight on my quarterdeck!" I shouted after
him. I grabbed him around the neck in a headlock and tried to
push him down between the camel and the pier, where he would
be crushed when the surge of the swells moved them together.
Two Seabees in my class had been walking up the pier and saw
what was going on. They didn't want me to kill the guy so they
both jumped me and tried to break it up. Finally I let go of him.
Both of them looked incredulously at each other and then at me.
"Jesus, Waterman, didn't you know we were on your back?"

"No, I didn't. Were you?"

They cast each other the same glance. "Hell, yes, you were a
crazy man. I'm glad it wasn't us who pissed you off." After that I
tried to control my temper a little more.

The rest of the time there passed without major incident. We
graduated and said good-bye to each other and I continued on to
my "new" command, Combat Camera Group. But by then, I
think, they had changed the name of it to Naval Audio Visual
Command, Atlantic. No more Combat Camera Group. The Navy
was becoming politically correct and somehow combat and
cameras were seen not to mix. Even so, we still called it "combat
camera."

One night, in early fall 1973, I got a call from Lane Briggs, the
owner of Rebel Marina and Rebel Marine Service. The clam-
dredging vessel *Christy* had hung its dredge down and then managed to get the towing line caught in one of its two screws. She
was effectively anchored in about seventy-five feet of water in
Chesapeake Bay. Lane wanted me to meet one of their other
dredges, the *Ocean View*, at the dock and go out and cut the thing
loose. They would buoy the *Christy*'s dredge off and go back
later to recover it. I told him I needed another man to go with me,
so I called Dick Johnson, the chief I had worked for at Combat
Camera Group. Dick brought tanks for both of us. We got our
gear together and headed to the dock where Miles Brothers
Clam Company kept its boats. The *Ocean View*'s skipper and one
of the crewmen helped us get our diving gear aboard and we

headed out. It was starting to get pretty snotty out on the bay and I wondered if it would be safe to dive; it was getting dark, and the wind was blowing about twenty-five knots. By the time we got on station I was puking my guts out in true seafarer style. Even so, I crawled into my wet suit and scuba gear. I brought along a hacksaw to cut through the huge polypropylene hawser. My plan was to go down to where the hawser was connected to the dredge and saw it in two. When they felt the hawser part, they were to move well away. I would count thirty seconds before surfacing. My grand scheme worked pretty well, although as I sawed, the swells kept tightening the hawser like a large black violin string until the last stroke of the hacksaw, when it simply parted.

When I surfaced I popped an MK-13 signal and the *Ocean View* came right to me. I had one hell of a job getting back aboard as the swells were level with the side of the boat. Finally they threw the boat out of gear upwind of me and I just let them drift to me until I could slide right over the coaming onto the stern deck. Dick was there to help me out of my gear. It was time to go home. We slept all the way back. I was worn out more from the puking than from the diving.

The next day I went to the dock and cut the hawser out of the *Christy*'s propeller. That was quite a job in itself. Later that evening Lane called me and said we needed to go back out and recover the dredge. It would cost about fifteen thousand dollars and take a long time to build a new one. I asked PH2 Larry Cregger and PH3 Ike Johnson, two members of the Combat Camera Group's Underwater Photo Team, to come along. We had worked together a lot on other diving projects and I felt confident of their abilities. I told them I would pay them fifty dollars apiece to come along and a hundred dollars if they had to dive. That was big money in those days. They agreed. We loaded our gear aboard another boat owned by the Miles Clam Company, the *Hampton Creek* or something like that. It was not a clam dredge, and the only piece of electronics it had was a VHF or CB radio. But the compass worked and I think the skipper had a chart. We put to sea and headed for the *Christy*. She went along ahead of us and had to locate the buoy the skipper had put on the end of his haul-back wire. In a couple of hours we were on-site. Cregger and I dived, so Ike stayed in the boat. We had to go down to the dredge and attach the haulback wire to it using a metal shackle made especially for the job. There were several holes in the bracket where it could be attached and Captain Ben of the *Christy* told us that it didn't matter which one we used. This cable was about an inch-and-a-half in diameter and I knew it was going to be a bitch to drag it over the bottom, so I told them I wanted a block (sheave) to tie onto the dredge. I had them lower that down to me with some line woven through it. I took that to the dredge and tied it off. Then I had them pull on the line, which was attached to the cable's end, and pull until it stopped. I went down and cut the rope and easily put the shackle on the dredge. That was all there was to that. I imagined what would have happened if we had tried to pull that big cable by hand over to the dredge. I'd still be out there screwing with it.

We headed back to the dock by Little Creek. By then it was starting to snow and cold as hell in the boat. I had climbed into the top rack in the wheelhouse bunk and Larry Cregger was in the lower. The seas were rough. Before long we were taking water over the bow. Ike had gone forward and down into the forecastle to try to get some sleep. The skipper of the *Ocean View* and Richard Miles, son of the owner of the Miles Clam Company, were at the helm. It was so rough that they fell down a couple of times and I thought we might not make it in. A fuel drum rigged on deck broke loose and went overboard and the stack for the galley stove was carried away. We hoped Ike was okay down in the forecastle. When we got back in, he said that he'd figured he wouldn't be any worse off there than anyplace else on the boat. At least he was dry, if not warm.

I went out clam-dredging a few trips on board the *Christy*. I quickly found out why guys who work on clam dredges had huge arms and the sixty-fathom stare. I think I had about two hours of sleep out of thirty-six and all of that was in fifteen-to-twenty minute naps on deck between tows. We shoveled clams into large baskets with aluminum scoops each time the dredge came up. I want to tell you, it is hard work.

Richard Miles and I became friends. He was a millionaire but worked harder than most fishermen I have met. Eventually, after Captain Ben died, he became the skipper of the *Christy*. Ben weighed in at around 450. He had to have a special table built for him down below so he could sit and eat, and brother could he *eat*!

Shooting the USS *California*

I had been back at Atlantic Fleet Audio Visual Command for a few weeks when we got a call that a team was needed at Atlantic Undersea Test & Evaluation Center (AUTEC) on the Bahamian Island of Andros. This was good news as we always used any excuse we could to go down there on a job. There was no problem getting volunteers because the water there is warm and clear and the beer is cold and cheap. There weren't any women available, but what the hell, two out of three ain't bad.

Chief Dick Johnson picked the team: "Mac" McCraw, yours truly, and a guy whose name I can't remember. We would also have some frogmen from UDT-21 as our swim buddies. The CO of Team-21 sent a new lieutenant, junior grade (O-2) as OIC of the frogs and told him he'd be working for us. The job was under Lt. Comdr. Chuck LeMoyne of Naval Ships Systems Engineering Command. I had met Chuck before, in Puerto Rico, but had never actually worked with him. Chuck was a UDT/SEAL officer and doing his time on shore duty to get his ticket punched on his way to admiral.

We arrived at the Fresh Creek International Airport (a dirt strip with remnants of aircraft lying about the perimeter) and a van came out to ferry us in. A platoon of civilian engineers was already there from another one of the naval engineering commands. Chuck was with them. During a little get-together we photographers didn't attend, the frog officer told Chuck LeMoyne that we, meaning the underwater photo team, were *just* photographers and that *they*, the frogmen, were the guys trained to do scary shit, and that they should be shooting the film and we should just be there to support them. Chuck put an end to that and things went on as planned.

The problem with the ship was, when it went above eighteen knots the sonar had such a high ambient noise level, the technicians could not hear anything over the passive sonar. The engineers believed the problem was being caused by cavitation along the sonar dome. Cavitation occurs when uneven pressures in the water, caused by irregular surfaces, pull air bubbles out of the water. When the bubbles collapse, noise is generated that can screw up the sonar signal. We had a boom-buoy system set up to give the helmsman of the USS *California* (a six-hundred-foot, nuclear-powered frigate) a target to aim for. The system was nothing more than a couple of floats on ropes leading down to weights at the end. A boom made of neutrally buoyant aluminum tubing kept the sides at a specific distance. The ship would pass between the buoys in the same direction each time.

We would have photographers stationed along the boom system. I would be halfway from the waterline to the keel on the starboard side shooting with a DBM-9 movie camera set at two hundred frames per second. Hanging off a large inner tube, we would wait on the surface until the ship started its run. At a certain point the ship would blow its whistle and the team would submerge and take up stations. When we got to ours, on Chuck's hand signal, I would start shooting film of him firing a .357 magnum bangstick[4] into a five-gallon can we had tied off on the buoy line. That gave the ship an acoustic marker for reference. From that point on I had to keep the trigger down on the camera to keep continuity. The ship came by at about twenty-two knots on the first run. I shot my film and noted that my distance seemed to be a little farther from the ship than I wanted.

Between each run all divers surfaced, then handed their cameras to photomates in the Zodiac inflatable for reloading. Chuck would put another round in his bangstick, and we'd hang off the inner tubes in the three-foot seas. We had all become acquainted the night before in the dimly lit interior of the Thousand Fathom Club. Being short of women to impress, we simply got drunk and were not early to bed. That was taking a toll on Steve and the crew. I started to get seasick. Before long I was puking and so was Chuck and a couple of the others. We couldn't wait for the damned ship to come back so we could go down where it was calm. By then the ship was supposed to be steaming by at thirty-two knots. I figured if they were going to have an observable cavitation problem, it would be on the last run and I'd be goddamned if I was going to miss it. That time when I went down, I worked my way out to the middle of the boom after I shot the bangstick. I looked back to check the distance from the line on my side of the boom system and realized, Oh, shit, I'm too far out, and started swimming back to where Chuck and another frogman were hanging off the line. Then, out of the gloom,

4. A bangstick is a device that resembles a pistol barrel on the end of a pole. A cartridge is inserted into it, it is shoved together, and when it strikes a solid object, it fires the cartridge into whatever you strike. They are used as a defense against sharks and for shooting large fish for food.

in the three-hundred-foot visibility, came the bulbous sonar dome of the USS *California*. I was just to the starboard side of the dome and was going to get run over by it. I kicked my young dumb ass into overdrive and just about broke the blades off my duck feet, all the while keeping the camera switch jammed down hard. If I survived, this would be some wicked footage. I swam at warp speed until the hull stopped getting wider and I realized I was safe, so I turned around and faced the hull. The ship was about ten feet from me and passing by at thirty-two knots.

I exhaled to get negative and started to drop below the bilge keel. I could see the screws churning through the water. I dropped below the hull and shot them from about thirty feet away as the ship blasted by overhead with the sound of a hundred locomotives thundering in my ears. I swam back into the prop wash, prepared to be slammed all over the Tongue of the Ocean. I wasn't disappointed. With the camera shoved against my face mask, I rolled up into a ball and waited for the blast of water. I felt like a pissant getting hit with a fire hose. It threw me all over the place like I was in a blender full of whipped cream. The water was nothing but a froth. When it cleared I looked around for my swim buddy, one of the frogmen who had wanted to do our job. He was about thirty feet below me. I think his eyeballs were bugged out right against the faceplate of his mask.

Later that afternoon, as we relaxed in the air-conditioned comfort of the Thousand Fathom Club, Chuck stood up with glass in hand. "I just want you guys from combat camera to know that we'll swim with you anywhere, anytime." That felt good to us "titless Waves," as photographers were often called.

Chuck LeMoyne made admiral some years later and died of cancer in 1996. I was sorry to hear that. He was a good man.[5]

I never did get to see my footage from that job.

CHAPTER EIGHTEEN

The SHAD Project

The crew at combat camera was PH2 Bob Hasha, PH2 Paul Whitmore, PHC Dick Johnson, PH2 Harry Kulu, and PHC Dave Graver. Graver had made chief, and PH1 Trotter, who had been there when I left for NSWG, had gotten himself into some kind of trouble. It was 1974 and there wasn't that much work for the underwater photo team, so I went to work drumming up some business. I called around and found out about a project called SHAD, Shallow Habitat Air Dive. The plan was to put a couple of divers on air in a chamber for thirty days at the equivalent depth of sixty feet. This would give them the effect of breathing a hyperoxic[1] mix of gas. There were plans to use air instead of the more expensive gases and equipment for saturation diving. They needed to find some guys dumb enough to volunteer for the project. I volunteered.

At first they were not going to take me as I was not a first class diver, but they decided that I would be okay as I had had a lot of experience. I am not *sure* that was the reason, but I didn't care.

I packed my gear and headed up the coast for Connecticut. I was driving a 1963 VW Bug with a sunroof and a six-volt system. It ran great but was basically a piece of junk, and at night the lights were not much brighter than kerosene lamps. I had no trouble with it making the trip up to Groton, though. When I got there, I signed in at Naval Submarine Medical Research Laboratory (NSMRL). There I met Dr. Claude Harvey, MC, USN, and a number of other doctors, medical and Ph.D. The crewmen that I would be working with were all first class divers and they didn't let me forget it. The place was pretty slack militarily, and everybody was on a first-name basis. We were surrounded by Ph.Ds and MDs and physiologists and shrinks. I felt right at

1. Higher than the normal partial pressure of oxygen found at sea level.

home. I was there under the guise of documenting it for the Naval Photographic Center, where the Naval Photographic Archives are located. I had my own personal cameras and Navy film. I was getting paid per diem also, which was still about fourteen dollars a day. When I checked in I stayed with Ray "Superfine" Fine, who was a hard-core diver and who carried a .44 magnum when he went on liberty. He told me he had to pull it out once when he was accosted coming out of a bar. Two men pulled him into an alley but he had the pistol shoved in the stomach of one of them by the time they had him around the corner and they realized they'd grabbed the wrong guy. They apologized and Ray didn't shoot anybody.

Ray was pretty intolerant of just about anything and anybody. Jack Welch, Burton, and Gary Seibert, the other three guys, were pretty decent to work with. Gary and Ray would be in the chamber and the three of us would be topside control subjects. The Navy, as usual, did one hell of a fine job of picking candidates for an experiment. I was the only one who didn't smoke at all and the others drank more heavily than me.

The experiment depended on having people live about the same on the outside of the chamber as those on the inside. That meant we were not supposed to smoke or drink, and we topside types had to carry a Clorox bottle around all day and every time we urinated it was to be collected in it. Ellie, "the pee lady," as we called her—an organic chemist or biologist—analyzed all the urine. Each morning we'd come in and trade our full bottles for new ones. A slight amount of hydrochloric acid in each bottle was used as a preservative and man, did it stink! Our eyes would water whenever we had to uncap that jug. For some reason, when we were carrying the bottles, we were not welcome in restaurants. We also had to chew a piece of paraffin and spit it into a bottle each morning when we got up. The doctors could get a bacteria count that way and determine if we had tendencies toward tooth decay. The project dentist said I was very close to being immune to tooth decay (according to the dentist, one out of five thousand people is immune to tooth decay). We also had to have samples of parotid fluid taken from the parotid glands, part of the salivary gland system, in our cheeks. Until then, I didn't even know there was such a thing as a parotid gland.

We all were administered EKGs under stress, and they had to measure our carbon dioxide levels resting and under stress.

Color vision, night vision, stereo vision, and tonometric readings were taken of the eye. The X-ray regimen began and we had X-rays taken of our knees, shoulders, hips, and chests. We were told not to eat ice cream, gelatin, or chewy candy bars, as they contain alginate, or hydroxi-proleen. This would give them the same readings as if we were losing bone mass. One room at the lab had a bed in it, and copper screen covered the walls, floor, and ceiling. That was where we went for EEG tests. The screen was to filter to ground any extraneous electromagnetic energy. Turned out none of us was a flat liner.

At exactly 1400 on 15 March 1974 the chamber was pressed down to sixty feet with Ray Fine and Gary Seibert inside. That night I went into the NSMRL to get checked out on the emergency backup generator that would be put on line to keep the compressors running if there was a power failure.

We were briefed on chamber emergencies. In the event of the failure of a fitting on the inside lock, where Ray and Gary were, the operator would jam on the air supply to override the loss and attempt to maintain depth. One of the other topside people would grab a toolbox with special plugs and a wrench and get into the outer lock and run it down to depth (sixty feet). Then the inner door could be opened. The two "divers" would come into the outer lock and the topside man would get into the inner lock and close the door. The outer lock would be maintained at sixty feet of equivalent depth. Now the inner lock could be drained and the fitting that failed would be replaced with a blank plug. Then the inner lock would be repressurized to sixty feet and the fittings would be tested with a soap solution and an ultrasonic device that could hear air leaks, no matter how small. When it was determined that the condition was safe, the inner door would be opened and the two "divers" would swap places with the topside man. He would go into the outer lock, close the door, and be brought back to the surface.

While looking over the chamber, I wondered about something else. When they had designed the hookup that would enable the men to take showers in the chamber, one thing had not been taken into consideration. They had two hot water heaters hooked up in parallel. There is a system to pressurize them to about thirty-five psi over bottom pressure. In most cases, water heaters receive cold water through the bottom and feed the hot water out the top. In that hookup they had things rigged so that air pressure could be added to the tanks. When it was put in, it was just blowing out through the discharge lines into the chamber and all the guys in there got was warm, moist air. I recommended that they switch the supply and discharge lines into the chamber, as we don't use a constant flow through the tanks.

Master Diver Jordan, a retired Navy chief, was in charge of the chambers and all ancillary equipment at the Naval Submarine Medical Research Lab. I casually mentioned it to him in question form.

"Gee, Chief, I wonder if they hooked that thing up the other way, if it would work?"

Next day I heard him telling Lt. Comdr. George Adams, the project supervisor, that they were going to reverse the input lines.

Another problem I wondered about. When blood was drawn, a needle was stuck in the patient's vein and on the other end of the little hose was another needle stuck into a vacuum test tube. That works great on the surface, but I wondered what would happen if they did that in the chamber. The equivalent vacuum would be around thirty psi, plus what the tubes were charged with. I asked one of the physiologists if that might cause a problem. He said it might, but they would cross that bridge when they came to it. Well, the first time they took blood using those vacuum-type test tubes they almost collapsed the guy's vein, and the blood shot into the tube so fast it turned to a red froth and the platelets were damaged. After that they just drew blood with large syringes and put it into tubes with the tops taken off. On the way up in the medical lock they would leave the tops slightly ajar, so the air could escape as it expanded. Things work differently under pressure.

As I figured they might, soon after the experiment began and Ray and Gary were in the chamber and pressed down, the other guys started going out and drinking and smoking and staying up late. Each morning we were required to sit for a blood sample. Dr. Roger Williamson, MD, was the guy who took our blood. After about a week of that, our arms were black and blue from wrist to elbow. I am sure some who caught sight of our arms accidentally thought we were junkies. The blood gases were all screwed up as the topside guys were smoking and the urine was a high volume because of the beer. I was the only one who tried to stick to the regimen. I wasn't a goody-goody, I just wanted the damned experiment to come out right. We ate the food that the guys inside ate and we were supposed to write down anything else we ate. An old black woman came in and cooked for the guys. I can imagine she had trouble making her kids leave home. It was great chow.

Feeding the crew required the use of the medical lock, a small protrusion on the end of the chamber. The operator would call into the chamber and tell them to secure the inner door. After that was done, we depressurized the lock through a valve on the outside and opened the door. Then food, books, or whatever were loaded into the lock, the outer door was closed and dogged, and the lock would be brought up to the pressure by opening a valve inside the chamber. Then the subjects would open the door, take out the supplies, and close and dog the inner door. Sometimes for breakfast a couple of us would lock in and eat with the chamber team. That required the larger outer lock door to be opened. We would walk in, close the door, and the outside tenders pressurized the outer lock until the inner door could be opened. Then we would go inside, sit down, and eat breakfast, which we usually carried in with us. The doctors would take blood and do whatever else was required as part of the day's procedures.

Dr. Claude Harvey was not especially adept at taking blood. He always had trouble hitting a vein. One morning when I was in the chamber, after we had eaten breakfast, he had Ray lie down on his bunk and was trying to get a blood sample. He missed the vein about three times. Finally Ray looked up at him and said, "You've got one more shot at hitting that vein and after that I'm gonna tear your fucking head off."

Claude backed away and had the corpsman do it. The corpsman hit it first try. After that he let the corpsmen draw all the blood from the guys in the chamber.

Dr. Ben Weybrew was the resident headshrinker. He was a short man with a good sense of humor, a basic requirement for psychiatrists working with Navy divers. We used to take him to town with us and he'd hang around and have a beer with the guys before they went into saturation. We took the MMM test and other personality profile exams. Mine indicated that I had the "fighter pilot" personality. Dr. Weybrew gave us an IQ test and all of the guys came back with above-average scores. Mine was good enough to join Mensa, which I did years later.

In addition to the psychological tests, we took tests for color vision, respiratory capacity, coordination, math skills under stress, and others. The day we were taking the color vision test, I mentioned to Dr. Saul Luria, Ph.D., that I thought this test would not be giving proper data because it was being given under abnormal conditions. He looked at me kind of funny and asked what I meant. I pointed up at the lights.

"What is the color temperature and composition of the spectrum of light coming from those?"

He slapped himself on the forehead. "Shit, that's right, there's excess green and not much red in there. All the tests we've given so far have been done under incorrect conditions."

Saul mounted a little Tensor reading lamp over the table and we all started getting nearly perfect scores after that. I would not have understood about light color temperature if I had not been a photographer.

The coordination and math tests were fun. We sat in chairs and with a joystick control we followed a little green dot around a screen with another green dot. The dots were the same size and color. We had to try to keep one dot on top of the other dot. The faster we went the faster it went, so we never could win. The math test was interesting. There were three rows of three-digit numbers. The subject was required to add the top two rows together and subtract the bottom row and punch in the answer from left to right, instead of right to left as normal. The more the subject got right, the faster they made it go until the subject made mistakes. They kept the pressure on, but we knew it didn't count for anything. Even so most of us tried to do our best.

We also had to shoot color slides of each other's retinas with a special fundoscopic camera, a 35mm camera on a long tube. There was a bright light in the end of the tube that we were required to look at. We stared into it until the photographer on the other end could see into the eyeball, then he would fire the shutter and take a flash picture of the inside of the eye. That way they were able to detect rupturing and abnormalities in the blood vessels inside the eye due to pressure or decompression sickness. Well, Ray and Gary had another version of this. When the first batch of photos came back from the processor, one of the naive doctors couldn't understand why the retina had hair around it. Ray or Gary had photographed the rectum of the other man. Some of the doctors had a sense of humor. Others, we found out, did not.

On some days the program required the men in the chamber to

make "excursions" to deeper depths. They were normally kept at the pressure equivalent of sixty feet, but were taken on "excursions" down to well over two hundred feet. Common sense dictates that a man at sixty feet will perform better mentally and physically than he will at deeper depths, where greater pressure and an increase in nitrogen narcosis should impair his mental capabilities. Not so Ray Fine. He did better on the math test and the coordination at over two hundred feet than he did at sixty feet. Nobody ever figured out why.

When I went to take the respiratory volume test, there was a problem. The test consisted of inhaling all the air our lungs could hold. We would then expel it into a bellows arrangement calibrated in liters of volume. That would measure our tidal respiratory volume. A little rod on the side of the bellows passed a gauge and the corpsman could read off the gauge how large a capacity our lungs held. When he did mine, the needle kept going off the scale. He kept having me do it until I thought I was going to pass out from hyperventilating.

"Hey, get in here, Doc," he called to a passing physician. "There's something wrong with the wedge spirometer."

The doctor came into the room and had me perform the test one more time. "Hell, there's nothing wrong with the equipment. This guy just has huge lungs."

It turned out that I had an eleven-liter lung capacity. Normal is from seven to nine. The researchers started giving me the third degree on where I grew up and if I had had any diseases or anything as a child.

Oh, shit, I thought, here goes my diving career down the tubes.

About that time one of the doctors spoke up. He said that whatever they learned there stayed there and would not be part of my medical record.

"I had asthma when I was a kid," I admitted.

They decided that this might be the reason for the large lung capacity and said I could not be a subject in the chamber. If nothing happened to me and did to others, it might have been because of childhood asthma or the other way around.

The project lasted two months, with the men in the chamber for the first four of the last five weeks. The last week, the researchers just did studies on the men who had been in the chamber.

I didn't think they had a good baseline on the outside or on the inside of the chamber. Gary, whose wife was staying in the area, had marital problems, and Ray was a mean, cantankerous bastard most of the time. Gary's wife would come in and talk with him over the headset and tell him about the latest affair she was having with some guy she had met at the club the night before. I just could not imagine that the results of this study would be reliable enough to base further experimentation on.

One day I decided to visit the base at Groton to find one of my classmates from 2d Class Divers School who had been transferred to the *NR-1*, the Navy's smallest nuclear submarine, which was used for "black projects." The sub was top secret and had a very small crew for a submarine. I walked down the pier and right up to the *NR-1*, which was tied off by itself. I was a little nervous about going aboard as I didn't have a clearance higher than "secret." I walked closer and shouted, "Hello aboard *NR-1*!" No answer. I stepped onto the brow and walked onto the deck and up to the conning tower. I called out again. Again, no answer. I walked inside the conning tower and over to the hatch, which was open. I could hear machinery noise coming from below and could look down into what I figured was probably the control room. Another shout garnered the same result. By then, knowing the capability and purpose of the sub (at least I thought I did), I was pretty nervous so I walked off the sub and went back to my car and left. I was amazed at how slack the security was around that black boat.

At noon on 12 April 1974, Ray and Gary came out of the chamber not much worse for wear and not smelling very good. There was a shower in the outer lock, but it just didn't do the job. I heard later that they were both quite weak for some time because their bodies had not been creating as many red blood cells as normal. Apparently, because of the hyperoxic environment of the chamber, the cells just weren't needed to provide oxygen. The last week after the chamber run there was not much to do, so we got our gear straightened out and checked out of NSMRL.

The next year they ran another SHAD dive. That time Burton was one of the men in the chamber. I heard that he was sick for almost a year afterward. It was decided to cut back the partial pressure of oxygen to about what a person would breathe on the surface.

My wife, Mary, took the bus up to Groton so she could help with the driving on the way back to Norfolk. I had been shooting Kodachrome all along and had all my film and camera gear packed and ready to go. We stayed a couple of days out at the motel where I had been living, and then headed home to Virginia Beach. As we were passing through New York, I decided we should stop to get some food. As we drove through an underpass we spotted a large station wagon pulled over at the side of the road. The hood was raised and a woman was standing there as if waiting for assistance. I drove by and we managed to get something to eat at a convenience store. On the way back to find the freeway, as usual, I got lost. We passed by the disabled car again. The woman was no longer with the car. It had not been twenty minutes since we had last passed this vehicle but we couldn't believe it; the car was already sitting on cinder blocks, the wheels were gone, and the seats had been stripped out.

At the time Mary was working as a layout artist at Haynes Furniture in Norfolk. Her job was laying out the ads using artwork produced on-site by a man named Paul Boatwright.[2] Paul had a degree in fine arts from Yale, and he and his wife, Kitty, became good friends of ours. Paul had a Cheoy Lee twenty-eight-foot sloop. I had never been sailing on a real sailboat before, but I'd had my share of time lobster fishing and had been messing around on the water my whole life. Paul asked us if we wanted to go sailing. So we went to where he kept the boat, Rebel Marina on Willoughby Spit,[3] and we cast off for an afternoon on Chesapeake Bay. It didn't take me long to catch the bug and before I knew it I was reading *Sail* and *Cruising World* magazines. Mary and I decided to buy a WestSail 32 sailboat and live on it. Lane Briggs, owner of Rebel Marine Service and Rebel Marina, told me I could keep the boat at the marina if I'd act as a sort of night watchman and do some diving to pay for the slip. It would be a good deal. I went to the bank and talked to the manager, retired Navy captain Lee Mather. I asked him if they would finance the boat as a residence if I was going to live aboard. He said they would and asked me where I was going to buy it. I told him I didn't know yet. He said it just happened that a good friend of his, Rear Adm. Jim Cobb, was the local representative and I should give him a call. He kept his boat over at

2. Some years later, Paul's artwork was used in the movie *Cape Fear* starring Robert DeNiro.
3. Willoughby Spit is a thin strip of land that runs along the coast of Virginia just north of Norfolk. The Hampton Roads Tunnel comes up there. The other end of it is in Newport News.

the Norfolk Shipbuilding and Dry Dock yard and was one hell of a nice guy. I was an E-6 and quite nervous about hobnobbing with a retired admiral because I hadn't had a lot of experience with anybody above the rank of lieutenant commander, but I called him up and asked when I could come down and look at a WestSail. He told me he'd be there on the weekend, so Mary and I went and took a look. We immediately knew it was the boat we wanted. It didn't look like a racer, in fact it looked bulletproof and was modeled after a Norwegian pilot boat, so I knew it was seaworthy, probably more so than we were.

Cobb turned out to be a very nice guy; I could not imagine a better person to do business with. The first day we met him, he invited us for lunch. He ate sardines and peanut butter crackers and washed his down with beer, but I drank a Coke with mine. He didn't want to use the head in the boat, so he had a plastic bottle to urinate in that he'd dump overboard later. The guy was a real person and Mary and I both liked him a lot. He became a surrogate father to us.

We came up with the thousand-dollar down payment to lock in the order and decided on the features we wanted on the boat. I chose the teak decks and a few other extras that would be easier to get from the builder rather than add on later. Jim took us sailing on many occasions and told us many sea stories about his forty-six years of naval service. He had quit high school, or been thrown out, and joined the Navy. An officer he worked for had seen potential in him and counseled him to get his GED and try for the Naval Academy. Jim did and got accepted.

Then he was accepted to flight school and flew PBY amphibious airplanes during World War II. He was stationed at Pearl Harbor during the attack and had made a bombing run on a Japanese submarine off Diamond Head the day before. He told me that the day of the attack, he jumped out of bed and pulled his socks on so hard he drove his feet right through the bottoms. He went out in the yard and shot at the Japanese planes with his .45. He said he never hit any, but it made him feel like he was doing something to help.

Later on he was flying the first plane to bomb an enemy ship by radar contact alone. Since PBYs didn't have bomb racks the crew would open the side door and throw bombs out by hand, so he always tried to get the strongest and biggest men on his flights.

A wild man in his younger days, Jim had flown a PBY under the Golden Gate Bridge and gotten away with it. Rear Adm. Jim Cobb had also lied about his age and about having asthma in order to get into the Navy. Decades later, he called up a friend, an admiral who was chief of the Bureau of Naval Personnel (BUPERS), and told him that a mistake had been made in his service record and that he was one year younger than was recorded. Then he told the BUPERS admiral about lying to get into the Navy. The admiral laughed and told Jim he'd made up for his crime by serving over forty years on active duty.

Not long after ordering the WestSail, Mary discovered she was pregnant. We decided to go back to Maine for a few days of leave, so we climbed in the old Datsun pickup and pounded our way up the coast. When we got there, we found out my neighbor's house was for sale. It had been built by my great-grandmother's brother in 1898 and had a great view of the Mussel Ridges. I could look right out and see Dix Island, where my great-grandmother was born in 1866.

I had approached my neighbor years earlier about buying it; he had been reluctant to put it on the market, but gave me first refusal on it. He'd inherited it from his best friend and didn't want the capital-gains tax burden right away. But this time he was ready to sell. We told him we'd take it.

I hated to go back to Jim Cobb and tell him about the house deal, but when I did he understood perfectly and did not blame me for buying the house instead.

"They'll be making Fiberglas sailboats a long time after they've quit making shorefront property in Maine," he said smiling, and wrote me a check for a thousand dollars, my deposit.

He told me that in the time that had passed since I ordered the boat, the price had gone up and he had people who would take my order.

I began working for him on weekends and taking people out sailing, and generally being the guy who kept his boat squared away. Jim gave me a hundred bucks a month and I got to take the boat out sailing whenever I wanted to. That fall I went up to the Newport boat show and helped sail a new WestSail 43 to Annapolis, Maryland, with Jim Cobb and an old friend of his, retired captain Buck James. We had a third man there, the guy who would become the new WestSail dealer when Jim Cobb moved into another line of boats. His name was Leif Oxaal, a Norwegian.

By then we had about ten thousand dollars in savings because we'd been looking forward to buying the boat and had stuffed every cent we could into the bank. Through Mary's getting rid of car payments, us paying off our bills, and our basically frugal living, we were rapidly building up a cash reserve. I had called up to Maine and talked to our local savings and loan there. They told me they would have no problem financing the house. I transferred our money into my checking account and had my sister drive me to the Greyhound Bus station. Heather had joined the Navy after finishing college and at the time was the classified-material officer at the naval weapons station in Yorktown, Virginia.

We arrived at the bus station. When I got to the counter, I broke out my checkbook and asked the ticket agent how much it would cost for a round-trip ticket to Rockland, Maine. She noticed that I was starting to write a check and informed me that I would have to speak to the manager before they would accept it. I thought nothing of it and walked into his office. He looked out from his glass enclosure through the little round window and asked if he could help me. I said I was going to Maine to close on a house and needed to write a check for the ticket. He asked me where I worked. I told him I was in the Navy. His exact words were, "Sorry, pal, we don't take checks from servicemen on weekends."

I went apeshit, to put it mildly. I started raving about how the whole goddamned Tidewater area of Virginia depended on us low-life servicemen to stay alive and the sonsabitches wouldn't even take a check on weekends. I made some remark about dragging his narrow ass through that little round window and stomping the shit out of him, but I decided to back off when he reached for the phone. I assumed he would call the police. A bus driver standing at the back of the room just grinned as I stormed out the door.

Heather had not left yet, so I threw my stuff in the car and we drove away. I had a couple of hundred dollars or so in my pocket in cash, but I was furious at the idea of that jerk not accepting my check. I told Heather to step on it as I was pretty sure he had called the Norfolk police. She drove me to the Chesapeake Bay Bridge Tunnel and I got out at the bus stop at the end of the bridge. In a while the bus came by and I got on board. It was the same driver. He grinned and told me that I could pay for the ticket at the first stop. I had calmed down by then and just put my brain in neutral until I got home. Mary flew up later and we closed the deal. Now we were making mortgage payments on a house in Maine and paying rent in Virginia Beach on the little house on Lauderdale Avenue behind Little Creek Amphibious Base.

Our neighbors Duke and Chele Leonard were among our closest friends. Duke had been a second class mineman in SEAL Team Two. He had served in Vietnam extensively and been awarded the Silver Star for saving a Vietnamese trooper and loading him into a hovering helicopter during a firefight in the middle of a river. Not a good place to be.

Duke had just left the Navy and was returning to college to get a degree so that he could go back into the Navy and become an officer with the SEALs. He needed a job. I called Beldon Little to see if he had anything going. He didn't have a steady job for him, but managed to get Duke some work now and then, and that relieved some of the financial strain while Duke went to school. Chele worked full-time at a bookstore. At the time the only "kid" they had was a large black Great Dane named Whiskey. He must have weighed nearly two hundred pounds and was pretty ferocious, or at least that's what we wanted people to think. He used to ride around town in the front seat of Chele's yellow VW convertible. She'd have the top down and Whiskey could look over the windshield if he wanted to. Not many people gave her any trouble. Of course we had a lot of good times and parties. We could have gone to a party every night if we wanted to.

We were also friends with Slator Blackiston and Bill Barth, guys who had gone through UDT training with Duke. Slator and his wife, Diane, had a nice house in a development some distance from the beach. We went there a few times for parties and they came down to our house on the beach. Chele's parents and brother came by and visited quite a lot. Chele's dad, Mike, was a hardworking, ex-enlisted sailor who had served on submarines in combat during World War II. Mike had retired from the Navy as a lieutenant commander. Chele's mother, Olga, who we called Ogie, was one of those people everybody wants for a mother. Both of her parents were great people and would do anything to help any of us.

The next house over toward the base from Duke's and Chele's was occupied by Guntis (John) Jaunzems, a SEAL who had immigrated from Germany when very young. Born in Latvia, he spent his teen years in Germany. John, as we called him, was a great guy and had an IQ off the scale. One night a bunch of German UDT guys were over at John's house getting drunk, and before the night was over Mary was there speaking German with them. She had thought she'd forgotten her German, but the beer made it come back. Another time I was up at a bar called the Casino. Another of my neighbors, former frogman Howard Blaha, was in there drinking beer. Somehow we ended up arm wrestling. I beat him every time, but just barely. We went back and forth, alternating arms until I had won ten times. It was very close each time. The next day I could not raise my arms, I was so damned sore. Howard was killed in a car wreck some years later.

My sister Cheryl, at the time a lieutenant in the Medical Service Corps, lived in the house on the other side of ours. She was stationed at the Portsmouth Naval Hospital. Cheryl had worked her way through college and had taken some money from the government for her internship so she had to serve her time in the Navy. She put in a total of twelve years' active and made commander in the Naval Reserve. Cheryl had sworn Heather in, and I photographed the ceremony.

Later that year I took a crew of underwater photographers to Newport, Rhode Island, and worked for the underwater sound lab on Gould Island, where we did more missed-distance testing on the Mark 48 torpedo exploders. By that time my sister Cheryl had been transferred to the Newport Naval Hospital. She had a fairly large apartment, so we borrowed two sets of Navy-issue bunk beds and converted one of her rooms into a bunkroom for the four of us. That saved us the cost of renting motel rooms, and we paid her for staying there. We had a kitchen and bathroom and we bought all the grub while we worked that job.

Joe Parker, an engineer from the naval ordnance lab in White Oak, Maryland, was in charge of the torpedo project, and we worked for him while on the island; Frank Deriso, a civilian engineer from the underwater sound lab, was our direct boss. Each morning we went to the pier and rode out to the island aboard a Navy utility boat. Our diving gear stayed on the island so all we needed to bring back and forth was lunch and dry towels.

We wore wet suits but mostly stood around waiting for the crew to fire torpedoes. One of the guys brought a .22 target pistol and we set up a range outside and practiced shooting at cans and pieces of roofing that had blown off the buildings. The place was in a pretty run-down condition but the huge compressor still worked, and we used it to fire the torpedo tube and rigged up a whip to fill our scuba tanks with the same air.

Our job was to rig up an underwater housing in which a Hasselblad camera would be mounted on an H-beam that was part of the target the torpedo would be fired past. The torpedo had a row of lights in its right side. When the crew had everything set, they would turn the lights on in the fish, open the shutter on the camera remotely, and fire the torpedo, in that order. The torpedo would flash past the camera, leaving a streak of light on the film, and then float to the surface some distance away. A torpedo-retriever boat from the base was standing by to pick up the dummy torpedo and bring it back to the dock so it could be used again. The purpose of the drill was to determine exactly how far away a torpedo could be from the hull of a ship and still trigger its warhead. Of course, there were no explosives involved here, and the electrical charge that would have set off the torpedo just made a mark on the engineer's oscilloscope instead.

The job was not exciting and Newport was a stuffy place with a mild to strong dislike of enlisted sailors. So on weekends we would pile into the rental car and drive up to Maine. There we would eat lobster and generally mess around like sailors on liberty. When the job was completed I turned in the rental car, and we all flew back to Norfolk. It was nearly June 1974.

CHAPTER NINETEEN

Italy

When we weren't on the road working at our trade, things got a little boring around the diving locker. We had some make-work projects like helping out in the pool, going to leadership school, attending meetings, and pulling maintenance on the air compressor and the two inflatable outboards. All of our underwater motion picture cameras used rechargeable batteries and they had to be constantly monitored to ensure that they did not discharge or leak and ruin the insides of the housing. So I put in for a slot at the Naval School of Deep Sea Diving, where I would become a diver, first class. My request went through the chain of command and was approved. School would start sometime in April 1975. In the meantime I needed to stay busy.

Not much was happening and we were getting a little antsy and wanting to get out and operate. I looked around for more work, but found none. Then one day Chief Dick Johnson asked if I had a passport. I told him I did not.

"What's the deal?" I asked.

"They need somebody to fly over to Naples, Italy, to do a job and you're the only one I trust to do it right. I'll check and see if you can get away with just a Navy I.D. card." He found out that I could, as long as I was traveling on Navy orders.

The USS *Cascade* was a destroyer tender that had been hauled out and painted in an Italian shipyard. The yard had been hired to paint the bottom with tin tributylin paint that was supposed to be extremely effective in keeping marine growth down. It had not been working. It was reported that workers had sprayed the paint on from distances of up to ten feet, and that there was no way they could have applied a proper paint job from that distance.

The *Cascade* was tied up in Naples and due to be towed home to be cut up for scrap. I guess the Navy wanted to sue the yard and recover some of the costs of the bad paint job. My job was to go to Naples and shoot underwater stills of the growth on the hull, which would be used in court to prove that the paint hadn't been applied per specifications.

I packed my diving gear. All I needed was a regulator, fins, mask, and my UDT life jacket, as the water there was said to be warm and the tender had plenty of weight belts and tanks. My choice of camera was a Leica M-2 body in an underwater housing built by E. Leitz of Canada. That housing was specially built for the Navy and the setup didn't require any focusing; the lens was the sharpest one I have ever seen. Once the camera body was mounted onto the lens in the housing and the flash synchronization cord was connected, the back cover was dogged on and I was in business. It was small and light. I packed a Sub-Sea Strobe and some film and was ready to go. I would travel and work in civilian clothes.

Mary drove me to the airport and I took off for New York, where I changed planes for Naples. The flight over was about as boring as one can get. We stopped in Rome to change planes. The appearance of young Italian cops—they all looked about nineteen years old—in uniform and carrying machine guns while they wandered around the airport did not give me great confidence.

PH1 Doug Keever of the AFCCG Naples Detachment picked me up at the Naples airport and took me to the small well-furnished house where I would be staying with him and another man from combat camera's Naples detachment. I unpacked my stuff and he gave me a ride to the *Cascade*. I told him I'd get a ride back to the photo lab, where he had made arrangements for me to process the film when I finished the job.

I walked up the brow, showed my I.D. to the officer of the deck, and was escorted aboard. The *Cascade*'s diving officer was a warrant officer. When I entered the diving locker, he was sitting at his desk. He looked up and then stood and shook my hand.

"Welcome aboard, Waterman. So you're the guy who's gonna try and shoot underwater pictures of our hull?" The smirk was not hidden in the tone of his voice.

"No, sir. I *am* going to shoot underwater pictures of your hull." He smiled and sat down.

"Tell me what you need for gear and I'll get you a swim buddy."

I said I needed only a set of tanks and a weight belt as I had all my other equipment. I changed into my trunks and we went out on deck and carried the gear back onto the pier, where some of the deck crew had rigged a ladder down to the water. My swim buddy was going to use a Jack Browne mask instead of scuba so he'd have a lifeline and communications to the surface. The mask he had was fitted with a communications mike so he could talk to the tender. I had loaded the camera with Kodak Tri-X film and made sure the battery was charged in the strobe unit. We jumped into the water—the ladder was for getting out—and made our way over to the side of the ship. I had not gone very far down the hull when I started seeing huge amounts of marine growth. It looked like a damned garden, with sea anemones the size of small apples sticking out from the hull. I shot some photos of them and continued to under the keel. My swim buddy had a flashlight that he used to point at where he thought the worst of the growth was. But there really wasn't any "worst"; it was all bad. The Mediterranean is a great place for marine growth, and without the protection of the bottom paint, the hull was like a fertile garden.

We returned to the side of the ship and climbed the ladder onto the dock. Just then a young officer walked up and asked if I could get some photographs of the underside of his destroyer. It was moored outboard of the *Cascade*. I told him I could. He asked if I could shoot them in color as they had put some red lead on something and wanted to show it in color to see if it was corroding. I had a few rolls of Ektachrome with me, which could be processed at the lab. I usually shot Kodachrome, but that has to be sent to Kodak for processing and takes a few weeks to get back. I wanted to see the results right away. Back in the diving locker, I dried off the camera and changed film, putting in the roll of color.

"Do you have any idea where this thing is we have to shoot?" I asked my swim buddy.

"Yeah, I can put you right on it," he answered. I wasn't sure that he could.

We returned to the pier, got into the water, and then swam under the *Cascade*, out the other side between the two ships, and then under the destroyer. Once we passed the turn of the bilge the visibility turned to zero. During the swim, my buddy's flashlight quit working and we moved along in the darkness by feel. After a while he grabbed my arm and put my hand on something on the hull over my head. With the other hand he squeezed my arm twice. I understood that to mean that the thing I had my hand on was what they needed photos of. I pointed the camera up where my hand was, moved my hand quickly, shot the photo, put my hand back, and did this several times, varying the f-stop. After the last shot I turned and gave him two squeezes on the arm and he led us out from under the destroyer.

Now for the good part. I wondered if I had made an ass of myself for being so cocky in front of that warrant officer. My swim buddy and I changed our clothes and he gave me a ride to the base photo lab. He didn't have to be anyplace, so I told him to hang around and I'd process the film and see what we had. I souped the black-and-white and looked at the negatives. Everything came out perfect! You could even see the little hairs in the sea anemone's structure. Every detail was there. While the negatives were drying we went to the gedunk and got a hamburger and Coke. Then we went back to the lab and I made five prints of each shot. Meanwhile, one of the guys in the lab ran the color film for me. I couldn't believe it, again I was right on the money. Most of the exposures were correct, and I even got the fitting I was photographing correctly framed.

It was hard to not grin when I laid those black-and-white photos in front of that warrant officer. He had a look on his face as though I had just hit him with a bat.

"I'll be damned," he said. "I can't believe you actually got pictures off the bottom of this tub in that sewer down there."

I remained humble and withheld any smart-ass remarks.

"Well, sir, there's a good reason why they sent me over here clear from Norfolk."

"Oh, yeah, what was that?"

"Cause they couldn't find anybody else." I laughed.

He thought that was funny, too, and started putting the photos into piles, separating them into stacks according to who they would be sent to.

"I guess you don't need me anymore," I said.

"No, but thanks a lot for doing this job. It will mean a lot to the skipper and the admiral."

The diver who had been working with me took the roll of color slides and said he would get them to the officer on the destroyer. He must have done it because some time later we got letters of thanks at combat camera from the captain of each ship.

I caught a ride back to the combat camera detachment with the diver and went up to the office. Only about a dozen people were stationed in the Naples detachment, and I thought it was a boondoggle. Their standard of living was high.

Art Cutter, the guy I had bad-mouthed when he made warrant

officer, was the officer in charge. He wasn't really a bad guy, I had just been spouting off the day I made my remarks. Sometimes people just took me too seriously. Art showed me his house and then we drove around Naples to see some of the sights. When we came back to the unit, I called Mary in Norfolk on the AUTOVON network (military and government phone network). She was pregnant with our first child and I wondered how she was doing. The connection was clear and I talked for a few minutes on Uncle's nickel.

Later that afternoon Doug Keever and I went back to his apartment. We cleaned up and got ready to pull some liberty in Naples. The car Keever had was a real junker. The passenger seatback wouldn't stay up so I had to lean forward while Doug drove us around. He said it was good for some things, but not much for riding around. We passed a couple of good-looking women, or at least I thought they were, on a corner. I asked Doug what the story was. He told me they were cross-dressed men. I didn't believe him, so we slowed down when we came to some more of them.

Doug leaned out the window and said, "Quanta costa?"—"How much?" in Italian. When one of them walked over to the car, I got the message; "she" had a slight five o'clock shadow. That took care of my questions. We then drove to the Silver Dollar, a local bar where many combat camera types hung out. The bartender, Jerry, spoke excellent English. We had a few beers, then drove back and hit the rack.

The next day I rode to the base with Doug and made the rounds of the exchange and some little shops nearby. For about fifteen dollars, I purchased a mandolin that seemed to be a good instrument for the price. I bought a pair of silver earrings for Mary and then hung around the combat camera spaces for the rest of the day. We shot the bull and talked about photography, the Navy, and women, as usual, but probably not in that order.

My flight was due to leave the next day, so I got my gear (what little I had) and crammed it into a small bag. My camera was in a small case that looked like a woman's compact. That's what I liked about that Leica housing. I wish I had one today. It was the best underwater camera I have ever used. Most of the underwater photos in this book were taken with one.

Doug ran me to the airport and we shook hands good-bye. I told him I'd see him in Norfolk as soon as he was getting ready to rotate back to the States.

I went through the usual routine to get on the plane. Security was fairly tight, but nothing like it is today. The same kids were running around with machine guns and looking like they were trained for anything. I checked my bag and carried my mandolin and camera case onto the plane with me. The seat I had was up against the bulkhead, so I had a lot of legroom. As I got comfortable, I looked around and noticed that everybody around my seat was a lot taller than me, and I am six feet three inches. After a while I asked the guy sitting next to me how tall he was.

"Seven-foot-six," he answered.

I glanced at the three guys sitting behind us. They were all about his height.

"You guys play a little basketball?" I asked.

"Yeah, we're semipros and play for a corporate league. We were just over here playing another company's team."

I can't remember the guy's last name but his first was Ron. He told me he'd been drafted by the Chicago Bulls, and was a school-teacher from Illinois. He was worried about not making the team because of an old knee injury. We talked for a while and the flight attendant announced that tax-free liquor could be purchased. I looked at Ron and asked him if he drank scotch. He replied that he did. So we purchased a liter of Johnny Walker Black Label from the flight attendant for about five dollars, and I asked her for two cups of ice. She gave me a little talk about it being against regulations to drink on the plane unless she served it. I told her that I understood the rules and we would make every effort to comply. As soon as she turned her back and waited on others, I cracked the cap and Ron and I poured out a couple of large slugs into our plastic cups. We managed to consume the entire bottle crossing the Atlantic. I barely remember getting off the plane.

When I passed through customs the inspector asked me where I had been, how long I had been there, and what I had brought back. I told him: Italy, three days, a mandolin, and half a bottle of scotch that was inside me. He was only slightly disgusted as he waved me through. "Three days in Italy and all you brought back was a bottle of booze. Get out of here."

My flight to Norfolk left from Kennedy. I had landed at La Guardia so I had to take a helicopter shuttle from La Guardia to Kennedy. That taken care of, I got on board the flight to Norfolk. I called Mary and told her what time my flight landed, then got aboard and ordered another drink—something I really needed.

When I arrived in Norfolk, I was in pretty good shape—I thought. When it came time to get off the plane, I staggered down the ramp and walked to the gate. Mary was there, really pregnant with our first kid, and had to help me walk to the baggage claim and then to the car. We got a lot of stares. I had a package with me that Ron had given me on the plane. He had bought some things in Italy and wanted me to have a gift to take to my wife. It was a small ceramic vase. I guess we had become good friends in our drunken state.

She poured me into the VW and drove me home. I went to bed and slept soundly for the remainder of the night. When I returned to the unit the next day there was a message from the staff in the Mediterranean to our command, thanking them for the great job I did. The skipper called me to the office and told me that he appreciated me taking care of that job. I told him that anytime he had an off-the-wall job that nobody else either would or could do, I would take it. It was a good feeling to be appreciated.

My next big adventure was attending race relations training. Once again I went over to Little Creek Amphibious Base for school. The course was supposed to last one week and make us aware that we were probably racist, bigoted, unthinking sons of bitches.

The first day of class we had to stand in a circle and tell everybody our name. The class met in a circle of chairs so that nobody got to sit at the end of the table and feel somehow superior as a result.

The petty officer who ran the class was a light-colored black guy with blue eyes who wore a 2d Class diving patch on his uniform. He also drove a Jaguar XKE. The first thing I did was ask him about his background.

"Looks like you are from the guts of the ghetto," I joked. "What does your father do for a living?"

"Oh, he's a thoracic surgeon out in L.A.," he answered.

"Yeah, and you bought that Jag on a second class's pay, right?" I asked. "Something tells me you ain't exactly what the Navy had in mind for this course, being a typical black guy and all that," I kidded.

He got the message. I knew that being the "race relations" counselor was a tit job and I wished I had something as good. As a matter of fact, I did, so I backed off and got along with the guy very well, as we were both divers.

When they got to the part about being prejudiced, I stood and made my speech.

"Well," I started, "where I come from, we don't have any black people, except a few that came up to Maine with the underground railroad during the Civil War, but they have been watered down by white people and we don't even consider them to be black anymore. When I was growing up, they had to have somebody to pick on, so they picked on the Finns because they spoke a foreign language and drank a lot. Pretty soon the Finns lost their accent and became lawyers and doctors and nobody could tell who they were anymore. We still need somebody to pick on, so I pick on people who are assholes. They come in all colors."

That got a round of cheers and laughter, which is all I lived for in these stupid politically correct schools. At the end of that class, I returned to Combat Camera Group for more underwater photography adventures.

One of the people I had met over the years was Jack Chappell. I haven't mentioned him to this point because we never *did* anything together, just talked. Jack was an ace underwater and topside photographer and one of the smartest people I ever met. He could also sell ice to the Eskimos. Jack and another man, Buck Rouzie, a commercial and salvage diver, had teamed up with Hyrum Mulliken, who owned the dive shop where most of us bought our gear. One day a fisherman from the Eastern Shore of Virginia dragged up a piece of gold bullion in his net. He took a Loran A bearing and marked the spot on his chart. Somehow, Jack and Buck had become involved and wanted me to be in the crew that followed up on the find. They felt the gold bullion had come from the steamer *Merida*, a 6,207-ton passenger freighter that was struck amidships and sunk by the SS *Admiral Farragut* on May 12, 1911, while steaming in a fog on a voyage from Mexico to New York, *Merida* was rumored to have had a large amount of silver and copper on board. Others had tried to recover the treasure, but if they managed to pull it off they had certainly kept quiet about it. The earliest attempt recorded was in 1917.

Jack and Buck came over to the house and we formulated a plan. There would be several teams. The salvage team would be in charge of setting up the diving operation and removing the metal from the wreck. The support team would oversee the diving gear, food, tools, and the rest of the equipment (radios, etc.). The photo team would do no salvage or support work but would document the operation from start to finish. It sounded like the project had the makings of a successful venture, but Murphy is always lurking in the background.

We planned to drive up the Eastern Shore, take a boat to the site, and make a preliminary dive on the wreck. I would go along for the ride, and Jack, Buck, and Hyrum would be there as observers and to oversee a dive that one of Hyrum's men would make to survey the wreck.

The ship lay in 210 feet of water so the working dives would require a serious diving operation. And we'd have to have a decompression chamber topside and medical personnel standing by.

The lot of us drove up there, climbed aboard the old fisherman's boat, and steamed out to the Loran A bearings he had written down. We got on-site and watched for the indication on the recording fathometer that showed us that we were above the ship. The bottom in that part of the ocean is mostly flat mud, so anything sticking up from it would have to be a ship. The skipper of the fishing boat nailed it right on target and we hooked into the wreck with the anchor. Our diver, a Navy first class diver taking some time off, strapped on a set of double tanks and jumped overboard. He followed the anchor line down to the wreck and stayed to his maximum bottom time. When he came up he assured us that it was the *Merida* and that it had been blasted flat. He was eager to make another quick dive, so, against our better judgment, he strapped on another set of tanks and went down for a quick look.

Apparently during the Second World War the Navy had depth-charged this thing until it was nothing more than a pile of scrap metal on the bottom. German U-boats had operated off the coast up and down the eastern seaboard, so *any* underwater metal got hammered by the surface craft. We also heard unsubstantiated rumors that the silver had been removed by one of several salvors attempting to get the riches off the vessel.

We went ashore and headed back to Norfolk. Later that evening our diver was stricken with decompression sickness and had to be treated in the recompression chamber at the dive school at Little Creek. That did not bode well for us, and we never followed through on that adventure, although Jack and Buck's company, DiveScan, was equipped well to do it.

CHAPTER TWENTY

Naval School, Diving and Salvage

Mary was getting big with #1 kid and she had made arrangements to go to the Portsmouth Naval Hospital to have the baby when the time came. We had made friends with her doctor, Lt. Comdr. Lee Artman, who would deliver the child. He used to come over to the house and have a few beers with us. Mary had quit drinking entirely (not that she had been a big consumer of alcohol) and cut her smoking way down while she was pregnant.

On March 14, 1975, quite late, Mary started to go into labor. I drove her to the hospital and went up to the "labor deck" with her. A nurse came and assigned her a bed. She got rigged for bed and climbed in. Of course I was a bit nervous but tried not to show it. As I was wandering about the room I grabbed the chart off the foot of the bed and opened it. The nurse, using the tact I would expect, snatched it out of my hand, saying, "You can't look at that."

Well, I felt my blood pressure go off the scale. She caught me at the wrong time and I really got pissed off.

"She's my wife, I guess I can look at the fucking chart if I want to," I shot back. That was the wrong answer.

"We'll have you removed from here if you don't behave," she replied.

"I'll take care of that myself," I said, and walked out the door. Over my shoulder I said, "Call me when she has the kid."

I stormed out of the hospital and drove home. At about 0630 in the morning I got the call from the hospital that I was the father of a little girl. We had decided to name her Emily Olga. Emily had been my great-aunt's and my great-great-grandmother's name. Olga came from one of my wife's friends and the mother of one of Mary's best friends. She was a healthy little girl. The date was March 15, 1975, just two weeks before my twenty-ninth birthday.

Paul Whitmore, one of our underwater photographers, had been discharged from the Navy and taken a job as a diver with AUTEC (Atlantic Undersea Test & Evaluation Center) in the Bahamas. The divers working there were all ex-military, and one of their jobs was jumping out of helicopters and picking up torpedoes that had been fired from submarines in the Tongue of the Ocean. It was an excellent place to have a torpedo range because the torpedoes were all live (except they didn't have warheads), and the nuclear subs could operate there as the water was a thousand fathoms deep.

Whitmore wanted a new outboard motor. He had a boat, but the engine on it was pretty old. He asked if we could smuggle one through customs so he could avoid having to pay the 30 percent or so duty on it to the Bahamian government. I told him we could probably handle that. He sent me a large amount of money in a cashier's check and I went to an outboard shop on Shore Drive, not far from Little Creek, and purchased what he wanted. I told the salesman that it had to be in a crate that would stand up to some abuse. He took a motor, checked it out, ran it, and had it repacked in a very heavy cardboard box. I also told him that I didn't want any labels or names on the box. He understood where it was going and cooperated fully. Then we borrowed a pickup truck and manhandled that big damned box back to the diving locker in Norfolk. We put a label on it that designated it as photographic gear, contents we knew the customs people wouldn't mess with. The Bahamians were used to us coming down to Andros and carrying lots of gear. We usually carried spearguns, too, which were illegal in the Bahamas. Of course the Bahamian customs guy liked to go spearfishing with us, so he didn't bother to look at our gear too closely.

We managed to get all the equipment packed and ready for the trip. It took a couple of trucks to get our inflatable boats and all the rest of the gear to the airport. We loaded it on a C-9 jet and blasted off for West Palm Beach. There we would have to change to a C-1A, a small, twin-engine prop airplane that belonged to VRC-40. The C-1As were used for COD, Carrier On Board Delivery. They had a lot of power and could carry a large amount of cargo.

The C-9 landed us in Palm Beach and the smaller plane was ready to take us across to Andros "airport," a dirt strip where only small aircraft could land and take off. By the time we had all the stuff jammed into the plane, I was trapped in the back by the door and the pilot had to climb in through the overhead emergency escape hatch to get into the plane. But he was a young lieutenant, junior grade and was up for the adventure. We made it to Andros in a few minutes and landed at Fresh Creek International Airport, as I called it. Once we were there, we called AUTEC and they sent a truck out to get us and our gear. We made it through customs and invited the customs guy to come down and have a beer with us when he had the chance. The equipment was taken to the torpedo shed, where the diving locker was located. We used a forklift to get Whitmore's crate off the truck, and he was quite happy to see his new outboard. Later that night we went to eat out at Papa Gay's in Fresh Creek, which is just across the Fresh Creek Bridge in Andros. Paul Whitmore managed to buy us a beer but the cheap bastard didn't even spring for the meal, even though we saved him several hundred dollars, not to mention the risk we took by smuggling an expensive piece of gear into the Bahamas. You never know, do you?

The trip was partly mission-oriented and partly training. We did the job that had to be done testing classified equipment. Our work consisted of photographing the hull with motion picture cameras as it went overhead. That took us part of a morning. Then we stayed about a week and did some spearfishing and scuba diving. Ellsworth Boyd, a writer from Maryland, came down to do a story on us for *Skin Diver* magazine. He was a decent guy and a lot of fun. The first day out on the water, Chief Johnson asked him if he was ready to dive with us. He just about choked and asked what Johnson meant by that. Dick told him to saddle up and get ready. It turned out that in all the time he had been writing about Navy diving units and other military service divers, Boyd had never been allowed to dive with them for some "official" reason. Dick figured the guy must have had as much time in the water as most of us and there would be no reason for him not to dive. Screw the regulations.

We even let him use some of our underwater photo gear to shoot pictures, but the guys from the underwater photo team shot all the photos printed with the story. It came out in the August 1975 issue of *Skin Diver*, I think.

We speared a few fish, filleted them for the freezer, then put our spearguns away. A vice admiral visiting the AUTEC facility wanted to dive with us. He was not a Navy diver, but he was close enough. After all, he had made vice admiral. So we took him out in one of the Zodiac inflatables to a place where there was a lot of coral and fish. We got to the area and I bailed out of the boat face first, without checking. I landed right on top of a branch of staghorn coral jutting up from the bottom some twenty feet below. It hit me in the shoulder and cut me some, but not badly enough to require medical attention. I still have the scar.

On another dive, one of the new guys, PH3 Ike Johnson, was feeding small grouper scraps of fish, or leftovers. The grouper he was feeding probably weighed fifteen pounds. He was holding the bag off to the side and out of his field of vision. Next thing he knew, a larger grouper had swallowed the hand with the bag in it clear to his wrist. In a panic he jerked his hand out of the fish's mouth, raking its teeth across the back of his hand. When we finished laughing, we took him to see Dottie, the nurse at the AUTEC sick bay. She fixed him up with antibiotic cream but had trouble seeing clearly because of all the tears in her eyes from laughing.

Since I would soon have to report in at the Naval School of Diving and Salvage, I caught a flight back to Norfolk and packed for the trip.

At the time there were probably three or four photographer's mates in the entire Navy who were first class divers.

I packed my gear once again into my old VW Bug and headed up the road to Washington, D.C. This time I took an additional piece of equipment that I hadn't needed to carry before, an automatic pistol. I had heard horror stories about the DC area and how unsafe it was, so I carried my Heckler & Koch HK-4 .380 pistol in a shoulder holster. I think I wore it once before I got tired of lugging the damn thing around. I figured I could talk my way out of about anything anyway, so the first weekend I went home I took it back.

In the Navy there are several different levels of diving qualification. The absolute lowest on the food chain is the scuba diver. He is qualified to dive with open-circuit scuba, the same equipment used by the sport-diving world. The next level is Diver, Second Class. Those men are qualified to dive any scuba or surface-supplied equipment that uses compressed air. Additionally, they are trained in salvage and underwater burning and welding.

The Diver, First Class has to have those levels behind him before he can attend school. At the Naval School of Diving and Salvage, the training involves air diving, mixed-gas diving, submarine rescue chamber operation, salvage, decompression chamber operation, diving medicine, treatment of decompression sickness, diving supervision, burning and welding, explosive demolitions, and waxing and buffing tile floors. That level brings the Navy diver closer to becoming a diving supervisor.

Some first class divers went to Point Loma to qualify as saturation divers. They had to learn a lot more about diving physiology, mixed-gas techniques, and a different set of equipment. A lot of them worked in black projects, diving from nuclear submarines on spy missions.

If a diver is a chief petty officer and has met certain requirements, he can then go on to become a master diver, but a lot of politics are involved in becoming one and the Navy has billets for only about fifty of them at a time. The responsibility that a master diver has on a diving ship is incredible.

There are a couple of other specialized diving ratings. One is EOD technician and the other is combat swimmer (UDT/SEAL). The EOD people were second class divers and trained in the nonmagnetic version of the Mark 6 semiclosed-circuit scuba. The combat swimmers took the standard scuba course and then went on to learn the Mark 6 and the pure-oxygen rebreather, the Emerson. The master-diver rating also was expanded to include a saturation master diver. Very few ever made that grade.

So, back to the story. I checked in at NSDS (Naval School of Diving and Salvage) in Washington and was assigned to a room on the ninth floor of one of the barracks at Bolling Air Force Base five or so miles away from the school. We were paid comrats (commuted rations), which meant we could eat wherever we wanted but if we ate in the chow hall, we would have to pay. I could live with that, but I had hoped to draw per diem and live off base in an apartment like a lot of the other men in classes.

My building had three elevators but at least one was always broken. The place was noisy and the air-conditioning was usually inoperative. I was in a room with two other guys who were in the class ahead of me. One was Bruce McLawhorn, from SEAL Team Two, and the other man was Spurling, who would be going back to a ship when he graduated. He was a PADI scuba instructor (Professional Association of Driving Instructors), and he traded me an advanced scuba card for a couple of rolls of Kodachrome. My other civilian certifications were gleaned in a like manner. My NAUI (National Association of Underwater Instructors) card cost me a color eight-by-ten of one of the SDVs we worked on in Puerto Rico, and my ACUC (American/Canadian Underwater Council) card was given to me by a Chinese guy from Canada in a Mexican restaurant in Orlando, Florida. So I had several. To me the only one that counted was the Navy card, but some scuba shop owners would not accept anything except civilian certification when somebody wanted to purchase compressed air or scuba gear.

Class started, and an MM1 Barefoot was assigned class leader. I was the senior person in the class, but he had told the administration officer that he had made chief and gotten out of the Navy. After he came back in they told him he would be advanced as soon as they got some things straightened out in his record. Meanwhile, I was standing watches and doing all the other stuff regular sailors do. In a couple of weeks the admin people found out that he would not be making chief, so I got the job as class leader. I didn't have to stand watches, but I had to run the class. There I was, an aviation rating in a diving school with bosun's mates, machinist's mates, enginemen, and hull technicians. My real job in the Navy had nothing to do with fixing broken ships or salvage, but I had done all that work on my own time. The fact that I was a photographer's mate did not affect the way my classmates treated me. The skipper of the school was Lt. Comdr. Tony Esau, an Annapolis graduate and former football player. I had heard stories about how he used to take care of problems with sailors on his ship and I didn't want to experience any of his ire firsthand.

McLawhorn and I used to travel home on the weekends sometimes in his camper pickup truck. One afternoon we got ready to go, picked up the usual six-pack of beer to nurse on the boring trip, fueled up the truck, and headed down the road. We had passed about the halfway point and were cruising down a deserted road in the boonies somewhere near A. P. Hill Training Area in Virginia, when the left rear tire blew. Bruce started to panic and hit the brakes. I screamed at him not to hit the brakes, just let it roll to a stop, but he was out of control and had the damned brake pedal all the way down. We were slowing down from 45 mph, but I could tell we were about to upset. The ditch was fairly deep and the road was narrow. There were trees on the right and a field on the left. In a matter of a few seconds, the truck flipped onto its left side and scraped noisily along the pavement. By that point, Bruce was screaming that we were gonna die. We slowed to a stop about fifteen feet from some trees and I looked back through the window and into the camper. I could see flames.

"We're on fire, Bruce, we better get out of this thing fast!" I shouted.

I stood on the driver's side door and lifted the passenger's side door. Then I climbed up and sat on the side of the cab. Bruce climbed up, over, and out. He never missed a stride, but stepped on my hand in the process and kept going until he was across the road and a few yards into the field. I went to swing my legs out of the cab and dropped the door on one of them. I had to reach back and open the door to free my leg before I could jump down to the ground. By that time the flames were following our spilled gasoline down the road. Sparks from the left rear tire rim scraping the road had ignited the gasoline.

I ran across the road to where Bruce was having a fit. All his uniforms and electronic repair tools and a couple of guns and ammunition were in the truck and he didn't have enough insurance to cover their loss.

The flames shot higher and higher. An old black farmer who lived in a house in the field came out and told us he'd called the fire department. I thanked him and he said we could use his phone when things settled down. Before long a truck showed up being driven by one fireman. We were so far out in the sticks, they didn't have anything but an old pumper truck and a volunteer fire department. I grabbed the hose off the truck and the fireman started the pump. He couldn't figure out which valve to turn to get me water, so I ran back and we finally got it set right. I started spraying water on the trees and the bushes to extinguish the flames while he made sure the water pressure stayed up.

"What about my truck, save it!" Bruce shouted.

"Screw the truck. If these woods catch on fire we're gonna have bigger problems than that truck." I figured it would wipe out half the state if the forest caught on fire.

By that time, aluminum was melting and running down the side of the road and ammunition inside the camper was cooking off like firecrackers. My wallet had been on the dashboard, as I had left it there after we stopped for gas and beer. It had had two hundred dollars in it. Gone. A sandwich that I had bought for

Mary at a place that made really outrageous sandwiches was also consumed by flames. I went up and tried to kick the windshield in to get at these things, but the flames were just too high to get close to it.

After the fire was out, Mac went across the street and called somebody who came and gave us a ride home. They dropped me off at my house. Mary's parents were there for a visit and I didn't want to upset them.

"How was the ride down?" she asked.

"Not bad, but I don't have your sandwich."

"What did you do, forget to buy it?"

"No, it burned up along with the truck and my wallet."

She thought I was kidding, then she saw the black charcoal stains on my pants and shoes.

On the way back Sunday night, Bruce and I stopped at the garage where they had taken the wreck. I shot a roll of film of it for the record. Later on, he managed to get some insurance money from his homeowner's policy and gave me the money I had lost.

One afternoon as I was driving back to the barracks with three other classmates in my old tan VW, I stopped at a four-way stop on Bolling Air Force Base. I looked to my right just as an official Air Force sedan rolled up to the corner. I was already stopped, so I just kicked her ahead and made a left turn. I drove along at my usual pace of about twenty or so miles per hour on base and noticed the sedan following me. I cut through the parking lot of the commissary and it followed me there. Finally I stopped to see what he wanted. I pulled over and an E-8 Air Force sergeant came up to my window.

"The colonel would like to see you, sailor," he said.

I hated being called "sailor," even though that's what I was. So I got out and walked back to where a colonel was sitting behind the wheel of his blue sedan. He never looked up at me once, but only talked to me like he had a microphone in the steering wheel.

"Sailor, it is people like you who make military life difficult, people [he didn't say men] like you who don't obey the rules and cause problems for others." He went on with more of his diatribe, but I don't remember it.

Finally he asked me, "Sailor do you live here on Bolling Air Force Base?"

"Yes sir, I do."

"Well then, Sailor, do you like living here on Bolling Air Force Base?"

"As a matter of fact, sir, I don't."

"Well then, I think we can do something about that. Sergeant, get this sailor's name and see that he doesn't have to live on Bolling Air Force Base any longer."

"Yes, sir."

That was the end of our conversation. I climbed back into the car and said, "What an asshole. At least when I get reamed by a Navy man, the son of a bitch will look me in the eye."

The following afternoon I was lying on my bunk in my skivvies in the sweltering, air-conditioning-free heat of Washington, D.C. Two Air Force men walked into the room, a captain (O-3) and an E-6 sergeant.

"You Waterman?" the sergeant asked.

"Yeah, that's right."

"We have orders to escort you from the barracks."

"I figured that might be why you're here. Any idea where I am going?"

The captain replied, "The Navy has found you a place over at the Anacostia Naval Station in the barracks where the misfits are housed until they are discharged."

Great, I thought to myself, this oughta be good.

"Oh, did the colonel tell you to rough me up or try to kick the shit out of me or anything like that?" I asked.

The two Air Force guys cast a sheepish look at each other and then the captain answered, "Well, the colonel did say we might expect some trouble."

The sergeant had been looking around the room and saw my dress blues hanging on the locker door. I had my Vietnam ribbons and jump wings and so on displayed on them.

"Oh, you been to Vietnam, I see," he offered.

"Yeah, I was there for one tour with underwater demolition team, and you can tell that little pissant colonel that if *he* had come to throw me out of the barracks there *would* have been trouble. I would have given that cocksucker flying lessons right out of his goddamned Air Force barracks ninth-floor window. By the time he got to the ground he would be even shorter than he is now. And you can tell him I said that."

Spurling and McLawhorn helped me carry my bags down to my car. The Air Force guys were apparently under orders not to lay a hand on my gear or in any way assist me. They escorted me across what used to be Anacostia Naval Air Station to the front of a two-story brick building, then they drove off. It did not look like a typical barracks to me. I humped my bags up onto the top step, where I could keep an eye on them from inside. I walked in and entered an office next to a communications center of some kind.

"You must be Waterman," said the petty officer behind the desk.

"Gee, how'd you guess?" I asked.

"News travels fast around here. We got you a room upstairs with a chief cook. He's never there, lives in Norfolk, but leaves his gear here, and there's a TV in there and the air conditioner works. I think he's even got a refrigerator, too."

"Ain't this the barracks where the misfits and homosexuals are housed until you discharge them?" I asked.

"Yes, but that's in the other wing, and the two are not connected. This wing is where the Navy men in the Old Guard live. Pretty squared away bunch. They are all young boots and pretty gung ho."

"So you told the Air Force that this was the barracks where the guys lived who were gonna be shitcanned?"

"I didn't, but when they called the chief and asked where they could put a first class petty officer who had wised off at the base CO, he knew the guy that did it had to be okay, so he stretched it a little. He wanted to make them think they were really shafting you."

"Well, tell him thanks a lot; I am not gonna give you guys any trouble, that's for sure."

The petty officer helped me carry my stuff to my second-floor room, which had two beds in it, the chief's TV, large lockers, and a table for my typewriter. When I walked in I had to turn the air conditioning down a little as it was *too* cold. I unpacked my stuff and put it in the locker, then went back downstairs. At the bottom of the stairs was that communications room. I walked in and asked the kid at the desk what type of work they did there. He told me they routed calls all over the base. I asked if it was hard to make a call to Norfolk on the AUTOVON system. He said not at all, and that the operators there would probably patch me through to a local number if I wanted. I thanked him and later on made good use of the system.

Just down the hall was a small Navy exchange where I could

buy things like soda, candy, canned goods, shoe polish, toiletries, and other odds and ends. It was open a few hours a day and in the morning on Saturdays. Hell, I wish I had gotten kicked off that damned Air Force base sooner. I even had a parking space! I thought of the story of Br'er Rabbit. "Please don't throw me in the briar patch!"

A couple of days later I was doing something in the chamber room when the CO opened his office door and motioned for me to come in.

"Have a seat, Waterman," he said. "Rumor has it you got thrown off Bolling Air Force Base."

"No rumor, sir; that's a fact."

"And did you make some remark about throwing the colonel out of the ninth-story window?"

"Yes, sir, I did. I also added a few more phrases after that."

Esau grinned. "I kind of figured that. Listen, I don't like that little son of a bitch any better than the rest of you guys, but we have to get along with those Air Force pukes. We can't afford to pay per diem to everybody, so tone it down a little. Got it?"

"Yes, sir. I'll work on it some. I like where I am now," I said, and I left his office.

During the training phase, we did all of our diving in wet pots, chambers inside the building that were full of water and capable of being pressurized to three hundred feet or so. We split and mixed helium-oxygen gas and made up our own mixes. We learned the theory and practice of using inert gases other than nitrogen, and had plenty of practice rolling heavy gas cylinders around the building to place them in the racks and remove them again for use.

One of the training evolutions we took part in was the "narc run" in the chamber. A half dozen of us at a time would be placed in the chamber with one of the instructors and we would be pressed down to 290 feet on air for a ten-minute bottom time. The idea was to give us a feeling of what it would be like to be at that depth and the resultant effects of nitrogen narcosis, "rapture of the deep." We took off our shoes to prevent dirt and oil from contaminating the chamber and crawled inside, taking seats along opposite sides. The instructor was near the speaker so he could talk to the outside tender.

"Ready to leave the surface," he said.

The air started hissing into the chamber as we were pressurized to the depth equivalent of 290 feet. It got very hot and everybody started sweating profusely. The air felt thick as syrup and you could not whistle. They had told us we would not be able to, but we all tried anyway. Most of the class started laughing uncontrollably and I just sat there staring at the depth gauge and tried like hell not to crack up. Eventually I joined in the laughter, but I had been trying to make myself think clearly in preparation for when I would actually have to make a dive to that depth, because we knew we would make a training dive in the pressure pot to 290 on air. We made our way back to the surface at the standard ascent rate of sixty feet per minute, and I think we had a decompression stop at ten feet. As we went up, the chamber got very cold and vapor formed in the air from all the sweating and then the lowering of the pressure. It covered us in a cold, clammy, wet fog. Then the chamber door clanked open and we all crawled back out and into our shoes.

We stayed around until the rest of the class had completed the "narc run," then went across the street to the classroom, located on the top deck of a floating barge. A machine shop on the first deck was where repairs were made to equipment and where suits and helmets were stored.

As we sat in the classroom filling out the dive report that would be sent to the Naval Safety Center, I noticed that when my hand went toward the right side of the paper, it disappeared. I closed my left eye and did a quick peripheral vision check. I could not see anything to the right of me, only straight ahead.

"Chief, I think I have a CNS hit in my right eye," I spoke up.

"What makes you think so?"

"I am losing peripheral vision in my right eye."

That was all he needed to know.

"Hey, Hill—you and Mills grab Curly here and walk him over to the chamber. I'll phone Doc and tell him he's coming."

Hill and Mills walked me over to the chamber. By the time I got there, in three minutes or less, they were standing by the chamber with their hands on the valves. The doctor and a corpsman were inside the chamber waiting for me. I kicked off my shoes once again, crawled inside, and lay down on a foam mattress on the floor. No sooner had I done that than we left the surface to level off at sixty feet. I was immediately placed on 100 percent oxygen by mask and the doctor was shining a flashlight into my eyes, alternating between them. The doctor asked if I could see anything. I told him that my peripheral vision was clearing up. When I looked with my right eye, flashes of vision occurred closer together—as if somebody was turning the lights on and off, except finally they just stayed on.

"I think we'd better extend this table five anyway for one O_2 breathing period, just to be safe," the doctor said.

"Yeah, it ain't gonna cost any extra and it might help," the corpsman said.

In what seemed like hours I was out of the chamber, and the duty driver was taking me to the Naval Ophthalmology Clinic at Bethesda Naval Hospital. I found the correct desk and checked in. An ophthalmologist administered a vision test to detect blind spots in my eye. My vision turned out to be normal so we drove back to school and I finished the rest of the day.

Another classmate, a Seabee by the name of Alley, got the bends in a jaw hinge on the same dive. After that the master diver drew a line through that particular dive on the decompression tables and they went to the next greater depth for the decompression schedule but used the same bottom time as before, ten minutes at 290 feet.

One of the more exciting parts of the class was when we went to Indian Head to the Explosive Ordnance Range for the demolition phase. As we were sitting in the classroom, smoking and joking, the instructor came in and gave each of us a stainless steel soup spoon and a sock of C-4 plastic explosive. Then we drew some shaped-charge canisters from a box at the front of the room and started making shaped charges by shaving the C-4 from the block and packing it into the little metal housings. Later that day we took our Play-Doh projects to the range and learned all about the Monroe effect, that is the science behind the way shaped charges work. With a very small piece of C-4, one about the size of a 35mm film can, one could make a shaped charge that would blow a hole straight through a piece of railroad track. The hole, except for some spattering around the edges, would look like somebody had drilled it.

We shot holes in steel plate and through the sidewalls of empty out-of-date scuba bottles. We learned how to tie in a trunk line and set up cratering charges in a road. It was a welcome respite from the smoke-filled classroom and heat of summer in Washington, DC.

One morning the word was passed that the diving detailer,

Master Diver BMCS "Red" White, would be coming to the school to talk to us about our diving careers. It would be our chance to see what was out there and maybe snag some choice assignments. Our small group filed into the classroom and Red White walked in. He was a large senior chief bosun's mate and had an imposing appearance. A lot of master divers are small, ratty-looking guys, but not him. He told us that anybody who got caught smoking dope or doing any kind of drug would be history forever in the diving community; there were no second chances. He also said that there were some billets here and there and told us a few things about dive pay and how they were going to raise it. We had heard all that a million times and read it in *Navy Times*, but it never seemed to materialize.

I asked Red how I could get to go to saturation school. He looked up at me and said, "Volunteer to go to the USS *Ortolan* and you can get it."

The USS *Ortolan*, ASR-22, was a ship about 250 feet long with a catamaran hull and two Mark 2 Deep Dive Systems. It was equipped to do saturation diving and was supposed to support the new DSRV (Deep Submergence Rescue Vehicle). The *Ortolan* was home-ported in Norfolk and didn't go to sea much. I asked if he was sure I would be able to get into saturation diving school if I volunteered to go to the *Ortolan*. He looked me in the eye and said, "No problem, just talk to the XO when you get there. He'll take care of you."

I thought about it some more and told him I would call him at his office. I called Mary that night and asked her what she thought. She figured saturation school would be a good thing to have under my belt, so she said to go ahead and take the billet. I called Red White and told him I would take the job. I felt a little bad about jumping ship from Combat Camera Group, as they had obtained the billet for me at school, but I had bailed out on them before when I went to Vietnam with UDT.

During our training in the wet pot we got to attend some of the officers' classes. It was there that I met a man who I would end up making friends with and being stationed with later on. His name was Edward Miller. He had graduated from the Naval Academy and was instrumental in finding the USS *Monitor* during Operation Cheesebox. Ed had been part way through college when he got an appointment to the Naval Academy. He took the appointment and found that he didn't have to take some of the courses he had already completed so he had the time to get involved in the search for the *Monitor*. When the USS *Monitor* sank off Cape Hatteras while under tow, there had been a red lantern hanging from the turret as a signal. Ed was in the submersible when that lantern was recovered.

One day he was in the tank doing his underwater cutting project, which we had to do against the clock. The object was to clamp a piece of half-inch-thick steel plate to the workbench and burn off part of it. Your time started when you struck the first arc and it stopped when the plate was broken off. Sometimes in underwater burning the cuts are not complete and you have to take a hammer and break the steel off because what are called spider webs hold it together. In this case we had a large crescent wrench in the tank to snap the piece off. When the students had the sheet cut all the way across, they would take the wrench, put it on the edge of the steel, and use it as a lever to snap off the burned-off piece. Well, Ed burned his piece most of the way through, but spider webs were holding it together, so the instructor got on the comm box and said, "Ensign Miller, finish it off with the crescent hammer." Ed picked up the wrench and instead of fastening it on the steel and bearing down, he started pounding away on it with the crescent wrench. The class was nearly rolling on the floor with laughter. It took Ed a while to live that one down. He had a good sense of humor and didn't let it get to him.

Two other officers I met were from the Middle East. One was in the Israeli Navy and one was in the Egyptian Navy. I could not imagine the administration that would put those two guys in the same general area. One day as I was standing on the comm box outside the wet pot while the Egyptian was diving, the Israeli officer came up to me and said, "Hey, you let me tend him and he not come up." We acted as though he was joking, but he probably was not.

After a few weeks we were ready to go downriver for the salvage project, which involved the actual salvaging of a ship sunk in the river. The steel vessel, about 125 feet long, was scuttled in forty feet of water alongside another of the same type. Since the classes alternated between ships, the class before us could not tell us where all the holes were that we would have to patch in order to raise the ship. We loaded all our gear and the clothing we would need onto the training barge and got under way downriver.

This project would take two weeks, and I was warned that the class leader always got the lowest grade in the class.

Each day we headed downriver on a crew boat at about 0600 and came back to the dock near the school in the afternoon just before dark. The days were long but went rapidly because we had a mission at hand.

The first day we had to set up the diving station on the wreck and start to determine where the leaks were. All diving would be done in the Mark V deep sea rig, and visibility was either zero or very close to it. The school had plywood and old fire hose for gasket-making material, and nails, hammers, saws, canvas, and anything else we would need for the project. As class leader I had to send in a SitRep (Situation Report) every day after school. I wrote it up and gave it to the instructor to place in the file.

About the second day one of the instructors, BMC Bamberger, walked out of the wheelhouse of the training vessel and started ragging me out about being behind schedule. He had done that a little on the first day, but now he was really putting it onto me. He said his ten-year-old kid could do better than we were, we would never get the damned thing afloat, and so on. I piped right up.

"Chief Bamberger, if your kid is so damned smart, why don't you bring the little bastard down here and we'll work for him. Maybe you can get your wife to come down, too, and cook us some decent chow while you're at it." He shut up and walked back into the pilothouse.

"Shit, you've had it now, Waterman," one of my classmates said.

"Yeah, I guess I got a little carried away. He's probably going in there right now to write me up or drop me from the school."

Bamberger acted as though nothing had ever happened. He would just come out, chewing on one of his unlit cigars, watch us from the deck of the training boat, then go back in and suck down more coffee.

We found all the holes and patched each with a toggle patch, a plywood patch with a bolt run through its center. We would push the toggle patch through the hole and then place a strongback, with the bolt running through that, on the inside and tighten it with a nut. Some holes required Tucker patches, which were similar to toggle patches but folded in the middle so we could get them through a round hole. Any other hole but a round one, we could make a toggle patch to fit.

In some places the doors or hatches had to be shored up with timbers and wedges. We had the ship all tightened up and ready to pump by Friday morning of the second week. Now I had to come up with a pumping plan. I had the blueprints to the ship and took them back to my room. I measured each compartment with a yardstick, as that's all I had, converted it to scale, and figured the cubic footage of the spaces, which I converted to gallons of water. There are seven and a half gallons of water per cubic foot. I knew the capacities of the pumps we would be using, and dynamic head, the pumps' height above water, would not be a consideration as they would be sitting almost at "sea" level.

I had the plan down. I figured the time and then threw in a little "Jesus factor" in case something screwed up.

The next day we rigged the pumps and started pumping. Sure enough, one of the electric submersible pumps failed and we had to alternate between two compartments with one pump. When we had pumped her dry and secured the pumping operation, I was ten minutes off the time I had estimated. Ten minutes early. Needless to say, I was more shocked that I was so close. We stripped out the remaining water with buckets and climbed down inside the wreck to see what it looked like. We were one bunch of happy sailors to see that test over with. Later that afternoon we pulled the patches and sank her back to the bottom again for another group to raise.

Before we left the project for good that day, Bamberger called me up into the wheelhouse of the training boat.

"Waterman," he asked in a somewhat gruff voice, "what kind of grade do you think you got in this class?" I started to feel a little weak.

"Gee, Chief, I don't know. But if I passed, that's close enough."

He was standing with the grade book open and had his hand over where my grade was written. He slid his thumb down and uncovered it. I had a 90. Then he spoke up.

"I never give anybody a ninety, especially the class leader. You drove me off the job that first day and showed that you were in charge. That's what I wanted you to do. On a salvage job there can be only one boss, otherwise people start second-guessing each other and men get hurt and gear gets destroyed. Good job."

Another situation where I couldn't get the grin off my face. I had to go back to the barracks and write an after-action report. I had decided not to go home that weekend as I was pretty tired, and they had steaks on special at the Petty Officers' Club on the base. So I got together my copies of the daily SitReps and formulated a salvage report, which I typed out on the old typewriter I had brought along after being evicted from the Air Force barracks. It may have taken me half an hour to write it, but I put in fluff about having to abandon the wreck before the tugs came to tow it as we were taking small-arms fire from the east bank of the Anacostia River—stuff like that. In reality some boys were firing BB guns at us from the shore and hitting the ship around us.

On Monday afternoon, one of the instructors told me the skipper wanted to see me in his office.

I thought, Shit, what have I done now?

I walked through the door of his office. Lieutenant Commander Esau was standing behind his desk with a coffee cup in his hand. He was an imposing sight. The man stood six-foot-six and weighed in at around three hundred pounds.

"Have a seat, Waterman. I read your salvage report." Silence. "Best one I've seen. How long did it take you to write it?"

I answered, "Oh, I don't know, about a half hour, I guess."

He gave me a quizzical look and continued, "I'm going to use it as an example of what these reports should look like and put it out to the salvage officers' classes. Those guys could use some improvement in their reporting."

"Well, thanks, Skipper. I was afraid you were calling me in here to chew my ass for something."

"Not this time." Esau laughed.

The rest of the week was spent making deep helium/oxygen dives in the wet pot and preparing to go downriver to Dahlgren, Virginia, to make our deep-qualifying dives. A master diver candidate, Chief Jim Starcher, would be along to mess with us. Two or three other master divers would be there to evaluate his performance.

We rode a boat down and stayed in barracks at the Dahlgren Naval Weapons Station. It was a run-down place pretty bare of essentials, but we were going to be there for only a week. Then, after one more week of school, we would graduate.

Each day we went aboard the boat and steamed to a point near the bridge that crossed the Potomac River near Dahlgren. The boat would anchor in about 180 feet of water. We had actually made our qualifying dives in the wet pot, but had to get that one in to satisfy a requirement for an open-water dive or something of that nature.

Each dive would be made with just one diver on the stage. We would dress in the Mark V Mod 1 rig with the helmet with the baralyme canister, etc. When fully dressed in that gear I weighed over five hundred pounds, with the eighty-pound belt and the eighty-pound set of shoes. The helmet and canister alone weighed 130 pounds. When a diver was dressed to dive and waiting to go, a rope was threaded through a becket in the top of his helmet. That went through a pulley arrangement so the weight of the helmet and breastplate could be lifted from his shoulders.

When it came time for me to dive, one of the evaluating master divers came up to me and started whispering in my ear. He told me that when I got to the bottom I should get off the stage, but when they told me to get back on, to say I was on but *not* get back on the stage. They wanted to see if Starcher, the master candidate, would be watching the gauges to see if I was actually coming up with the stage.

The tender closed and dogged the faceplate of my helmet and the hissing of the helium/oxygen mixture was all I could hear as I climbed clumsily onto the diving stage and prepared to be lowered to the bottom of the river. I went down, then felt the stage hit bottom.

"Red Diver[1] on the bottom," I reported in the high-pitched nasal tones of one breathing helium.

"Roger, Red Diver, get off the stage."

"Red Diver getting off the stage."

I reported in a moment, "Red Diver off the stage."

"Roger, Red. Get back on the stage and stand by to leave the bottom. Let me know when you are on the stage and ready to leave the bottom."

I waited a few seconds. "Topside, Red Diver on stage and ready to leave the bottom."

At this point I stood up to my thighs in the muddy bottom of the Potomac River in total blackness, my helium suit blown up

1. The Navy uses a color system to identify each diver. There are usually Red, Green, Yellow, and Black. The helmets have a color swatch on them as do the breastplates. The canvas covering on the diver's air hose is also painted a specific color. That prevents communication problems during dives and doesn't require the tender to remember who is in each rig when there is more than one diver in the water.

to the point where if I relaxed, my arms would extend out from my body. At that point, the Michelin Man was just a thin version of me. The Mark V Mod 1 helmet requires that gas be blown through a venturi in the back of the helmet where the canister of baralyme is mounted. In order for the gas to flow correctly and the carbon dioxide to be scrubbed out, there has to be constant overpressure in the suit, and that causes the diver to be almost blown up all the time.

The stage started to lift and I kept my hand on it until it went out of reach.

"Red Diver are you on the stage?" came the voice over the comm speaker.

"Negative, topside, I fell off the stage. Bring it back down."

Now, I knew that I would have a problem if that damned stage came back down and drove me further into the mud. I had trouble enough moving around already.

The stage came back down and, sure enough, landed on top of me, even though I had not moved. Now I was almost up to my waist in the mud.

"All stop, the stage is on top of me," I reported.

"Roger that, taking the stage up."

"Just lift it up slowly, about three feet," I ordered.

I tried to hang onto the stage as they pulled it up a few feet so I could pull myself out of the mud. It didn't work and I had them lower it again. This time I guided it so it came down right in front of me. I bent over and put the top half of my body, which wasn't in the mud, onto the stage and then had them lift it up a few feet. Once I was clear of the mud, I stood back up and hung on as they raised me. I arrived at the surface and climbed off the stage. I was undressed quickly by my tenders and got dressed to take my turn topside. Jim Starcher came over and asked me what the hell happened to me. I told him that I had done what the guys told me to do. He understood then that it had been a drill. Starcher made master diver and went on to his next command.

We finished the week making qualification dives and were tied up alongside the school at the Navy yard by Friday afternoon. The next week we would do the course on the McCann Submarine Rescue Chamber.

On Monday we started the classroom sessions for the McCann rescue chamber. This device was used to rescue submariners from a submarine on the bottom in water over six hundred feet deep. The bell was one atmosphere—that is, it was not pressurized internally—and had an upper and a lower section. The lower section is open at the bottom, and in the floor of the upper section is a watertight hatch.

The McCann Submarine Rescue Chamber requires two operators and can carry six passengers per load. There is a hatch in the top of the chamber, also, that enables the persons operating the chamber to climb into it once it is sitting in the water. The inside piping system had twenty-two valves that controlled various ballast tanks and the air supply. The umbilical to the surface carried air down to the bell and also allowed the chamber air to be exhausted to the surface.

When the bell was mated to a downed submarine, the operators of the bell could vent the sub and give it enough fresh air to last between runs to the surface with rescued submariners. By the time we went into the chamber to make dry runs, we had to understand the operation of the bell and be able to explain what all of the valves did.

On an actual chamber run the scenario is as follows:

The submarine releases the sub rescue buoy, which is attached by a cable to a bail on the submarine's hatch. There used to be a telephone in the emergency buoy, which could be used to talk to the men in the submarine. The buoy phone has since been replaced by the UQC wireless underwater communication system.

When the buoy is released in an actual emergency, smoke grenades can be fired from the submarine by remote control to show the buoy's location to the rescuers. The ASR (Auxiliary Submarine Rescue ship) finds the buoy and runs a race track pattern around the buoy while setting out the four mooring spuds, huge steel buoys with wooden chafing gear on them. They are anchored to the bottom with chain. When all four are set, the ASR sends out its boat to secure mooring lines to the spuds and the ASR is maneuvered alongside the sub's emergency buoy. The men on the ASR cut the cable and connect the end to the chamber's air winch. When this is done, the crane on the ASR lowers the bell over the side and the operators climb in. The bell's umbilical (hose, safety, and power cable combination) is faked down on deck so that it will run out freely. This umbilical is about six inches in diameter and it takes every free hand in the diving gang and a few others to handle it. In the water, it is nearly neutral, but it is still damned heavy to handle on deck.

The chamber operators flood the ballast tanks until the chamber is slightly positive. Then the winch is activated and they start winching the chamber down to the submarine. Once they get to the sub and make the "Kittredge seal," and equalize the upper and lower chambers at atmospheric pressure by venting the pressure in the lower chamber to the surface through the exhaust hose (part of the umbilical), one of the operators opens the hatch in the bottom of the upper section of the chamber. He taps on the submarine hatch and the submariners slowly open it. Once they are secure in the knowledge that all is well, the total weight of the men to come up into the bell is passed to the operators. The same amount of lead ballast must be handed down into the submarine to offset the weight of the men who will be coming aboard. As soon as that is accomplished, the rescued submariners can climb into the chamber. The sub's hatch is closed, the lower chamber hatch is closed, the chamber is flooded by letting seawater into it through a valve, and the operators allow the winch to free run slowly back to the surface. Once on the surface, the chamber's ballast tanks are blown full of air and the upper hatch is opened. The submariners climb out and lead pigs take their place. The whole evolution is repeated until the remainder of the sub's crew is taken off.

The school had a McCann Submarine Rescue Chamber outside the classroom on a concrete pad. A ladder was rigged up to it and permanently attached as each class used it for chamber week. The only operating we did with the chamber was to go inside and talk our way through what each valve did and why we were turning it. During one of our classes on that piece of gear, it was mentioned that a certain procedure when docking the chamber to a bottomed submarine was called the Kittredge seal. I asked how it came to have a name like that. Was it a procedure or a piece of hardware? The instructor said it was a procedure named after the old submarine skipper who had perfected it.

I told the class that I knew Captain Kittredge and that he was my neighbor. "Aw, bullshit, Waterman" was the only answer I got. I really do know him; he grew up about two miles from where I lived in Maine and retired from the Navy two years before I joined. He was a World War II sub skipper and built midget submarines after he retired.

The next time I went home on leave, I asked him exactly what the Kittredge seal was, as I had not paid that close attention in class. Captain Kittredge explained it to me:

> The chamber has ballast tanks in it to give it positive or negative buoyancy. The old system required you to put a strain on the downhaul cable, and that would pull you down to the sub's escape hatch. Then you tried to hold the chamber down with the downhaul winch while you blew the water out of the lower part of the chamber where the bell mated to the submarine. It did not work. What we did was get down as tight as we could. Then we would open the valve between the lower chamber and the ballast tank. That would instantly suck the chamber onto the seat around the sub's hatch and make the Kittredge seal. We set the record for the deepest operation of the McCann Submarine Rescue Chamber while I was COMSUBDIV 11. The USS *Coucal*, ASR-19, was the ship we used and the USS *Tang*, SS-563, was our "victim." The sub lay on the bottom and we took the chamber down to it. We made the seal and I went aboard the submarine for the ride back, and a torpedoman first class from the *Tang* rode the chamber back to the surface in my place.

During the week, I had gradually been packing up my clothes and gear so I could bail out after I graduated on Friday. We were going to have a small party at the club afterward, but most of us wanted to get on the road and out of DC. The traffic would be bad and the heat even worse.

On Thursday afternoon we took the written test on the rescue chamber and everyone passed easily. There was no final written exam, as we passed through each phase as the course progressed. They probably didn't think we would be able to remember the material that long anyway.

By noon we were ready to graduate. The diplomas were handed out and the base photographer took our picture on the front steps of the school with Lt. Comdr. Tony Esau and Lieutenant Duignan, the training officer. According to my final grade I was number one in the class.

After the little ceremony we went to the club and had a few beers. Then I headed down the road for home as I had put all my gear in the car that morning. I was beginning to rethink my stupid decision to volunteer for the *Ortolan*.

CHAPTER TWENTY-ONE

USS *Ortolan, ASR-22*

When I checked back in at Combat Camera Group, I didn't tell anybody I had volunteered for the *Ortolan*. I knew it would come out soon enough. Perhaps the orders would appear out of the blue and the unit would think that it was just my turn in the barrel. As I did more and more checking into what types of things went on aboard the *Ortolan*, I realized that I had made a mistake. However, perhaps getting a chance to attend saturation school would make up for all the bad stuff.

We had a few interesting jobs, but nothing out of the ordinary came up. The regular guys were still at the unit. Bill Curtsinger had been discharged some time back and became a contract photographer for *National Geographic* magazine. Frank Stitt was out in Hollywood, ostensibly making documentary films. Whitmore was still in the Bahamas working as a diver for AUTEC, jumping out of helicopters to snag practice torpedoes. Harry Kulu was back in Hawaii, I guess, and Trotter was either in jail or in some kind of trouble that might land him there.

We made it through the winter in the usual fashion, trying to get things lined up in the islands so we could dive where it was warm. It didn't always work out.

By spring we had some small jobs going and managed to wangle a training trip to Andros Island for a couple of months. I was hoping my orders would not come through for the *Ortolan* before that trip was over. The *Ortolan* was in the Philadelphia Naval Shipyard getting work done on it, and I had heard horror stories about that place.

Finally, about a week before we were scheduled to go back to Norfolk from Andros, the message came down that I had a set of orders to the *Ortolan*. The command told me that I had a month to get there, and if I wanted to take any leave I would have to come home right away. I told them I would finish out the trip and not take any leave. That met with approval.

We ended our trip to Andros and loaded up the equipment and flew back to Norfolk. This time we caught a ride from West Palm Beach to Norfolk in a Navy P-3 submarine hunter. They had to go to Brunswick, Maine, first to drop off some torpedoes before they circled back to Norfolk. We had only our summer clothing, as it had been pretty warm when we left Norfolk, so when we landed in Brunswick, where there was snow on the ground, we did not spend much time off the plane. The aircraft made a quick turnaround and soon we were in Norfolk with the gear: compressor, boats, outboards, underwater cameras, diving equipment, and personal items.

I cleaned out my locker at the gym and the one at the underwater photo team. It was not like I was leaving forever, but just going on another adventure to another command. It did not turn out that way. I would never come back to Combat Camera Group except as a visitor from then on. It was a turning point in my life caused by a decision I have long since regretted.

The *Ortolan* was home-ported in Norfolk at the Destroyer and Submarine Piers, only about two miles from Combat Camera Group, or Atlantic Fleet Audio Visual Command as it was then called. I checked out of the unit and went home to our little place on the beach behind Little Creek.

Taking out a sea bag and a duffel bag, I packed my Navy-issue wet suit and other gear I might need. Mary helped me pack my clothes and I made arrangements to get a flight from Norfolk to Philly, or Filthydelphia as we called it.

Perhaps I should have had a better attitude, but I just couldn't make myself look forward to going to the *Ortolan*. I had been hearing more and more stories about what a piece of junk it was, and I was about to see firsthand.

I had the phone number of the quarterdeck at the *Ortolan*, so I called the OOD and told him when I would be flying in to Philly. He said he'd send somebody to pick me up. I got off the plane there and walked to baggage claim. I was in uniform, so not too hard to spot. A small senior chief petty officer walked over to me and asked if I was Waterman. "Sure am, Chief. Is that good or bad?" I joked. "I don't know. I'm Senior Chief Apodaca," he said. "I'll give you a ride to the ship. Where's your gear?"

We made small talk while I waited for my bags to come around on the conveyor.

"How's the work going on the ship?" I asked.

"Not too bad, but as usual, we are behind schedule—the sand crabs[1] are too busy buying cigarettes in the ship's store and taking breaks to get any work done, but we should be out of here in a couple of weeks. You can square away the photo lab and get supplies while we do this."

"How many duty sections are we in?"

"Four, but it's pretty slack. It's fairly easy to get somebody to take your duty on weekends or Friday night if you want to go back to Norfolk. I go down every weekend if you need a ride."

"Gee, Chief, that would be great." I rode home a couple of times with Apodaca and chipped in for gas.

Apodaca drove me back to the shipyard and dropped me off at the brow. He said he had some other errands to run. I thanked him again for the ride and walked up to the brow.

The Philadelphia shipyard was like a giant gray, steel ghost town with hundreds of ships tied up there in mothballs. It was like visiting a graveyard where the bodies are all above ground. Our ship was moored by a huge hammerhead crane that jutted out over it where it lay alongside a pier. Steam lines were hissing and blowing all over the place and the smell of rotten food in the Dumpsters reminded me of every Navy base I had ever been at.

One of the seamen on watch helped me carry my gear to the photo lab, which was on the 0-2 level and right at the stern of the large catamaran *Ortolan*. As I walked across the bridge crane deck, which was the low part of the ship under the huge bridge crane used to move the DSRV (Deep Submergence Rescue Vehicle) around on deck, I noticed that the deck was slick with oil. I asked the seaman about that.

"Oh, shit, that's always like that. The damned bridge crane leaks hydraulic oil all the time. Sometimes you almost have to wear a raincoat out here on deck."

Great, I thought. Now I will have the added pleasure of falling on my ass in this stuff when I forget it is here.

The photo lab had two rooms. The outer room was the "finishing room" and the inside one was the darkroom. In the outer room was a large Navy-issue, stainless steel refrigerator, where

1. Civilian shipyard workers.

film, paper, and other essentials were kept. I found there was also plenty of room for sodas and containers of yogurt. There was a large Pako drum print dryer in the corner and a Polaroid camera on a stand for doing I.D. photos. Roll-up background paper on one wall served as a backdrop for shooting "official" portraits. Under the finishing table were several cases and in the darkroom under the large stainless steel sink were some more. This was the only place for storage in the compartment. There was a standard, hinged household-type door between the darkroom and the finishing room, and the outer door was a watertight steel door with a central dogging lever. It had a place for a padlock. The lab was kept locked whenever nobody was there.

The entire space was clean and neat and well-lit. The kid who had been running it, a Seaman Rivera, had an interest in photography and had been put in charge of the lab pending somebody's taking his place. He was not a diver and had no designated rating. I wondered why he had not changed to airman so he could strike for photographer's mate. I never asked him why, as I soon found out he was not the most popular person on board.

My first duty was to check in with the administration officer, the XO, and the skipper. I went to the admin office and walked in. YN1 Sherby Hart stood up to greet me. He was a short guy, somewhat older than myself. He shook my hand enthusiastically and introduced me to the other man in the office, PN2 Hosea. I'd always thought Hosea, usually spelled Jòsé, was a strictly Spanish name, but it wasn't. Sherby took my records and orders and called on the phone to the XO and asked if he was busy. Then he turned and motioned for me to follow him up to the next deck.

The XO's office was up in officer's country; that's where the officers lived and worked. He had a small room on the port side of the ship. I walked in. Lieutenant Commander Dix, the XO, was an ex-enlisted man. The CO was a redheaded commander whose name I have forgotten. The XO made some small talk about how it was good to finally have somebody to run the lab and also to have another diver on board. He then took me in to meet the CO.

"Welcome aboard the *Ortolan*, Waterman. We're glad to finally have a real photographer on board. Well, I guess there's not much I can tell you about this ship. One of the divers will show you around. Sherby will get your diving pay started, and I guess it will take you a few days to get squared away with a rack and get to know your way around the ship. Good to have you aboard."

I thanked him and walked back to the XO's office for a second. "By the way, Commander Dix, Red White told me that I could get a set of orders to saturation school if I volunteered to come aboard here."

Dix turned around and smirked. "Shit, Waterman, he tells everybody that."

I suddenly had the feeling that this tour of duty was not going to be much fun at all.

As I walked down the passageway, LTJG Ed Miller came out of his room.

"Well, I heard you were coming aboard. Glad to see you." He smiled while pumping my right hand. "When you get settled in, come on up to my room and I'll bring you up to speed."

"Good to see you, sir. I imagine I'll run across you again before long," I said. "You're probably not too hard to find."

Two other officers, Lt. Wolfgang Knueppel and the engineering officer, Lieutenant Moen, were also there and greeted me warmly. Both were former enlisted men.

These guys seem okay, I may be all right here after all, I thought. After all, we are in this together.

It didn't take me long to get squared away and get my gear stowed. I left my diving gear and personal camera equipment in the photo lab and got a rack two decks down with the guys from the engineering division. It was there I met HT2 Drew Ruddy, a hull technician and saturation diver with a college degree in biology and eyesight much worse than mine. He wore contact lenses. They made him squint and that made him look like a mole. He was good friends with Ed Miller and they used to go diving together on weekends when they could get away. Both were interested in underwater archaeology.

One of my first duties on the *Ortolan* was to inventory all the gear, film, chemicals, and paper. I knew that we had a tight budget, but I wanted to be able to stock the lab so it would not be a constant hassle to get consumable materials later on. According to Rivera, a great camera store nearby did business with the Navy, and we could get whatever we needed there if we had the proper paperwork.

In looking over the gear and checking it against the custody cards, I found that two items were not on the cards. One was a twenty-thousand-dollar Milliken DBM-9 underwater camera, and the other item was an underwater Leica housing built by E. Leitz of Canada. When I put them on the custody list, it turned out that the naval supply system had no record of them either, and that they could have just walked off the ship and nothing would ever have come of it. I was just too damned honest—or too damned scared of getting in trouble.

The levels of consumables were getting low, so I drew up a list of what I thought we should have and ran the paperwork through supply. The supply officer was a warrant officer who had been a storekeeper when he was enlisted. He helped me with the forms and it didn't take long to get the proper requests filled out. Rivera and I took the duty vehicle, drove to the camera place, and bought all the stuff. We used bulk film that we reloaded into cassettes for the 35mm cameras and bought photographic paper by the five-hundred-sheet box. We would take out only the amount of paper that we could fit into a paper safe so we would not ruin the entire box if some curious person should open the paper safe, upon which the words DO NOT OPEN IN WHITE LIGHT were written in large letters.

In addition to the black-and-white materials, I purchased some chemistry and film for color slides. At the time the Kodak process for Ektachrome was the E-4 process. We had the large stainless sink and a thermostatically controlled faucet, so I knew we would be able to process color slides. I ordered a Sen-Rac roll film dryer, the kind we had had in the naval special warfare lab, and that fit nicely onto one of the walls.

In a couple of weeks we got under way and steamed back to Norfolk. I had not driven my car to Philly as it would have been a hassle to get it back home again. The photographic work on the *Ortolan* was nothing very exciting. Grips and grins and broken parts—lots of broken parts. Groovy graphs (unofficial pictures about anything) I also shot, just to hand out to the crew and the other divers. Photographers, wherever they go, are usually welcome, provided they produce pictures for others to send home. I made sure I took lots of photos for the boys.

When we were getting under way or docking, my station was as a telephone talker on the bridge. I was to pass the word between the bridge and the damage control stations and other stations on board. In docking maneuvers I would pass the word between the wings of the bridge and the helm if the weather was windy and the helmsman couldn't hear the OOD. When

Lieutenant Moen had the conn, I would often have to help him maneuver the ship, especially at sea when we were making four-point moors. He had taken me aside and told me that he had very little experience above decks, as he had been an engineman his whole career. Many times when we were maneuvering on a four-point moor or to pick up one of our mooring spuds, I would give him the proper engine and helm commands. My experience on fishing boats prior to joining the Navy helped a lot. I would say the commands in a low voice and he would then say them back to me loudly and I would pass the word over the sound-powered phones. Afterward he'd give me a thumbs-up and wink.

One extremely windy day I was on the bridge when we took a new pilot aboard for the docking. Being a friendly sort of guy, I asked him if he had ever docked the ship before. He said he had not, so I asked him how many tugs he had for the docking. He said he had two. I advised him that he should have three or four if he could get them. He looked at me like I was a piece of dirt and made some remark about knowing what he was doing. I simply grinned and told him, "We'll see, won't we." I hated being a smart-ass, but the guy deserved it. Before the day was over he wished he had listened to me.

You see, I knew something that he didn't. This ship was about as seaworthy as a shoe box. It stuck up out of the water and offered as much windage as a kite. The northwest wind was blowing through the channel past the D & S Piers at fifteen to twenty-five knots and the tide was coming. We started our swing into the dock. We would be mooring port side to the dock so that the wind would have a tendency to keep us off the dock. As we made the turn toward the dock, the tugs could not keep us from sliding toward a destroyer tied up on the opposite pier to our starboard side. I knew what would happen next. One of the tugs went forward and started pushing on our port hull to move us against the dock, but to no avail. The wind had picked up and we were now rubbing against the old destroyer. With a metallic grinding sound we broke off boat davits and scraped along, tearing lifeline stanchions down. No real major damage was done. Petty Officer Sabat, one of the divers, who had a home movie camera, came out on deck and started shooting pictures of the collision. The skipper of the destroyer shouted to him, "Hey sailor, rig some fenders!"

Sabat shouted back, "You are our fenders!"

You can rest assured that went over well. Fortunately for Sabat, the captain of that ship never figured out who he was. Sabat was the one who had stolen a brand new Mark V helmet in Washington in diving school. They had searched our cars every day when we left the base. We all suspected he had taken it, but never found out how he got it off base. One day I asked him how he did it.

"I just moved it about ten feet from where it was normally kept and stuck it in a closet under some diving suits that were stored in there. Nobody thought to look around the area for it. They all figured it had been carried off base. They searched all the vehicles at the gate for about a week. When things cooled off, I just put it in the trunk of my car and took it out the gate."

He had also jumped off the barracks over at Bolling with his hang glider. He didn't get caught or he probably would have been thrown off the base, as I was.

Meanwhile back home, Mary and I found that the place we were living in was getting pretty small. We had one kid and two dogs and were paying rent there as well as making a house payment in Maine. A friend of ours told us about some townhouses being built on Pleasure House Road, named for the whorehouse there in previous times. We checked the places out and I talked with the guy who was building them. He was an Italian who looked and talked like somebody out of *The Godfather*. The man representing him as a real estate broker was Elton Lee, a real southerner from Hopewell, Virginia. He got us all lined up with the financing through the VA and told us to forget we owned the place in Maine. We signed all the papers and moved in. It had two bedrooms, a bathroom upstairs, half bath downstairs, a kitchen, living room, and a backyard with a chain-link fence, where we could let the dogs out without tying them. The place had central heat and air-conditioning. We paid $36,000 for it and the payments were $300 a month with no money down. We had some good neighbors in the other townhouses, mostly either military or retired military. One of them was a Marine captain and his wife, but we didn't hold that against them. I was always getting junk mail addressed to "Occupant" so Elton Lee gave us a door knocker with The Occupants on it for a name. We mounted it on the door and left it there the entire time we lived in that house.

When I didn't have anything else to do on board ship I hung

out in the diving locker and shot the bull with the divers. We all had sea stories to tell, some of us more than others. One friend of mine, Kulzicki, got tired of people making Polish jokes about him so he had his name changed to Culley. He was an easygoing guy and a decent diver. Many of the guys were saturation divers and some had worked in Vallejo, California, on special projects. We knew their job involved working on nuclear subs and locking out of them, but they were not permitted to talk about their adventures, and we didn't ask. Once in a while we would get a new guy aboard who was already rated and had served on a submarine. One guy in particular was in a rating very much in demand on subs. He tried to get a transfer off the boat, but the CO wouldn't let him. So he got himself caught smoking pot. Once that happened he was automatically disqualified as a submariner, but could serve on board surface ships. So the submarine squadron commander transferred him to the *Ortolan*. The acronym 'ASR' was sometimes said to stand for Assholes and Submarine Rejects, and it lived up to its name on occasion.

The *Ortolan* had two hulls, with two engines in each hull. There was only one propeller on each hull, with the two engines clutched together, in line. They were ALCO diesels made by the American Locomotive Company. The things were huge and made a loud rumbling sound that reverberated throughout the ship whenever we were under way, which wasn't very often. Many times we went to sea and came right back in because some piece of gear broke down. I had heard stories about the ship being designed to carry a certain amount of weight and berth a limited number of people. After the model tests were completed at the David Taylor Model Basin in Maryland, they changed the plans and added a hundred tons of weight. We could turn only about ten knots, much less than the design called for. The ship was pretty scary in heavy seas. The seas would pound up under the flat portion between the hulls and it sounded like it would break in half. When the ship was new they had taken it out for sea trials and the forward chain locker had flooded. The ship had to be brought to the shipyard in order to sister up all the frames on the inboard sides of the hulls. The twisting motion of the two hulls trying to work against each other, combined with the added weight, would make the ship basically a floating coffin for about two hundred men if we ever got into a serious weather situation. I think the Navy knew that. Ten of these white elephants were supposed to be built but only two were before they spent all the money allocated for the rest. The other ship was the *Pigeon*, ASR-21, stationed in San Diego. I envied the guys on the *Pigeon* compared to what we had to put up with. At least the weather there was warm.

I didn't stay in the berthing compartment very long. I decided I would move up into the photo lab. In the compartment I had a head and shower on the same deck, but when I moved up to the lab, I had to go down two decks. That was not a problem. I grabbed an extra mattress, some sheets, a pillow and blanket, and made my bed on the floor of the darkroom. I rolled the mattress up and stuffed it under the cabinet during the day. If I had to take a leak at night, I just went in the darkroom sink and rinsed it down, or if we were under way, I stepped out to the rail. I kept my wet suit in the darkroom in a parachute bag. There were times in high seas when I thought I would be better off wearing it. The ship would pound badly on a wave and shudder throughout. I would tighten up my guts and just wait for the next one. The seas would slam up under the flat underbody of the superstructure and shake the teeth almost out of my head. It woke me more than once while I was sleeping up there.

The guys in the compartment next to the photo lab were all electricians. Tim Noble was one of them. The ship was so crowded that Noble and another guy built a couple of bunks in the electricians' shack. The ship had been designed to berth about 120 men and we had nearly 200 on board. Noble's father was a retired Navy diver who worked as a diving supervisor with Taylor Diving Company of New Orleans. Tim planned to get out of the Navy and work in the Gulf or somewhere in the oil patch when his time was up.

I had no plans to get out. I had taken the chief's test several times and always made the board, but never got my "hat," so I decided to apply for the warrant officer program again. I had tried twice but had not made it in spite of high recommendations. Now I would go up for warrant photographer and warrant boatswain. I asked Admiral Cobb to give me a write-up in the boatswain field and had a couple of photo officers recommend me in the photographer rating. I thought I could get it in one field or the other.

As time passed I became familiar with the operation of the ship and got to know the deep dive system to a degree. As a first class diver, I was not required to know every valve and nut and bolt of the system, as that was not part of my area of expertise, but it helped to know some of it. When we put people in the chamber for dry runs, all the divers had to stand chamber watches. Usually I was in charge of temperature and humidity, areas quite critical if the dive is on helium/oxygen, when the temperature has to be kept in the nineties. Only a very narrow temperature range is bearable when diving on helium, because it sucks heat from the body. On deep dives the breathing gas has to be heated or the divers will get cold too quickly.

We made training dives once in a while, but I figured out that the master diver was "gundecking" the diving log. Master Chief Winter was a damned good master diver and a good chief, but he was under the gun to make it look like we were diving more than we were. The ship was always broken down and we just could not get to sea to get our qualifications in. A few of us who hated the damned *Ortolan* went to the Naval Investigative Service with this information and might as well have pissed into the wind. It went nowhere. At that point, happy that our rat-fink status had not been compromised, we just fell in with the status quo and kept drawing our unearned diving pay. Men were taking their discharges or volunteering for special projects. We even had a couple of them drop their diving qualifications in order to get off the ship. I was not ready to throw away $150 a month. When I asked the skipper what would happen if I dropped my diving qualifications, he said he would guarantee that I got a set of orders to an aircraft carrier that never saw land. I told him, "Never mind."

I asked again about saturation school, and again I was told that there were only so many billets and that I was way down the list. In hanging out in the diving locker, I learned about all sorts of jobs on the outside. BM2 Chuck Penn was going to work for some "oil patch" diving company, Culley was getting out, Milnes was going to take his discharge until he found out he was going to make chief, then he decided to stay. They were all good men and really knew their stuff, but the Navy was wasting them on that rattrap of a ship.

I also heard horror stories about the lack of "oxygen clean" procedures on board. When equipment is installed or overhauled that will be used with pure oxygen, strict protocols *must* be adhered to. Any hydrocarbon, such as oil, or other material that comes in contact with pure O_2 can cause an instantaneous fire. Chief Dan Dodd had saved the ship once by crawling on his hands and knees through fire to shut valves to the O_2 storage tanks after an oxygen-transfer pump had blown up and caught fire. He received a medal for that and after his burns healed, he was back on the job. But I saw no reason for the fire not to reoccur; the Clean Room was not oxygen clean, and that kind of talk went round and round.

While we were off Hampton Roads training and laying a four-point moor one day, the supply officer, who was the designated aft safety officer, got the hell knocked out of him when a spud mooring line surged, tore a P-250 fire pump out of its storage rack, then nailed him with it. He and a seaman got sucked around a bollard by the line and ended up in the Portsmouth Naval Hospital. Neither was hurt seriously, but it showed that a lack of training and knowledge was rampant on the ship. In particular, a supply officer had no business being safety officer on deck; due to lack of experience, he could not see an unsafe situation in the making.

Some time later we were out in Chesapeake Bay making training dives. We made Heliox dives on the first day. When I made my mixed-gas dive that day, LTJG Ed Miller was my partner. We left the open bell and traveled all over the bottom, gathering up as many scallops and clams as we could find. We stuck them in a mesh bag we'd tied to the bell so we could take them up and cook them later. We were down at 180 feet, so it was not a deep dive, but we still had to spend time decompressing on the way back to the surface. The open bell made it a fun trip because if we had a failure of a band mask, we could go back to the bell and take off the mask, stand up, and breathe in the bubble trapped there. We were diving hot water suits, so we were not even cold. The hot water suit is just a loose wet suit with little capillary tubes throughout the inside. Hot water is pumped down through the suit from the surface and that keeps the diver very warm in even the coldest water. I had already told the topside crew that if anybody shut off my hot water as a joke, they would suffer some sort of physical injury when I got topside. That little trick was sometimes pulled on divers, but they didn't pull it on me. That time.

On a dive later that day one of the chiefs passed out on the stage at about 160 feet. He regained consciousness and we didn't have to do anything to help him or treat him, but it was scary for a while. Later he said that he had had too much to drink the night before but because it was a Heliox dive, I always wondered if the atmospheric mix was screwed up. The other diver had no trouble, so it probably *wasn't* that.

The weather was calm, so the skipper decided to stay out and make some air dives in the Mark V rig the next day. The first few teams completed their dives without incident. ET2 Singer was a new guy, fresh out of school, who had not dived yet aboard the ship. I was one of his tenders. As he was being brought up to the thirty-foot decompression stop, I heard him say to the tender on the comm box, "Topside, my legs are tingling like they are going to sleep." The master told him to go ahead and just move around and keep breathing normally. I could tell from his voice that Singer was scared.

A few minutes later, after he had been brought up to the twenty-foot stop, Singer said, "Topside, I can't feel my legs, they are numb." Clearly he was suffering from a CNS (central nervous system) hit in his spine and could end up paralyzed.

I couldn't stand it any longer. I was only a first class petty officer, but I understood decompression sickness and probably had as much or more knowledge about it than many on the ship.

I walked up to the chief corpsman and said, "Doc, I know it is not in the protocol, but you gotta shift him to straight O_2. But fuck the protocol; we'll all back you up if anything goes wrong. His life is at stake here."

"Can't do it without approval from a medical officer," he said.

There might have been the consideration that the air hoses were not oxygen clean and there might be a fire, but I doubt this would have happened.

"Jesus Christ, Doc, if that was me down there, I would be begging you to do it. He's not that deep now and there is no problem with O_2 toxicity."[2] But they would not shift him to oxygen, which might have alleviated the symptoms and enabled us to treat him on the surface with no permanent damage. By then,

2. Oxygen poisoning can occur if you are working hard while breathing O_2 below about thirty-three feet or if there is something in your physiological makeup that causes you to be susceptible to O_2 toxicity symptoms. All Navy divers are tested for that and must pass or they cannot become divers.

Singer could not stand on the stage so he was sitting crumpled up and the other diver, who had no problem, was making sure he didn't fall off the stage.

The master and the corpsman decided to skip the ten-foot stop and bring both divers up and treat them together. When the divers were brought to the surface, the tenders stripped off their suits and helmets in a hurry and I and the other tenders walked Singer and his partner to the chamber on the port side of the vessel. They were immediately pressed down to sixty feet on oxygen. The other diver had no symptoms and was treated only for the first part of the table; he was locked out of the chamber prior to extending the table.

The *Ortolan* got under way as soon as we had the divers in the chamber. They treated Singer on extended tables with extra oxygen breathing periods, to no avail. His legs did not regain their feeling. When we reached Norfolk, an ambulance took him to Portsmouth Naval Hospital, where they put him in the neurology clinic. We went to sea again for a few days and when we came back, a couple of the divers went to see him. They said he was still paralyzed from the waist down and wearing diapers. He'd been married only a couple of weeks. I heard later that he had recovered nearly completely, but the Navy still gave him a medical discharge with retirement.

When the ship was under way, the seas came sloshing up through the center well of the ship, the open space between the hulls where the DSRV would be lowered if we had one. The rumors said that the DSRV had been redesigned with new fuel cells and that it would no longer fit the ship because it was about fifteen feet longer. I wondered why they didn't get to work right away extending the area where it was to be stored. The divers used to talk about it all the time. Finally one of them came out and said that the *Ortolan*'s mission was just hot air; our real mission was to make the parents and relatives of submariners think that their loved ones could be rescued if they ran into trouble. We all knew the realities of the operations of nuclear submarines.

And so, obviously, did the submariners. They laughed at the prospect of being rescued. One of them told me, "Hell, if we are at a depth where you guys can help us, we can just 'blow and go' with a Stanke Hood." That's a flotation device that looked like an inflatable life jacket with a hood attached. There was a clear plastic window in the hood. In the escape trunk, the submariners would inflate the things with compressed air. The trunk would be pressurized to ambient depth and they would simply float up to the surface. The air escaping from the jackets dumped into the hood and then blew out around the bottom of that. There was no need to breathe because the submariners would be exhaling all the way up due to the expansion of air in their lungs. I am not sure how deep they used these in training, but the Brits used a modification of this. On Project Upshot they encompassed the Stanke hood in a suit that allowed them to escape from depths to around a thousand feet.

Rivera, my assistant in the lab, became a problem. I suspected that he was stealing from the crew. One day I was going through the clothing hanging on hooks in the lab and I found a peacoat with another sailor's name in it. I went to the personnel office and asked what department the guy was in. Sherby told me and I looked him up.

"Have you got a peacoat?" I asked him.

"I did have, but I lost it somewhere while we were in the ship-yard," he said.

"Well, I found it up in the photo lab. Why don't you come up and ask Rivera how he came to have it."

Nothing ever came of it. Rivera gave it back and made up a story about thinking it was his or something so nothing was done. He started wising off to me whenever I asked him to do something. His time was up soon after that and he was discharged. He was not replaced. On the rest of the ship the seamen did the swabbing and waxing of the passageways. Outside the photo lab I was the one to do that while junior petty officers and nonrated men came by and made cute remarks about having a senior petty officer swabbing and waxing the deck.

In the summer of 1976, Comdr. Tony Esau relieved the red-headed commander. I thought things would improve because Tony was a hands-on kind of guy who took no bullshit. He liked to get things done, and I thought he would be able to get some operating money and fix things that were wrong with the ship. Wrong again. I think he realized that the *Ortolan* was a career-buster. The change-of-command ceremony took place in the hot sun of June 1976. I was now thirty years old, and a significant number of men my age in the diving Navy had made chief and some had been advanced to warrant officer.

Before I had left Combat Camera Group, PH1s Eddie Dotson, Doug Keever, and Dave Harris had been promoted directly to ensign in the LDO (Limited Duty Officer) program. This would enable them to serve only in their specialty, photography, so they would be stationed in photo labs or on board aircraft carriers as the photo officer in charge of the lab at that installation. I, of course, was not on the list. Mary might have been correct, perhaps my bout with the shrink back at Naval Special Warfare was having a bad effect on my career. I didn't think so, but it was always in the back of my mind. Eddie Dotson had been court-martialed for attempted murder at one time, and Doug was famous for being a wild man when he was drinking. I had none of that in my record and had excellent write-ups, but I had not taken college courses to get an associate's degree, and that may have made the difference.

The change of command went off smoothly and nobody passed out from standing on the hot steel decks in the blazing sun. There was not a breath of wind that day, and we couldn't wait to get the hell out of there. Tony Esau made a speech about how he was happy to be there and looked forward to serving on board. I had heard that same speech at every change-of-command ceremony I'd ever attended.

We broke from there, had some cake and punch down on the mess decks, and secured for the day, except for the duty section.

In August it was time for the promotion examinations to be given. I was eligible, as were a number of others on the ship. John Cantale and I sat together for the test, which was given on the base at the Educational Services office. He was an electrician's mate. We blew right through the thing, as all of us had been studying. When you are a chief on a ship, you have your own quarters with the other chiefs. Up to that point, you are just meat along with all the other sailors on board, at least that's how it was on the *Ortolan*. It would be a few months before we got the results.

BMC Raesman, one of the divers on board, had put in for warrant officer. We all *knew* he would be selected because he was a sharp chief and everybody liked him. I had some connections and decided to see if either one of us had made it. I made the call and learned that he was on the list and I was not. I hadn't had my hopes up very high anyway. I went to the uniform shop and purchased a set of warrant officer bars and the appropriate insignia for his specialty. We were due to go back to sea for more training. I had told the CO that Raesman had made it and asked him not to tell him. I gave the chief the bars and told him he would probably need them pretty soon. He didn't think he'd made it and I didn't tell him I had the word in advance. I really don't think he believed he had made it. He was already a chief, so if he was advanced all he had to do was pin the things on his collar after he had removed the chief's insignia. We didn't have a hat for him, but I got the insignia for his "piss cutter," as we called the Boy-Scout-looking hat that chiefs and officers wore aboard ship. When the word was "officially out," the skipper called him to his office. He gave him the hat insignia that I had held back and told him to go ahead and pin it on. Raesman was really surprised and happy.

By the time Christmas rolled around we were still in port with no mission. The list came down and I found out I had passed the test with a high score and would be advanced to chief petty officer. About three hundred had taken the test for PHC and only about sixty had made it. I was number thirty-two on the list.

I was doing something in the photo lab on 31 December 1976 when I got a phone call from HMC Shirley, one of our corpsmen. He told me he needed to see me in sick bay right away. I walked in and he told me to lock the door. I did and when I turned around he handed me a tin cup full of some orange liquid. He and HM2 Andy May were sitting there sipping the stuff already.

"Drink this," he commanded.

I took a drink and it about killed me. It was a mixture of pure medical alcohol and Navy-issue canned orange juice. Once the fire went out a little, I kind of liked it. We had a few more, the dicksmiths (the divers' name for corpsmen who are qualified divers) said "Happy New Year," and I left for home. The drive home was not too bad; I didn't have any symptoms of being drunk. I knew I had a slight buzz on, but otherwise seemed okay. But by the time I pulled into the yard and parked my VW, I was hammered. The stuff had taken hold and was really nailing me hard. I made it through the door and started taking my shoes and jacket off. I went up to the bathroom and the next thing I knew I heard this little faraway voice saying, "Steven, are you all right?"

Mary didn't know that I had been drinking, as I had been in pretty good shape when I came through the door. I lay there for a while and got up and went to bed. Jesus, that grain alcohol was some powerful stuff. I never had occasion to drink any again.

The *Ortolan* was like a fire department, except we "firemen" knew there would never be a fire. Morale on board was low and divers continued to leave one after the other. We had no purpose in life other than to draw our pay and hope that somebody would either decommission the ship or find a use for it. There were plans for a cruise to St. Croix in the Virgin Islands to use the Mark 2 Deep Dive System, the PTCs (personnel transfer capsules), and all that stuff. Guys would go into the chamber, transfer to the PTC, be lowered to some deep depth like four hundred feet or so, make an excursion, then be brought back up in the PTC. It would mate up to the chamber, and they'd decompress in there.

I had talked the future over with Mary and we decided I would probably get out of the Navy when my time was up in June 1977. I would have to turn down chief to do that so I waited until the last possible moment to tell Sherby Hart in the admin office. We spent a lot of time talking about it. Mary was pregnant with #2 kid and Emily was growing rapidly. I really wanted my kids to grow up in Maine, where they belonged. Compared to South Thomaston, Maine, the crime rate around places like Norfolk was pretty bad and there were too many distractions. I have been around Navy brats and noticed that some had turned out good and some had turned out bad. Also, I was afraid that if I stayed in for twenty years, my ambition, what little I still had, would be stifled because I'd be getting a sure-thing retirement check every month. I'd probably end up working at the post office or selling insurance or used cars like so many retired military personnel. No, I would get out and jump naked right into the civilian world, where I had never really been before. I had been corresponding with Capt. George Kittredge, USN, Ret.,[3] the man who had thought up the "Kittredge seal," and he offered me a job running sub schools. He was starting up a school to teach people how to operate his one-man dry subs.

---

3. Captain Kittredge had started a school to train people in the use of his one-man dry subs. He felt that he could build a customer base if he offered training in his subs, even to people who did not yet own one.

One of my friends in the diving locker was MR1 Jim Hutchinson, a saturation diver. Hutch was not too happy about some of the safety practices on board the ship and we used to have long discussions about them. He had been at special projects in Vallejo, but had left. Somebody told me he had become a conscientious objector or had other beliefs that would not allow him to take part in what could become combat situations. I didn't ask him about that as I knew missions at special projects were highly classified. Anyway, Hutch and I were both going to leave the Navy, so we decided it was time to do something about the shoddy conditions on the ship. I knew my congressman, David Emery, because we had gone to high school together and he had gone on to become the youngest congressman in Washington. Hutch was from Wisconsin, so he figured that Sen. William Proxmire would be his best bet to get some results. We formulated a plan. I called Dave Emery on a Friday and asked him if he could meet with us Saturday morning. He said to call him at his home in DC when we got there and he'd come down to the Cannon Office Building to meet us. We were just to make ourselves at home until he got there.

Hutch and and I donned our dress "canvas" with all our ribbons and pins and drove up to Washington, DC, the next Saturday morning. We wondered if we were doing the right thing. We knew that the guys on the ship were really looking forward to going to St. Croix and the warm water and liberty that they would enjoy there. We would be going with them, but it just made us nervous knowing that the things we had heard about and pretty much knew to be factual concerning the safety of the ship could kill some of us. We had told Ed Miller and Lieutenant Moen what we were going to do, and they wished us luck but could not get involved as it would mean the end of their careers. We understood their situation. We had already committed to getting out. Hutch had about the same time in as I did, so we had over twenty years between us.

We arrived at the Cannon Office Building and walked in. The guard there asked us who we were and what we needed. I told him that we were there to see Congressman David Emery from Maine and that he was expecting us. The security guard called Dave's office, got the okay, and then told us to go ahead.

One of Dave's assistants in the office pointed us to the coffeepot and we made some small talk. In a half hour Dave walked in wearing blue jeans and a flannel shirt, much the way he would be dressed back in Maine.

We shook hands and I introduced Dave and Hutch.

"Well, I guess you guys have some stuff to tell me. I have been catching up on some of it through the assistant you have been talking with. Fill me in."

We took turns rattling off the points we were trying to make about the safety, morale, and uselessness of the ship. He sat there with his chair tilted back and his fingertips pushed together in front of him. After a while he spoke.

"Steve, you know how to type. There's a ream of paper, a typewriter, the coffeepot is over there in the corner, and if you need anything to eat, let my assistant here know and he'll run out and get it for you. I'll talk to you next week."

Dave left and I started pounding the IBM Selectric. Hutch would make a point and then I would. We hammered away until I had created a ten-page document listing all the defects and dangers that we were aware of aboard the USS *Ortolan*. We tried not to make it sound like we were whining or just bitching, as both of us were professionals and had a genuine concern for the welfare of our fellow divers and friends. When we finished, I handed it to Dave's assistant and he put it in an envelope. Hutch and I drove back to Norfolk with the feeling that we had just stepped in a huge pile of dogshit with both feet.

The next day on the ship there was no sign that anything had happened. We told a select few of our friends what we had done. They agreed that it had been the correct thing to do.

A week passed and then the word came down through ComSubLant. The admiral had asked Commander Esau who the two sailors were on his ship who had jumped the chain of command and gone to a congressman. The skipper never said anything to us about it, as he may have been advised not to. I called Dave's office a couple of days later and found that the secretary of the Navy had been pretty upset over the report. Of course, there had been a rebuttal. There had been no attempt to write this off as just disgruntled sailors bitching, as we were both what they considered career Navy men. I was very surprised that they didn't try to "kill the messenger" on that one. I fully expected to be court-martialed or otherwise punished as a result of having jumped the chain of command. But the skipper never even referred to the report and everybody treated us pretty much the same as they had before. One thing I remember is that Lieutenant Moen was walking down the passageway one day and Hutch and I were coming the other way. He smiled and gave us a vigorous thumbs-up, and as he walked by us said, "You guys sure have bigger balls than I do. Good job." That was the last he made reference to it.

The *Ortolan* took on stores to get under way for the Virgin Islands. We had plenty of breathing gas on board for diving as we had hardly used any since I had been there. We set sail for St. Croix and the whole crew was looking forward to going there, if only just to get the hell out of Norfolk for a change.

The ship was about eight hundred miles from St. Croix when a message came. We were to turn back and go to Charleston Naval Base and tie up alongside the tender. They had the capabilities to inspect the oxygen system and render it oxygen clean and up to standards. Hutch and I quickly became quite unpopular with the crew and suffered many dirty looks. Both of us were over six feet and rumors had circulated that I was nobody to piss off, so we had no physical confrontations. The divers didn't treat us badly, as many of them had had the same concerns, they'd just failed to voice them to the proper authorities. LTJG Ed Miller was my friend and he said that we had done the right thing. He never said that in front of the other officers. No officer ever talked to us with other officers within earshot.

The ship pulled into Charleston, steaming past a nuclear submarine that had run aground on the side of the channel. The technicians from the tender came aboard and, with the help of some of our divers, started tearing the system apart and inspecting it. I didn't have much to do there as no photography was needed, so I painted the walls in the photo lab and cleaned things up, logged some negatives that I had been meaning to get to, and generally kept busy.

One afternoon Hosea from the admin office called me on the phone and asked if I was going on liberty that evening. I told him that I might go to the bowling alley and get a hamburger and a few beers or something. I told him to come up when he got ready to go and we'd walk up together. We spent a few hours there, had supper, and drank a few beers. On the way back to the ship, in total darkness, I stepped in a hole in the pavement and wrenched the hell out of my right ankle. I hobbled back to the ship and it felt worse and worse. In the morning I could not put any weight at all on it, so I called down to the sick bay and asked Doc Shirley to take a look at it. He came right up and, after examining it, told me that it should be X-rayed.

One of the guys in the duty section drove me to the hospital, where I sat around until they had a chance to X-ray my ankle. When that was finished, the doctor called me into the examining room. He looked at the X-ray and said, "Well, there is a break here, but it is an old one. This is just a real bad sprain."

"Well, Doc, I am on a ship and the head is two decks down and the chow hall is all the way forward. The frigging decks are always covered with hydraulic oil and we are heading for the Virgin Islands to do some diving. Can you put a cast on it and tell them I am unfit for shipboard duty?"

He looked at me a minute. "Are you Cheryl Waterman's brother?" he asked.

"Yes, how did you know that?"

"We were stationed together at Portsmouth and she talked about you being a diver on some ship. I just figured it out when you told me about the ship. Yes, I think that ankle will heal a lot faster if it has a cast put on it."

He sent me in to the cast room and the cast was put on. He told me to have it removed in a few weeks—to make it look good—and to take it easy on it for a while. I thanked him and made sure I had his name to give to my sister when I talked with her again.

When I went back to the ship I told Sherby Hart that there was no way I was going to be able to handle any of my shipboard duties. By now they all knew that I was getting out as I refused to extend the obligated service required to be advanced to chief.

"I'll have the XO transfer you back to the squadron and you can just do light duty there until we get back," he said.

There is a God! I thought.

Sherby prepared the necessary paperwork, got me lined up with a TR (travel request) for a plane ticket, and I flew back to Norfolk. The next day I had my neighbor, who had the day off, drive me in to the squadron. They were in the process of having their office renovated and had all their desks and equipment in a trailer. I hobbled in on my crutches and talked to the chief, who told me to stay home and call in at 0800 each morning.

I went home. Mary was about to have our second child and I would be able to be home when it was born. I also was getting ready to take the test for my ham radio and Coast Guard captain's licenses and that little vacation would give me the chance to study for them. Things went along quite well. I called in every morning for muster, took the ham radio tests up to the advanced class and passed them, and even got my Coast Guard "six-pack" license. Admiral Cobb, my employer in the yacht business, had signed off on my sea time, and the rest of it was just book work and practical knowledge.

On 18 March 1977, Mary went into labor. I had the cast on my leg and could not drive, so my sister Cheryl, by then lieutenant commander, drove her to Portsmouth Naval Hospital. A few hours later she delivered our second daughter. We named her Nellie Marie after my great-grandmother. Nellie had helped me learn to read before I was old enough to attend school. Later on she went blind and I read to her, recipes when she was cooking and letters when she got mail from her friends. She died in a nursing home at the age of ninety-four.

When the *Ortolan* returned to Norfolk, I reported back aboard. All I had to do was take some clothes as I had left all my gear on the ship. Rivera had long since been discharged, so only Sherby Hart had a key to the photo lab. I had given it to him when I left even though there was a spare locked away in the office key cabinet. I'd told him to help himself to the Coke and yogurt and other stuff I had in the official photo lab refrigerator.

Things returned to normal on board the ship. I was invited to move into the chief's quarters, the "goat locker." The word had not gone out that I was leaving the Navy because the guys in the admin office did not believe I would go through with it. One of the chiefs, EMCS Powell, who had heard the rumors, called me into the goat locker one evening when we had the duty together. He was black and one of the real professionals on board the *Ortolan*. He was not a diver, but was in charge of the electrical gang. Powell was a class act all the way.

"Waterman, I hear you are getting out of the Navy," he started. "I want you to know that you are doing the right thing. It is not the Navy we joined, and you're a smart guy. You'll make out all right in whatever you decide to do. Don't let them talk you out of it. I know you've given it a lot of thought."

Then he went on to tell about how he had to "bust his ass" to get where he was and that the young black kids coming into the service figured the world owed them a living. They looked at him and thought he'd had it all handed to him because he was black.

"I don't need that shit anymore," he said. "My wife has a good job as a teacher and I own a farm down South. I want my kids to grow up in one place. I'll have twenty-two years in when my time is up. I'm going home."

We had a good conversation there in the chiefs' quarters, and I appreciated him taking me aside and speaking with me. I'd had some trepidations about getting out, with almost thirteen years in service. I had made chief—a major stumbling block to a lot of people—and all of a sudden I would be getting the respect and perks that were accorded chiefs, even though some of them didn't rate it. I still might have been able to pick up a commission, but I doubted it; I was too much of a rogue and had a tendency to put the men before the mission. Lately the mission seemed to have changed to getting your ticket punched and never taking chances.

In the third week of May, the *Ortolan* was due to go to sea again and would be gone through the time of Tim Noble's and my discharge dates. Hutch had already left the Navy and had procured a job designing anesthesia equipment for a medical supply company. Before its departure, the ship transferred Tim Noble and me to the transient barracks at the Norfolk Naval Station.

I cleaned out all my equipment and clothing from the photo lab. Then I went and said good-bye to the XO and the captain. Commander Esau said there were no hard feelings about what we had done to the ship and that he hoped all would go well with me in civilian life. I thanked him and wished him luck with the ship. Then I walked to the office, got my records, saluted the fantail, and walked off the ship for the last time.

Tim Noble's job was running road crews who picked up trash along the road to the base. Mine was counting heads in the chow hall. We attended some meetings where we were told how to convert our military life insurance to a civilian policy and how to take advantage of G.I. benefits and the procedure to follow to join the Reserves. I got my discharge and Tim and I said good-bye to each other. I never expected to see Tim or any of the other people I had served with again.

I drove to Little Creek on the way home and signed up to join the Naval Reserves there. A few weeks earlier I had told the chief at the Reserve Center that I would be going home to Maine as soon as I got out and sold my house. He advised me not to tell him that, and said he would sign me up the day I got discharged and *then* I could tell him I was going home to Maine. I guess he needed the numbers for his recruitment quota. That was the end of my active-duty naval career. The date was Friday the thirteenth, May 1977.

I had a job lined up working for Captain Kittredge teaching people to operate dry subs and working as the skipper of his sub tender, the *Aquatic*. I didn't think it would last, but it would get me started.

IN MEMORIAM

MRC Charles D. "Tobacco Lew" Lewis, USN (Ret.)
July 28, 2000

We'll see you on the other side, Lew.

Index

A-6A Intruders, 22, 44, 62–63
Abney, Steve, 130, 132
Abourjille, Bill, 186
ACUC (American/Canadian
  Underwater Council), 238
Adams, George, 212
Algeo, Doc, 144
Allen, Bosun's Mate First
  Class, 3–4
Ames, Adelbert, 17–18
Anacostia Naval Air Station,
  241, 242
Andrea Doria, 89
Andrews, Hoot, 159
Antiwar movement, 171
Apodaca, Chief, 257–258
Apollo 12, 158–159
Aquatic (sub tender), 280
Archuleta, Frank, 36–38
Armed Forces Qualification
  Test, 4
Artman, Lee, 233
ASR (Auxiliary Submarine
  Rescue ship), 253
Atlantic Fleet Combat Camera
  Group (AFCCG), 66, 68,
  76–90, 77, 165, 168–190,
  202, 203, 257
Atlantic Undersea Test and
  Evaluation Center (AUTEC),
  90, 206, 234–236
Azores, 95–104

Badger, Pat, 197
Bamberger, Chief, 248, 249
Barbata, Brian, 194
Barber, Skip, 180
Barrett, Everett, 197, 199
Barth, Bill, 72–73, 221
Basic Naval Aviation Officers'
  School, 12, 16, 22–30
Bataan Death March, 36
Bay King (tug) 179–184

Beechcraft, 25–26
Bell, Ron, 165, 166
Bender, Jay, 170–171
Blackfin (yacht), 96, 97
Blackiston, Diane, 221
Blackiston, Slator, 69, 221
Blaha, Howard, 222
Blazer, Linda, 188
Bloom, Lieutenant
  Commander, 22
Boatwright, Kitty, 217
Boatwright, Paul, 217
Boehm, Roy, 159
Boles, Wesley, 88, 89, 105
Bolling Air Force Base, 237,
  240–241, 243
Bomar, Frank, 115
Boot camp, 9–16
Boot leave, 19–21
Boyd, Ellsworth, 235
Boyles, Lou, 158, 165
BRAT Team (Beach
  Reconnaissance Amphibious
  Team), 48
Briggs, Lane, 179, 203, 204,
  217
Brigman, Lem, 176, 177
Broderick, Patrick, 135
Brown, "Bubba," 95, 97, 102
Brown, Tom, 46–47
Browne, Jack, 92
Bryan, Acey, 88
Burton, 210, 216
Busby, Pat, 22, 27, 34–35
Butler, Chief, 22
Byrd, Chief, 37

Call, Jim, 171–172
Ca Mau Peninsula, 136, 146
Camp Barry, 10
Campbell, John, 135
Camp Magsaysay, 146–147
Camp Porter, 14

Camp Tien Sha, 125
Cantale, Jim, 271
Carley, Norm, 201
Chamberlain, Joshua, 17–18
Chappell, Jack, 231–232
China Wreck, 176–178
Christy (clam dredge),
  203–205
Civil War, 17–18
Clark Air Force Base,
  Philippines, 125, 145, 152
Clausen, Judy (*see* Waterman,
  Judy Clausen)
Clausen, Rosalyn, 164–165,
  167
Cobb, Jim, 217–219, 265, 278
Combat Camera Group (*see*
  Atlantic Fleet Combat
  Camera Group [AFCCG])
Company 242, 12
Company 303, 12
Condon, Bob, 66
Conklin, Chuck, 67, 68
Conolan, Peter, 150
Cooper, David, 6
Cooper, Winola, 6
Craig, PR2, 165, 166
Cregger, Larry, 185, 204, 205
Cronin, Gary, 127–128
Cubi Point Naval Air Station,
  Philippines, 118
Cumbie, Commander, 22, 52
Curraco, Ray, 176
Curtis, Charlie, 168, 169
Curtsinger, Bill, 78, 80, 90,
  168, 169, 256
Cutter, Art, 78, 227–228
Cyr, John, 62

Dahlgren Naval Weapons
  Station, 250
Daigle, Dwight, 135
Dalrymple, Kevin, 36

Da Nang, 125–126, 133, 145
Davis, Hershel, 59, 201
Davis, Rex, 174
Davis, Riley, 176, 177
Decompression sickness, 82–83, 268–269
DeLorme, YN1, 119, 149, 150
Dennis, Irving, 56
Dentice, Jim, 154, 156
Dentry, Ned, 14–16, 29
Deriso, Frank, 222
Dilbert Dunker, 80
DiMartino, Joe, 197, 199
Din, Sham, 200–201
Dix, Lieutenant Commander, 259–260
Dodd, Dan, 267
Dolginger, Clifford, 187
Doss, Dale, 51
Draft dodgers, 18
Drinkwater, Sonny, 2
Drinkwater, Tint, 7, 20
Dropp, Joe, 49
Droz, Don, 134
DSRV (Deep Submergence Rescue Vehicle), 246, 258, 269
Duchene, Dave, 16, 29, 31, 38–39
Dudley, Seaman, 163, 164
Dumeuse, Ken, 96–97
Duong Keo River, 133
Dyer, Bruce, 136, 138, 141

Eisenhower, Dwight, 64
Emery, David, 274–275
EOD (explosive ordinance disposal), 70, 73
Esau, Tony, 238, 243, 250, 255, 270, 271, 275, 279
Eyes Under the Sea (movie), 169–170

F-4 Phantoms, 22, 46–47
Famuliner, Charlie, 47–48, 50, 58, 59, 62, 67
Farmer, Lance, 135
Farrington, Fred, 172, 173
Fine, Ray "Superfine," 210–216
Flud, Al, 146, 149–150
Fort Benning, 154
Fort Bragg, 201
Fort Story, 65, 76
Frogsville compound, 125, 127, 133

Gagliardi, Gene, 165
Gallagher, Bob, 119

Gamage, Bruce, 2
Garlick, Chief, 75
Gaulin, Ed, 43
GED (General Education Development) test, 30
Genovese, Vito, 89
George, Jerry, 185
Giberson, Art, 31
Gladding, Ray, 74
Glasscock, Jerry, 69
Gluhareff, Gene, 67, 68
GMS (guided missile school), Dam Neck, 64, 65, 68, 69, 83
Gordon, Joe, 95, 102
Gore, Jim, 125
Graver, Dave, 78, 80, 87, 91, 95, 96, 102–104, 110, 111, 209
Great Lakes Naval Recruit Training Center, 10–16
Grumley, Terry, 196
Guzman, Marine Sergeant, 36

Hale, Al, 70
HALO (high altitude low opening) school, 201
Hamilton, Dave, 160–163
Hamilton, Ron, 77, 80
Harjula, Arthur, 9, 10
Harper, Jim, 197
Harris, Dave, 271
Hart, Sherby, 259, 270, 273, 277, 278
Harvey, Claude, 209, 213
Hasha, Bob, 209
Hawkins, Tommy, 197
Heide, Dave, 37
Heinlein, Joe, 59
Hendricks, PH1, 43
Hewitt, Pappy, 75
Hinckley, Harry, 72
Hinson, Ricky, 134
Hollow, Lieutenant, 123–124
Holloway, Tom, 134
Hong Kong, 124
Hooten, Bill, 98–102
Horner, Al, 201
Hosteter, Dave, 147
Hummer, Tom, 66, 114, 115, 153
Husman, Don, 195, 200
Hutchinson, Jim, 274–276, 279

Indian Head Explosive Ordnance Range, 245
Iovino, Charlie, 46

Jahncke, Ernie, III, 141*n*, 159
Jakubowski, Bill "Jake," 130, 132, 133, 160

James, Buck, 219
Janecka, Stan, 59, 201
Jaunzems, Guntis (John), 222
Johnson, Dick, 77, 80, 87–90, 110, 112, 168, 169, 203, 204, 206, 209, 224, 235
Johnson, Ike, 204, 205, 236

Kaczmar, Joe, 70
Katala, Adam, 60–61
Keener, Fred, 174
Keever, Doug, 225, 228, 271
Kennedy, Gus, 78, 85–86
Kennedy, Jack, 49, 58, 61
Kerr, Jim, 35, 40, 43, 88
Kinne, Jane, 187
Kirby, John, 69–70
Kittredge, George, 254–255, 273, 280
Knueppel, Wolfgang, 260
Korn, Jerry, 55
Kuhn, Rich, 71, 73
Kulu, Harry, 79, 80, 84, 85, 90, 209, 256

LaPointe, Robert "Frenchie," 23, 30
Lapping, Harry, 132
Larsen, Kent, 124
Lawson, Liz, 22
LDO (Limited Duty Officer) program, 271
Leace, Donald, 62
Lee, Elton, 263
LeMoyne, Chuck, 198, 206–208
Leo, Joe, 60, 192, 193
Leonard, Chele, 221
Leonard, Wellington (Duke), 72–73, 221
Lewis, Bob "Machine Gun," 141, 142
Lewis, Charlie "Tobacco," 121–122, 124, 280
Leyden, Corney, 197, 200
Light, John, 67
Lisle, Bruce, 70–71
Lister (schooner), 176–178
Little, Beldon, 55–57, 107–108, 175–182, 184, 221
Little Creek Amphibious Base, 174, 188, 189, 201, 230
Logan, Carl "Flack," 46–47
Lomas, Chris, 118, 134
Lowry, John, 134–135
Lucas, George, 77
Luria, Sam, 214

Manning, Bill, 175
Marks, Don, 55
Mark 48 torpedo, 184, 187, 222
Martin, "Moki," 135, 146
Mason, Rick, 169–171
Mather, Lee, 217
Maury, Chip, 120
May, Andy, 272
McAffrey, Chief, 61
McCann Submarine Rescue Chamber, 252–255
McCraw, Eugene "Mac," 173–174, 206
McCraw, Jeannie, 173
McDaniel, Neil V. "Mac," 51–52, 60
McIntyre, Carl, 171
McLawhorn, Bruce, 237–241
McLean, Scotty, 191–193
McLellan, Bill, 48–49, 55, 57–58, 67, 175–177
McLellan, Joyce, 48
McLenny, Denny, 95, 97, 101, 102
McNair, "Chicken," 114
McNeil, Mike, 6
Merida (steamer), 231–232
MeWha, Kent, 194
Middleton, Don, 185
Miles, Richard, 205
Miller, Edward, 246–247, 260, 267, 274, 276
Miramar Naval Air Station, 163, 164
Moen, Lieutenant, 260–262, 274, 276
Montgomery, Chief, 43, 52
Morse, Denny, 89
Mouse, 125–126
Muehlenback, Terry, 165
Mulliken, Hyrum, 79, 231–232

Nachtsheim, Dick, 77
Naples, Italy, 224–228
Nash, Steve, 119, 120, 122–125
National Oceanic and Atmospheric Administration (NOAA) divers, 49
NAUI (National Association of Underwater Instructors), 238
Naval Air Station, Barber's Point, Hawaii, 118, 157
Naval Air Station, Oceana, 40–41, 43–68
Naval Air Technical Training Unit (NATTU), 22, 30–40

Naval Audio Visual Command, Atlantic, 203, 257
Naval Aviation magazine, 47
Naval Experimental Manned Observatory (NEMO), 169
Naval Inshore Warfare, Atlantic (NAVINSWARLANT), 202
Naval Ordnance Unit, Key West, 80–82
Naval Reserves, 279
Naval School of Deep Sea Diving, 224
Naval School of Diving and Salvage, 236–255
Naval Special Warfare Group, Atlantic (NavSpecWarGruLant), 188–203
Naval Special Warfare Photographic Laboratory, 158
Naval Submarine Medical Research Laboratory (NSMRL), 209
Naval Underwater Sound Lab, 184, 222–223
Navy magazine, 169
Neal, Stanley, 127
Nelson, Oliver Dean "O.D.," 140, 144
Nichols, Stephen, 40
Nichols, Tim, 141n
Noble, Tim, 265, 279
North Island Naval Air Station, 115, 117
Noyes, 31, 39

OCAN (Officer Candidate Airman) program, 23, 29–30
Ocean View (clam dredge), 203, 204
Olson, Norm "Stormin Norman," 59, 201
Ong Doc River (Song Ong Doc), 133, 136–140, 144
Operation Cheesebox, 246
Owl, Everett, 70
Oxaal, Leif, 220

Pacuirk, "Doc," 197
Painter, Tommy, 7
Palma, Luco, 141n
Panama City, Florida, 91–95
Parker, Joe, 222
Parrish, John, 36, 37
Pearl Harbor Naval Base, 157
Penn, Chuck, 266
Pensacola Naval Air Station, 12, 22, 29

Perry Oceanographics submersible, 169
Peterson, Bob, 119
Philadelphia Naval Shipyard, 256, 258
Phillips, "Filthy Phil," 199–200
Photo school, 31–36, 38–40
Phu Quoc Island, 133, 144
Pikula, Walt, 96
Piper, William "Randy," 134
Polaris missiles, 65
Pond, Nate, 105
Ponson, Pierre, 201
Poppenhager, Paul, 108, 109
Powell, EMCS, 278–279
Pozzi, Bill, 158
Project Tektite, 110, 111
Project Upshot, 270
Proxmire, William, 274
Puller, Lewis B. "Chesty," 120
Pulley, Jerry, 64, 77, 78, 190
Pulse, Joe, 59

Raesman, BMC, 271–272
Raising of the Queen (Korn), 55
RDT&E (Research, Development, Testing and Evaluation), 194–200
Rebikoff, Dmitri, 81
Regulus missile, 128–129
Renaud, Charlie, 159
RFPFs (Regional Forces and Popular Forces), 136–138, 140–143
Rhodes, Dusty, 59
Riter, Jim, 115n
Rivera, Seaman, 259, 270, 278
Roberts, Walter "Mole," 130–132
Robertson, Robbie, 125, 129, 132
Rock, Steve, 64
Roll's Farm Drop Zone, 159
Rouzie, Buck, 231–232
Ruddy, Drew, 260
Ruiz, Art, 134
Ryan, Mike, 49–50
Ryder, 191, 192

Sabat, Petty Officer, 262–263
Sager, Dan, 124
St. Jorge (minesweeper), 98, 100, 101, 103
Salvage balloons, 92–95
Sanborn, Lew, 105
Sandlin, Mike, 134
San Miguel Naval Station, 145

284 Index

Schmidt, Fred, 43, 47, 50, 52, 61

Schnoebelen, Al, 48, 57, 58, 62

Schulke, Flip, 170

SDV (swimmer delivery vehicle), 128–133

SEALAB program, 80

SEAL Team One, 76, 115, 121, 135, 137

SEAL Team Two, 37, 61, 70, 198, 221

Seibert, Gary, 210–212, 214–216

Seifert, Volker "Hasi," 169

SERE (survival, evasion, resistance, and escape) school, 83, 115

SHAD (Shallow Habitat Air Dive) project, 209–216

Shearer, Bill, 130, 132

Sheehan, Don "Bud," 61, 64

Shelf Diver, 169

Sherman, Gary, 40, 43

Shirley, Doc, 272, 276–277

Singer, ET2, 268–269

Slaughter, Scotty, 195

Slayton, Deke, 72

Smith, Jerry, 176, 177

Snow, Bert, 6

Snyder, Steve, 108, 109

Soland, Richard, 135

Song Bo De River, 126

SOT (special operations technician), 75

Special Forces, 147

SS Lusitania, 67

Stachiw, Jerry, 169

Stamey, Bobby, 59

Starcher, Jim, 250–252

Starr, Al, 155

Stauffacher, Dick, 196

Steffens, Tom, 201

Stenger, Bob, 9, 10

Stitt, Frank, 63, 78–79, 256

Subic Bay, Philippines, 115, 117, 119, 125, 144–146

Sutherland, Davy (Diamond Dave), 59

Sutherland, Tommy, 59

Swanson, Bill, 1

Taylor, José, 84

Taylor, Medford, 186

Thede, Bill, 192

Theorine, Larry, 176–178, 180, 181, 183

Thrift, Bud, 59

THX-1138 (training film), 77–78

Tidewater Navy Skydivers, 59

Travis, Skinny, 108

Trimble, Don, 36, 37

Trotter, Howard, 78, 91, 95, 96, 102, 110, 111, 209, 256

Underwater Demolition Team-13, 114, 118–144, 154, 158, 159

Underwater Demolition Team Replacement Training, 36–38, 50, 61, 64

Uniform Code of Military Justice (UCMJ), 39

Upton, Pete, 127, 134, 150–152

USS California, 206–208

USS Cascade, 224–227

USS Cook, 119–120, 124, 125, 149

USS Hermitage, 111

USS Monitor, 246, 247

USS Ortolan, 246, 255, 256–279

USS Spiegel Grove, 95, 97, 100

USS Tang, 255

USS Terrell County, 133, 135, 137, 138, 143

USS Tunny, 128–133

USS Westchester County, 133, 135, 137–138

UWSS (underwater swimmers school), 66, 69–76

Van Horn, Donald, 43

VF-11, The Red Rippers, 46–47

Viet Cong, 29, 123, 124, 126, 127, 133–135, 137–144

Vietnam war, 16, 51, 54, 67, 111, 117–144, 166

Wade, Dick, 77

Walsh, George, 159–160, 163, 164

Ware, Iva, 41

Ware, Mary (see Peterman, Mary Ware)

Ware, Roland, 5, 14, 20, 26, 41

Waterman, Cheryl, 2, 7, 19, 41, 222, 277, 278

Waterman, Emily Olga, 233, 273

Waterman, Harry, 19, 57

Waterman, Heather, 2, 7, 19, 41, 220, 222

Waterman, Judy Clausen, 165–168, 172, 173, 178, 179, 184–185

Waterman, Mary Ware, 5, 7, 14, 19–20, 26, 41, 60, 67, 105, 116, 145, 165, 175, 188, 193, 196, 197, 200, 216–219, 221, 222, 228–230, 233, 246, 257, 263, 271–273, 277

Waterman, Mr., 2, 14, 19, 41

Waterman, Mrs., 2, 7, 14, 19, 41, 42, 57, 178

Waterman, Nellie, 19, 278

Waterman, Nellie Marie, 278

Welch, Jack, 210

Weller, Joe, 58

Wendell, Butch, 43

Wettack, Tim, 135, 136

Weybrew, Ben, 213

White, Red, 246, 260

Whitehead, Larry, 126, 141

Whitmore, Paul, 209, 234, 235, 256

Whydah, 178n

Wilkerson, Rodney, 72

Williams, Doc, 141, 142

Williams, Larry, 141

Williams, Lieutenant, 191, 194, 199, 201

Williamson, Roger, 212

Willis, 31, 39

Willits, Peter, 71

Wilson, Jim, 145, 154, 155, 166

Winter, Tom, 126

Wolf, Dick, 75–76

World War II, 18, 33, 36, 64

Worthington, Robert Leroy "Doc," 114, 134

Wright, Bill, 70

Yelinek, Fred, 108–110

YFNB-17, 49–50, 174–175, 202

Yocum, Gerry, 36

Zellers, Ty, 59–60, 201

Ziv, Shaoul, 198, 201

Zmuda, Dan "Mud," 59, 201

Zuchra, Norm, 63